SPOKEN
HAWAIIAN

SPOKEN

HAWAIIAN

by Samuel H. Elbert

Illustrated by Jean Charlot

UNIVERSITY OF HAWAII PRESS

HONOLULU

Contents

CONTENTS

Illustrations

Preface

This volume is a result of two decades' efforts in teaching Hawaiian. The objects of the book are to present the principal conversational and grammatical patterns and the most common idioms, and to prepare the student for a final reward: the capacity to read and enjoy the rich heritage of Hawaiian traditional legends and poetry.

Over the years, the reasons cited for studying Hawaiian have been diverse. Some students are merely curious or hopeful for easy credit; some have an emotional dedication to Hawaii's past. Some have practical aims. They want to teach the language or culture of Hawaii. Some want to become translators of the vast storehouse of as-yet-untranslated materials. Some wish to prepare literary materials for primary or secondary education levels, or to write novels. Some want to do anthropological fieldwork or any other work that will take them to the South Seas where mastery of closely related languages is so essential. Students majoring in linguistics want to probe deeper into the structure of the Hawaiian language. Some students wish to speak Hawaiian to grandparents and other native speakers still found on Niihau and in scattered communities on other islands and even in Honolulu. The Hawaiian language is *not* dead, and, to judge by the number of persons under twenty fluent in the language, it will be around for a long time.

A justification for the rather drastic limitation of vocabulary in this text to about eight hundred items is that new words are of little value until the student knows how to fit them into the patterns of the language; ability to speak is seriously retarded if the student dissipates his energy in memorizing words before he knows what to do with them. The words have been chosen on the basis of frequency of use in classroom situations, in general conversation, and in legends and songs—samples of which are generously supplied throughout the text. No attempt is made to provide Hawaiian names for everything in a supermarket, as few, if any, students today will make their purchases in Hawaiian.

Following the suggestion of Theodore Andersson, new words are not entered in vocabularies at the ends of lessons but are introduced in italicized phrases and sentences so that the student learns them with a minimum of pain, in *context,* and not as isolated citations. When a word has been used in four lessons, it is starred in the fifth lesson to warn the student that he should now have mastered it. The English in the dialogues is primarily a key to facilitate memorization of the Hawaiian; hence, it is sometimes awkward and unidiomatic.

The book was illustrated by Jean Charlot, professor emeritus of art at the University of Hawaii, who generously supplied drawings that serve as conversation pieces and make grammar lively and stories meaningful. Fred Kalani Meinecke made suggestions about the lessons and Helen H. Hamada drew the figure on page 181.

As in everything that I have attempted to do in Hawaiian, the deepest appreciation goes to my teacher and collaborator, Mary Kawena Pukui, who for more than three decades has shared so generously her profound knowledge of Hawaiian language and culture.

S. H. E.

Suggestions for Learning Hawaiian

The objectives of the Hawaiian course are: (1) ability to speak and (2) ability to read.

Learning to speak is often called the oral-aural approach to language learning. This is because speaking (oral) also involves understanding what is heard (aural). Learning to speak first demands mastery of the new melody and the new sounds. Hawaiian melody is not like English melody. There are fewer ups and downs in pitch, fewer variations in stress levels, and often there is a slight rise before a pause. Proper melody and speed are even more important than good pronunciation of individual sounds. If the melody and speed sound Hawaiian, slight mispronunciation of individual sounds will not be noticed. The difficult sounds in Hawaiian include the "pure" vowels (without accompanying glides), the only slightly aspirated *p* and *k,* and the glottal stop.

Understanding comes from hearing Hawaiian. For this the laboratory is supremely helpful, as is every opportunity that can be found to practice with Hawaiian speakers and with fellow students. The student is to mimic the tapes and the Hawaiian he hears. Local persons will have little difficulty, but mainland-reared students will have to break with many English habits.

The patterns that constitute the language must be memorized, the dialogues repeated—out loud—until they can be reproduced flawlessly and effortlessly. We admire the skill of a tennis player who seems to perform without effort. First attempts of even brilliant students at dialogue are halting, but with repetition comes ease and finally a nativelike sound.

The keynote to success is participation. You do not learn to swim by reading about it in a book or by wishful thinking, but by getting into the water. Any skill comes after practice and involvement. And so with language learning.

Learning to read Hawaiian is easy for one learning to speak. Because the writing largely follows the sounds there is no difficult alphabet to learn.

Here are some study suggestions.

Any fear of public display is fatal. Verbosity, use of clichés and banalities, exhibitionism, and other traits that you may ordinarily deplore are invaluable in attaining fluency. Shyness and pride must be overcome;

one must not mind making mistakes or showing ignorance. Scoffers eventually respect intelligent perseverance.

Babble to yourself in Hawaiian. Put even the most banal thoughts into Hawaiian. Do not translate them from English into Hawaiian. Think in Hawaiian. Use tried-and-true patterns.

Speak Hawaiian with your classmates, outside of class as well as in. This gives you oral training and ear training. Hawaiian can be a "fun language" that your outside friends will not understand, and that you may prefer to use on a telephone party line.

Space your homework, laboratory hours, and classes. Thirty minutes' study a day is more effective than an hour every other day, but snatches of conversation several times every day with deliberate application of new patterns is better still. The least effective procedure is postponing study and cramming before examinations. Such foolish techniques make little provision for oral training and none at all for ear training.

Keep up with the class. If you fall behind you will be uncomfortable and will hold back the entire class.

Writing out Hawaiian is a good aid to memory. Vocabulary cards, with the Hawaiian phrase or sentence on one side of the card and an English translation on the other, speed up learning. Carry these cards or slips around with you. Study the as-yet-unmastered phrases several times a day, while riding the bus, eating, or even while brushing your teeth. Above all, learn the new words in *phrases and sentences,* not in isolation.

Review unceasingly.

Three ways in which Hawaiian differs from English cause special difficulties: (1) A common word order is VERB plus SUBJECT plus OBJECT. (2) Adjectives follow nouns. (3) Abstract and frequently mass nouns take articles (the beauty, the God, the Sunday, the school). Concentrate on these special difficulties.

A language is a set of habits. Habits are acquired by repetition. Language learning is repetition. It is not intellectual but muscular. Repeat and repeat. The only key to success is *overlearning*. If you speak a word four times on four occasions, and hear it on four occasions, it is usually mastered.

May this be true of your Hawaiian: I will be METICULOUS yet GARRULOUS.

Here is your first lesson in Hawaiian:

'A'a i ka hula. Waiho i ka hilahila i ka hale.
Dare to dance. Leave embarrassment at home.

E kaupē aku no i ka hoe, e kō mai i ka hoe, e hoe.
Put forward the paddle, draw the paddle toward you, paddle.

Pronunciation of Hawaiian

The Hawaiian phonemes are listed below. English examples are approximate. The Hawaiian vowels are "pure," i.e., without glides. They are of either short or long duration. The consonants *p* and *k* have less aspiration (i.e., they are "harder") than similar English sounds in initial position. (Pairs distinguished by single phonemes follow descriptions in parentheses.) Long *a* (ā) is longer than the other long vowels.

i as *ee* in *keep (lohi, lohe; wai, wae)*.

e as in *bet*. Long *ē* suggests the English *a* in *tame*. Final short *e* approaches the *i* sound in *bit*.

a as a̱ and o̱ in *above*. Long *ā* is like the lengthened *a* in *father*.

o as in *only (malo, malu, pao, pau)*.

u as the *oo* in *moon*, with well-rounded lips.

p, h, l, m, n about as in English *paper, hill, lame, me, no*.

k as in *kodak*. On Niihau, *k*, except at the beginning of a sentence, is frequently replaced by *t*.

' glottal stop, a consonant similar to the break between vowels in fast pronunciation of *oh-oh (kou, koʻu)*.

w after *o* and *u* usually a lax *w* as in *well (auwe)*; after *i* and *e* usually a lax *v*, less tense than English *v* in *veil (ʻewa, iwi)*. Initially and after *a*, some people use the *w*-like sound and others use the *v*-like sound, and many use both variants, but to Hawaiians the two variants are one and the same sound.

A glide sound that suggests English *y* may separate *e* and *i* from following vowels. In Hawaiian this glide makes no difference in meaning and therefore is not written. Similarly, a *w*-like glide may separate *o* and *u* from following vowels (iʸā, Mauʷi).

A before *i* and *u* sometimes assimilates to *e* and *o*: *kaikaina* is usually *keikeina*, *ikaika* is *ikeika*; *mau* is sometimes *mou*. *A* is probably shorter before *i* and *u* than before *e* and *o*.

Neighboring vowels may also be separated in slow speech by slight hiatus, in which case there is no intervening *y*- or *w*-glide and neither vowel is influenced by the other (*ka + uka*, the uplands, *kauka*, doctor; *kana + ono*, sixty, *kaona*, hidden meaning; *ka + inoa*, the name, *kaikaina*, sibling;

he + inoa, a name, *heihei,* race; *ia,* he, *ali + ali,* clear; *loiloi,* criticize, *ilo + ilo,* maggoty, *ho'o + ilo,* winter; *hou,* new, *ho'o + una,* send).

All long vowels (shown by macrons) are stressed (*wǎhíne,* women, *wahíne,* woman; *kǎúa,* we two inclusive, *kǎúa,* war, *kǎuwǎ,* outcast). Here and in other words, the last stress (ˊ) is commonly somewhat louder than preceding stresses (ˋ). In general, stress is on the next-to-the-last syllable and on alternating preceding syllables, except that in five-syllable words the stress is commonly as in *ˋelemakúle,* old man. *Ei, eu, oi, ou, ai, ae, au, ao* without intervening hiatus are considered diphthongs and the stress is on the first member. All monosyllabic words (but not particles) are stressed.

Words in Hawaiian are of two main types that may be called content words and particles. Some of the latter express grammatical relationship rather than lexical meaning. Particles are frequently short (*'o, i, e, a, o*), and this makes their mastery difficult. Some of these particles occur *long* near final pauses.

Fast speech differs from slow speech in the following ways in addition to those previously mentioned:

1. After a pause (however slight, but not after the hiatus indicated above by a plus sign) word-initial vowels other than *u-* are preceded by nonsignificant glottal stops that are not written. Within an utterance, such glottal stops are clearly heard.

2. Adjacent like vowels commonly fuse into a single vowel: *aloha 'ia aku,* having been greeted, is *alòha 'iáku; e hele ana au,* I am going, is *e hèle anáu; nā ali'i,* the chiefs, is *nǎ lí'i.* The first of like vowels separated by a glottal stop is frequently lost: *Hawai'i* may be *Hawa'i; pua'a,* pig, may be *pu'a; ka mea e loa'a ana,* whatever is found, may be *ka mea e lo'ana.* Adjacent unlike vowels in different words may fuse into diphthongs: *he aha ia mea,* what does this matter, becomes *he ahàia méa;* the poetic name *'Aù-i-ke-kài-lóa,* swim in the distant sea, becomes *'Aui-ke-kai-loa.*

In summary, the spelling used in this book differs from conventional spelling in indication of glottal stops and long vowels, and in the separation by hyphens of parts of proper names. This helps the student pronounce unfamiliar words, but for fast speech he must imitate his teacher and apply some of the above suggestions.

SPOKEN
HAWAIIAN

ʻEKAHI

A. Hawaiian words used in English. You already know many Hawaiian words that are commonly used and mispronounced in English in the Hawaiian Islands. Many of these words have meanings in addition to the meanings in English. (For example, *kamaʻāina* is commonly used as a verb meaning "to know thoroughly.") The common meanings of these words used in English are listed below, and it will be assumed that all the students know these words. Additional meanings of these words will be introduced gradually in the lessons.

akamai	smart	laulau	steamed leaf
aloha	love, affection,		package of food
	good morning,	lei	lei
	good-by	lōlō	stupid
hana	work	lūʻau	Hawaiian feast
haole	Caucasian	luna	foreman
hapa		mahalo	thank you, thanks
haole	one of Caucasian	makai	towards the sea,
	and Hawaiian		seaward
	ancestry	make	dead
heiau	ancient temple	malihini	visitor, tourist,
holokū	gown with a train		newcomer
huhū	angry	malo	loincloth
hula	hula	mauka	towards the moun-
imu	earth oven		tains, inland
kāhili	feather standard	muʻumuʻu	gown without a
	of royalty		train
kahuna	priest	ʻono	delicious
kamaʻāina	native-born person	Pākē	Chinese
kapa	tapa	pali	cliff
kapu	taboo	pau	finished, over
kōkua	help	pāʻū	sarong
kuleana	private property,	pilau	rotten
	responsibility	pilikia	trouble

pohō	out of luck	pupule	crazy
pōpoki	cat	wahine	woman
puka	hole (perforation)		

B.   Work phrases. For reference: memorize these important words as soon as you can. They will enable the class to be conducted in Hawaiian.

Courtesy phrases

Please. E 'olu'olu 'oe (be kind you).
Thank you. Mahalo.
Excuse me. Kala mai ia'u.
How are you? Pehea 'oe?
Fine. Maika'i nō (good indeed).

Classroom questions

What? He aha? Pehea?
I have a question. He nīnau ka'u (a question mine).
How do you say in Hawaiian _____? Pehea ka 'ōlelo Hawai'i _____? (What's the word Hawaiian _____?)
What's the meaning of _____? Pehea ka mana'o o _____?

Classroom commands

Let's sing. Mele kākou (sing we).
Look at the English side. Nānā i ka 'ao'ao haole.
Look at the Hawaiian side. Nānā i ka 'ao'ao Hawai'i.
Read. Heluhelu.
Mimic. Ho'opili.
Repeat. 'Ōlelo hou (speak again).
Speak English. 'Ōlelo haole.
Speak fast. 'Ōlelo 'āwīwī.
Speak Hawaiian. 'Ōlelo Hawai'i.
Speak loudly. Leo nui (voice big).
Speak slowly. 'Ōlelo lohi.
Take the part of Frank. 'O 'oe 'o Palani.
It's the same. Like pū.
Continue. Go on. Ho'omau.

End of class

Enough. Lawa.
Class is finished. Pau ka papa.

C.   Hawaiian words from English. The many words taken from English into Hawaiian will be easy if you remember the most important sound shifts:

English	*Hawaiian*
p, b, f	p
t, d, th, s, z, sh, ch, j, k, g	k
l, r	l

Every introduced word ends in a vowel (often *a*), and adjoining English consonants are either separated by a vowel, or one of the consonants is dropped.

The words in the first ten lessons from English include: Kepanī, Kōlea, kula, palaoa, pepa, pia, Pilipino, pipi, Pokoliko, puke, Pukikī.

D. Ke ana ʻekahi (first pattern):
HE + NOUN SUBJECT + DEMONSTRATIVES

This is the first pattern, and one that you will use every day. Practice reading the Hawaiian side without looking at the English, thinking the English translation to yourself. Then cover up the Hawaiian, look at the English, and reproduce the Hawaiian. Do not be satisfied in your study until you can reproduce the Hawaiian without hesitation. Sentences containing new words are in italics. This is to help you to learn these words in phrases, and to facilitate reviewing. New words not in italics need not be memorized. *Keia* is also pronounced *kēia*.

(1) *He pepa keia.*
He kanaka keia.

He penikala keia.
He puke keia.
He wahine kēlā.

(2) He kanaka kēlā.
He pepa kēnā.

He penikala kēlā.
He wahine kēnā.
He puke kēlā.

(3) *He wahine maikaʻi kēlā.*
(*Maikaʻi* is often pronounced *meikeʻi.*)

He puke maikaʻi kēnā.
He puke hou keia.
He hale hou keia.
He penikala hou keia.

(4) *He puke pono kēlā.*

He kanaka pono keia.

(1) *This is a paper* (a paper this).
This is a person/man (a man this).
This is a pencil.
This is a book.
That (far away) is a woman/ lady.

(2) That (far) is a person.
That (near the person addressed) is a paper.
That (far) is a pencil.
That (near) is a lady.
That (far) is a book.

(3) *That (far) is a good woman* (a woman good that).
(Note that the adjective follows the noun.)
That (near) is a good book.
This is a new book.
This is a new house.
This is a new pencil.

(4) *That is a righteous/honest book.*
This is a righteous man.

He hale nui keia.   *This is a big house.*
He penikala nui kēnā.   That (near) is a big pencil.
He wahine nui keia.   This is a large woman.

(5) *He aha keia? He aha*   (5) *What is this? What is*
     keia mea? He puke.   *this thing? A book.*
He aha kēlā? He pepa.   What's that? A paper.
He aha keia? He penikala.   What's this? A pencil.
He aha keia? He kanaka pono.   What's this? An honest man.
He aha kēlā? He wahine.   What's that? A lady.

(6) He aha keia? He wahine   (6) What's this? A good woman.
     maika'i.
He aha kēlā? He puke hou.   What's that? A new book.
He aha keia? He hale nui.   What's this? A big house.
He aha kēlā? He penikala hou.   What's that? A new pencil.
He aha keia? He kanaka pono.   What's this? A righteous person.

E.   ADVICE. It is not easy to write Hawaiian. It is especially hard to remember to write glottal stops and macrons (long marks over vowels). Copy carefully the Hawaiian in this and other lessons. This is a good way to memorize.

F.   A Hawaiian alphabet song composed by Mary Kawena Pukui for her eldest grandson, La'akea (for reference).

E nā hoa kamali'i,   O fellow children,
E a'o mai kākou   Let us learn together
I pa'ana'au ka pī'āpā.   Till we've memorized the
     alphabet.

'Ā, 'ē, 'ī, 'ō, 'ū,   A, e, i, o, u,
Hē, kē, lā, mū, nū.   H, k, l, m, n.
'O pī me wē nā panina   P and w are the last two
O ka pī'āpā.   Of the pī'āpā.

'ELUA

A. Conversation.

This and all other conversations in the book should be memorized. The student should be able to take both parts in the dialogue. He should practice until he can say the Hawaiian as rapidly as the English, with the Hawaiian side covered.

Haumana.	*Aloha kakahiaka.*	Student.	*Good morning.*
Wahine.	Aloha kakahiaka.	Woman.	Good morning.
H.	He aha keia?	S.	What's this? (S shows book to W.)
W.	He puke.	W.	A book.
H.	*Maopopo iā'oe ka puke?*	S.	*Do you understand* the book?
W.	*Maopopo ia'u.*	W.	*I understand.*
H.	*Maika'i anei ka puke?*	S.	*Is the book good?* (*Anei* indicates that the utterance is a question that can be answered by yes or no; its use is optional.)
W.	*'Ae, maika'i.*	W.	*Yes,* (it is) *good.*
H.	Maika'i keia penikala?	S.	Is this pencil good? (S shows pencil to W.)
W.	'Ae, maika'i.	W.	Yes, (it is) good.
H.	*Maika'i anei keia noho?*	S.	*Is this chair good?*
W.	*'Ae, 'olu'olu.*	W.	*Yes,* (it is) *comfortable.*
H.	*'Olu'olu keia 'āina?*	S.	*Is this land cool?*
W.	'Ae, 'olu'olu.	W.	Yes, (it is) cool.
H.	*Aloha kāua.*	S.	*Good-by.*
W.	Aloha.	W.	Good-by.

B. Idioms.

Maopopo ia'u. I understand (understand to-me).
Maopopo iā'oe. You (singular) understand.
Aloha kākou. Greetings/farewell (more than two people).

Aloha ahiahi. Good evening.
Aloha kakahiaka. Good morning.

C.   Review of *he*, "a." HE precedes nouns!

(1)   *He 'ai maika'i kēlā.*   (1)   *That is good food/poi.*
      He 'ōlelo maika'i keia.   *This is a good speech/*
                                              language.

      He haumana hou keia.   *This is a new student.*
      He puke hou keia.   This is a new book.
      He 'āina nui kēnā.   *That* (near) *is a big land.*

(2)   *He ali'i au/wau.*   (2)   *I am a chief.*
      He haumana *(haumāna)* au.   I am a student.
      He Hawai'i au.   *I am a Hawaiian.*
      He wahine au.   I am a woman.
      He ali'i maika'i 'oe.   *You* (singular) *are a good*
                                             chief.

(3)   *He noho 'olu'olu kēlā.*   (3)   *That is a comfortable/cool*
                                             chair.
      He Hawai'i keia.   This is a Hawaiian.
      He hale kēlā.   That is a house.
      He haumana maika'i 'oe.   You are a good student.
      He kanaka pono 'oe.   You are an honest person.

D.   Ke ana 'elua (second pattern):   maika'i au, I am well.
                                      maika'i ka puke, the book is good.

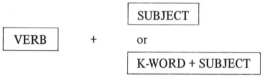

The sentences in *ke ana 'ekahi* all begin *he*. They might be called
VERBLESS sentences. *Ke ana 'elua* illustrates a sentence with a verb.
The first word (not a particle) in such sentences is by definition a verb,
regardless of what we may consider such a word in English.

(4) *Maika'i au.*   (4) *I am well/good/handsome.*
     Maika'i 'oe.   You are well/good/handsome.
     Maika'i ka puke.   The book is good.
     Maika'i ka penikala.   The pencil is good.
     Nui ka hale.   The house is big.

(5) Maika'i ka pepa.   (5) The paper is good.
     Pono ka puke.   The book is moral.
     Maika'i ka 'āina.   The land is good.
     Maika'i ka ha'awina.   *The lesson is good.*
     Maika'i ka 'ōlelo.   The language is good.

E. *K*-words.
Certain words beginning with *k-* are called *k*-words. Thus far we have
learned *ka, keia, kēnā, kēlā.* In the *he-* pattern, these words (except *ka*)
follow the noun because they do not directly qualify the noun. When
they directly qualify a noun (this man, this book), they precede the
noun.

(6) *'Olu'olu keia ali'i.*   (6) *This chief is polite/kind.*
     'Olu'olu keia 'āina.   This land is cool.
     'Olu'olu keia noho.   This chair is cool/comfortable.
     'Olu'olu kēlā 'ōlelo.   That speech is polite/kind.
     Pono kēlā wahine hou.   That new woman is honest.

(7) Maika'i ka haumana.   (7) The student is good/well.
     'Olu'olu ka noho.   The chair is comfortable.
     Pono ke kanaka Hawai'i.   The Hawaiian man is honest.
     Maika'i keia puke.   This book is good.
     'Olu'olu kēlā haumana.   That student is polite.

F. Dinner phrases (for reference).

A lāua 'o B.   Ūi!   A and B.   Halloo!
Haku hale. Mai mai mai mai!   Host. Come come come come!
  Komo mai!   Come in!
A lāua 'o B.   Ūi!   A and B.   Halloo!
H.   Mai mai! E 'olu'olu 'oe   H.   Come come! Please, sit in
      noho i keia noho.   this chair.
A.   Mahalo.   A.   Thank you.

H. E Pī, e 'olu'olu 'oe, noho
   i keia noho.

B. Mahalo.

H. O B, please, sit in this
   chair.

B. Thank you.

(The following are typical questions that H might ask.)

H. Makemake 'oe i wai? Make-
   make 'oe i kope? Lama? Pia?
   Pa'akai? Pepa? Palaoa? Pipi?
   Poi? 'Uala? Puna? 'Ō? Pahi?
   Kī'aha? Pā? Kōpa'a? Kalima?

H. Do you want water? Do
   you want coffee? Rum/
   liquor? Beer? Salt? Pepper?
   Bread? Beef? Poi? Sweet
   potatoes? Spoon? Fork?
   Knife? Glass? Plate?
   Sugar? Cream?

A. 'Ae. Makemake au i wai.

A. Yes. I would like some
   water.

B. 'A'ole. 'A'ole makemake i
   kope. Lawa.

B. No. Don't want coffee.
   Enough.

A. Pehea kēnā pipi?

A. How's that beef?

B. 'Ono keia pipi.

B. This beef is delicious.

A. Pehea kēnā palaoa?

A. How's that bread?

B. Maika'i keia palaoa.

B. This bread is good.

A. Pehea kēnā kī?

A. How's that tea?

B. Anuanu keia kī.

B. This tea is cold.

A. Pehea ka i'a? Ka mea 'ono?

A. How's the fish? The cake?

B. 'Ono ka mea 'ono. Hauna keia
   i'a.

B. The cake is delicious. This
   fish smells bad.

A. Pehea ka pia?

A. How's the beer?

B. Wela loa.

B. Very hot.

A. E 'olu'olu 'oe, hā'awi mai
   i 'uala, pa'akai, pepa.

A. Please, give me sweet potatoes, salt, pepper.

B. Hiki.

B. Okay.

A. Auwē! Mā'ona! Mahalo.

A. Boy! Full! Thank you.

G. Names. Choose a Hawaiian name if you don't have one. Suggestions:

'Au-i-ke-kai-loa, swim/travel
   in the distant seas
Ehu-nui-kai-malino, great spray
   calm sea
Hina, name of a goddess
Ka-lani, the heavenly chief

Ka-lī-o-ka-lani-'ōlapa-ka-uila-
   ku'i-ka-hekili-i-ka-maka-o-
   ka-'ōpua, the chill of heaven,
   the flash of lightning, the
   roar of thunder in the face
   of the cloud bank

Ka-makani, the wind
Kanaloa, name of a major god
Ka-ua-noe, the misty rain
Ka-ulu-kukui, the candlenut
  grove
Ke-ao-makani, the windy cloud
Ke-ehu-iki-awakea, little spray
  in the afternoon

Ke-kai-malu, the peaceful sea
Kinilau, great quantities
Lei-aloha, beloved child
Maile-lau-liʻi, small-leafed maile
Noe-lani, mist of heaven
Pele, volcanic eruption
Pili-aloha, loving comrade
Pua-nani, pretty flower

Names from English: ʻAlapaki, ʻAnalū, ʻElikapeka, Helena, Kale, Kamuela, Kāwika, Keoki, Keoni, Kimo, Kini, Kōleka, Kona, Lahela, Likeke, Lopaka, Luke, Makaleka, Mele, Palani, Pila, Poloika, Wiliama.

H. Nominative ʻo and vocative e.

Ke-koa. E Mēlia, maopopo iāʻoe ka puke?

Mēlia. Maopopo. E Ke-koa, ʻo wai kēlā haumana?

K. ʻAʻole maopopo, e Melia.

M. E ka malihini, ʻo wai kou inoa?

Malihini. ʻO Leo-lani. ʻO Leo-lani koʻu inoa.

The-warrior. O Plumeria, do you understand the book?

Plumeria. Understand. O The-warrior, who is that student?

T. Don't know, Plumeria.

P. Say, stranger, what is your name?

Stranger. Royal-voice. Royal-voice is my name.

ʻEKOLU

A. Review of *he* pattern.

(1) He wahine ʻoe.	(1) You are a woman.
He Hawaiʻi ʻoe.	You are a Hawaiian.
He haole ʻoe.	You are a haole.
He haumana ʻoe.	You are a student.
He aliʻi maikaʻi ʻoe.	You are a good chief.
(2) He noho kēlā.	(2) That is a chair.
He ʻāina kēlā.	That is a land.
He ʻōlelo kēlā.	That is a speech/language.
He kanaka kēlā.	That is a person.
He puke hou kēlā.	That is a new book.
(3) He wahine au.	(3) I am a woman.
He haumana au.	I am a student.
He Hawaiʻi au.	I am a Hawaiian.
He pepa kēnā.	That (near) is a paper.
He noho nui kēnā.	That (near) is a big chair.
(4) He noho ʻoluʻolu keia.	(4) This is a cool/comfortable chair.
He hula maikaʻi keia.	This is a good hula.
He kanaka maikaʻi keia.	This is a good person.
He ʻai ʻono kēlā.	That is delicious food.
He kuleana hou kēlā.	That is a new kuleana.

B. Ke ana ʻekolu: ke aliʻi, ke kanaka, ka wahine.

Ke and ka both mean "the" and are k-words that *always* precede nouns. Ke is used before all words beginning with a- and k- (ke aliʻi, ke aloha, ke kanaka) but usually not before words beginning ʻa- (ka ʻai). Ke is also used before words beginning with o- and e- (but not ʻe-). Ka is used before words beginning with other letters.

(5) *Noho au ma Honolulu.*	(5) *I live/stay in Honolulu.*
Noho ka haumana ma Mōʻiliʻili.	The student lives in Mōʻiliʻili.

Noho ka wahine i Lā'ie.   *The woman lives at Lā'ie.*
Noho ke ali'i ma ka hale.   The chief stays in the house.
No ka haumana i Ulu-kou ma   The student lives at Ulukou
  Waikīkī.   in Waikīkī. See page 48.

Hawaiian has two words for "at, in, on": a definite locative *i* and a vague indefinite locative *ma*. English makes no such distinction. *Ma* is always correct unless one wishes to specify a particular spot.

(6) *'Ai ka haumana. 'Ono ka 'ai.*

   'Ōlelo ke kanaka: aloha kākou.

   'Ōlelo ka wahine: aloha
    kakahiaka.
   'Ōlelo au: *aloha ahiahi.*
   'Ōlelo Hawai'i kākou.

(7) *Hele ka haumana.*
   Noho ka haumana.
   Hele ka wahine i Waikīkī.

   Noho 'oe ma Waikīkī?
   'Ae, noho au ma Waikīkī.

(6) *The student eats. The food is delicious.*
The man says: hello everybody.
The lady says: good morning.
I say: *good evening.*
We/let's speak Hawaiian.

(7) *The student goes.*
The student stays.
The woman goes to Waikīkī.

Do you live at Waikīkī?
Yes, I live at Waikīkī.

C.   Review: ke ana 'elua.

    VERB + K-WORD + SUBJECT

(8) Is the chief well?
   (Maika'i ke ali'i?)
   The chief is well.
   Is the student new?
   The student is new.
   Is the chair comfortable?

(9) Is the food good?
   The food is good.
   Is the house big?
   The house is big.
   Is the person courteous?
   The person is courteous.

D.   Review: he.

(10) This is a good chief.
    (He ali'i maika'i keia.)
    This is a new student.

That (near) is a new chair.
This is a good man.
That (near) is a good land.

(11) This is good food.
That (far) is a big house.
That (far) is a courteous person.

This is a good pencil.
This is a polite Hawaiian.
That (far) is a kind student.

E. Contrasting two patterns.

VERB + K-WORD + SUBJECT   HE pattern

(12) Is the student new? The student is new.

This is a new student.

Is the chair comfortable? The chair is comfortable.

That (near) is a comfortable chair.

Is this land good? This land is good.

This is a good land.

Is the house big? The house is big.

That (far) is a big house.

Is the student kind?

This is a kind student.

F. Substitution drill.

He noho hou kela.
haumana
ʻoluʻolu
ʻāina
maikaʻi
keia

He haumana hou kēlā,
He haumana ʻoluʻolu kēlā.
He ʻāina ʻoluʻolu kēlā.
He ʻāina maikaʻi kēlā.
He ʻāina maikaʻi keia.

ʻEHĀ

A. *He kamaʻilio ʻana.*

A. *A conversation.*

The teacher appoints students to take parts, saying, *ʻo ʻoe ʻo Palani, ʻo ʻoe ʻo Hina.* Students reply *hiki,* okay.)

Palani. E ʻoluʻolu ʻoe, ʻo
wai kou inoa?

Frank. Please, what is
your name?

Hina. ʻO Hina.

Hina. Hina.

P. He Pākē ʻoe?

F. Are you Chinese?

H. ʻAʻole. He Hawaiʻi au.

H. No. I'm Hawaiian.

P. Noho ʻoe ma Waikīkī?

F. Do you live at Waikīkī?

H. ʻAʻole. ʻAʻole maikaʻi
ʻo Waikīkī.

H. No. Waikīkī is not good.

P. Noho ʻoe ma Maui?

F. Do you live at Maui?

H. ʻAʻole. Noho au ma
Kahoʻolawe.

H. No. I live on Kahoʻolawe.

P. *ʻŌlelo haole ʻoe?*

F. *Do you speak English?*

H. ʻAe. *Mākaukau.*

H. Yes. (I'm) *clever/proficient.*

P. ʻŌlelo Hawaiʻi ʻoe?

F. Do you speak Hawaiian?

H. ʻAʻole mākaukau loa.

H. Not very well (proficient).

P. ʻŌlelo Kepanī ʻoe?

F. Do you speak Japanese?

H. ʻAʻole ʻōlelo Kepanī.

H. (I) don't speak Japanese.

P. ʻŌlelo Pākē ʻo kēlā
haumana?

F. Does that student speak
Chinese?

H. ʻAʻole ʻōlelo Pākē kēlā
haumana. *ʻAʻole ʻike. ʻAʻole
ʻoia ʻōlelo Pākē.*

H. That student doesn't speak
Chinese. (He) *doesn't know
how. He doesn't speak
Chinese.*

P. ʻŌlelo Pākē ʻoe?

F. Do you speak Chinese?

H. ʻAʻole au ʻōlelo Pākē.
ʻAʻole au ʻike.

H. I don't speak Chinese.
I don't know how.

P. Hula ka wahıne?

F. Does the woman hula?

H. ʻAʻole ʻoia hula.

H. She doesn't hula.

B. *'A'ole* (no, not) is commonly pronounced (but never written or sung) *'a'ale,* and occurs in three positions:

(1) By itself:
Hele 'oe? *'A'ole.*   Are you going? *No.*

(2) Followed by verb phrase ± noun phrase ± noun phrase (± = with or without):
'A'ole hele.   Not going.
'A'ole hele ka Pākē i Hawai'i.   The Chinese is not going to Hawai'i.
'A'ole 'olu'olu ke kumu.   The teacher is not kind.

(3) Followed by pronoun subject + *e* (non-past) or *i* (past) + verb:
'A'ole lākou e 'ike.   *They don't know/see.*
'A'ole lākou i 'ike.   *They did not know/see.*
Ho'oma'ama'a (practice):
'A'ole helu nā haumana.   *The students don't count.*
'A'ole au e helu.   I'm not counting.
'A'ole au i helu.   I didn't count.
'A'ole nui kēlā hale.   That house is not big.
Practice, using the same patterns:
The students don't speak, eat, go, love.
I (you) don't speak, eat, go, love.
I (you) didn't speak, eat, go, love.

C. Use *i* or *ma,* or both.
You live at Waikīkī.
You live at Ulu-kou in Waikīkī.
I live at Wai-luku on Maui.
I live at the Ala Wai in Waikīkī.
You live at Hilo on Hawai'i.

D. Substitution drill.

'A'ole i hele ke kanaka.
ka haumana   'A'ole i hele ka haumana.
e   'A'ole e hele ka haumana.
au   'A'ole au e hele.
'oe   'A'ole 'oe e hele.

ʻELIMA

A.	He kamaʻilio ʻana.	A.	A conversation.

Keaka.	*Aloha kāua.*	Jack.	*Hello* (we two).
Lani.	Aloha kāua.	Lani.	Hello (we two).
K.	ʻO wai kou inoa?	J.	What's your name?
L.	ʻO Lani Keawe.	L.	Lani Keawe.
K.	E Lani, noho ʻoe ma Mānoa?	J.	Say Lani, do you live at Mānoa?
L.	ʻAʻole. Noho mākou ma Lāʻie.	L.	No. We live at Lāʻie.
K.	*Auwē nohoʻi e! ʻAʻole kokoke.*	J.	*Goodness! Not near.*
L.	*ʻAʻole pilikia.*	L.	*No trouble.*
K.	*Pehea kou makuahine?*	J.	*How's your mother?*
L.	*Aloha ʻino! Maʻi kō mākou makuahine.*	L.	*Oh dear! Our mother is sick.*
K.	*Pehea kou makuakāne?*	J.	*How's your father?*
L.	Maikaʻi kō mākou makuakāne.	L.	Our father is fine.
K.	*Hele ʻoe i ke kula?*	J.	*Do you go to school?* (Hawaiian: THE school.)
L.	*ʻAe, hele nō.*	L.	Yes, just go (go indeed).
K.	*ʻO wai ke kumu?*	J.	*Who is the teacher?*
L.	ʻO Kamika.	L.	Smith.
K.	*He kumu mākaukau?	J.	Is (he) a qualified teacher?
L.	ʻAe, mākaukau loa.	L.	Yes, well qualified.
K.	He kumu Kepanī?	J.	Is (he) a Japanese teacher?
L.	*Tsa!* Kamika. *ʻAʻole ia he inoa Kepanī!*	L.	*Oh!* Smith. *That's not a Japanese name!*
K.	He inoa Pākē?	J.	A Chinese name?
L.	*ʻAʻole loa!* He kumu hapa haole.	L.	*Certainly not!* (He) is a hapa haole teacher.

*The asterisk (*) has been used throughout this book to emphasize a word which has appeared in at least five lessons. The student will be expected to have mastered thoroughly the starred word.

K. Pehea ke kula? He kula maika'i?

J. How's the school? A good school?

L. 'Ae, maika'i ke kula, maika'i nā noho, nui nā puke, maika'i *nā papa'ele'ele,* akamai nā haumana, *maika'i nā lole, hou nā kāma'a.*

L. Yes, the school is good, the chairs are good, there are many books, *the black-boards* are good, the students are smart, *the dresses are good, the shoes are new.*

K. Auwē noho'i e! Hou loa?

J. Man! Very new?

L. 'Ae, 'olu'olu nā noho, pono nā puke, akamai nā haumana, mākaukau nā kumu.

L. Yes, the seats are comfortable, the books are morally suitable, the students are smart, the teachers are qualified.

K. He kula maika'i loa, 'a'ole anei?

J. A very fine school, isn't it?

L. 'Ae. He kula hou. He kula maika'i.

L. Yes. A new school. A good school.

Nō, an intensifier, may be translated freely as *very, quite, indeed.*

B.   Inclusive and exclusive pronouns.

Inclusive forms (including the person addressed)	Exclusive forms (excluding the person addressed)
kākou we	*mākou* we
kō kākou our	*kō mākou* our

Translate the words for *we, our, us* in the following. Translate nothing else. Think over each sentence and determine whether the inclusive or exclusive forms are needed. The speaker is addressing a kama'āina friend whom he has not seen in a long time. 1. *We* (my wife, children, and I) want you to come over to *our* new house. 2. *Our* cook is sick, so *we'll* all just eat what *we* can find. 3. *Our* kitchen is modernized. 4. But *we* are not good cooks. 5. *We'll* take pot luck. 6. *We* all hope you can join *us* (same as *we*) and *we'll* have a good time in *our* new house even though *we* don't eat much.

C.   Ke *ana ʻelima: nā (plural article).

Nā indicates "the" before nouns to be translated by English plurals. Unlike other monosyllabic particles, *nā* is always stressed, regardless of position.

Noho nā Kepanī i Oʻahu.	*The Japanese live on Oʻahu.*
Noho nā haole i Maui.	*The haole/Caucasian people live on Maui.*
Noho nā Pākē i ka *hale.	The Chinese people stay in the house.
*Maikaʻi nā lole hou.	The new dresses are fine.
Maikaʻi nā hula hou.	The new hula dances are good.

D.   He _____ keia?

D.   Is this a _____ ?

Kū. He pepa Pākē keia?	Kū. Is this a Chinese paper?
Lono. ʻAe, he pepa Pākē kēnā.	Lono. Yes, that's a Chinese paper.
ʻAʻole he pepa Pākē kēnā.	That is not a Chinese paper.
K. He muʻumuʻu Hawaiʻi *kēlā?	K. Is that a Hawaiian muʻumuʻu?
L. ʻAe, he muʻumuʻu Hawaiʻi kēlā.	L. Yes, that's a Hawaiian muʻumuʻu.
ʻAʻole he muʻumuʻu Hawaiʻi kēlā.	That is not a Hawaiian muʻumuʻu.

(The dialogue continues in the same vein. Kū points to shoes, blackboard, book, dress, chair, etc. and Lono answers.)

ʻEONO

A. Pronouns.

This is the only table you are asked to memorize. Say the pronouns aloud over and over until you can say them from memory both vertically and horizontally without hesitation. Note particularly the macrons. This is one of the most important pages in the book.

Person	Singular	Dual	Plural
1	au/wau (I)	kāua (we, inc. 2)	kākou (we, inc. 3)
		māua (we, exc. 2)	mākou (we, exc. 3)
2	ʻoe (you, 1)	ʻolua (you, 2)	ʻoukou (you, 3)
3	ʻoia (he/she)	lāua (they, 2)	lākou (they, 3)

Explanations.

1. The dual is used for two people. The element *ua* is found in every dual term. It is probably related to *lua* (two).

2. The plural is used for more than two people. The element *kou* is found in every plural term. It is probably related to *kolu* (three).

3. The inclusive-exclusive distinction is made only in the first person dual and plural. *Kā-* is always inclusive, *mā-* exclusive.

4. No distinction is made between *he* and *she*. The *ʻo* in *ʻoia* is the subject marker. One can say *ia* but *ʻoia* is more common.

5. Note: All pronouns beginning with *ʻo-* have an initial glottal stop. All other pronouns (except *au/wau*) have macrons.

(1) *Maikaʻi lāua.*　　　　　(1) *They (2) are well.*
　　Maikaʻi lākou.　　　　　　*They (3) are well.*
　　Maʻi mākou.　　　　　　　*We (exc. 3) are sick.*
　　Maʻi māua.　　　　　　　*We (exc. 2) are sick.*
　　ʻAi nui lākou.　　　　　　*They (3) eat a lot/plenty.*

(2) *Hauʻoli ʻoia.*　　　　　(2) *She/he is happy.*
　　*ʻOluʻolu loa ʻoukou.　　　*You (3) are very kind.*

Nani lāua.	*They* (2) *are pretty.*
Hele kāua.	*We* (inc. 2) *go.*
Noho lāua.	They (2) stay.

The dancing pronouns

B.   Ke ana 'eono: nui nā (there are many).

Nui nā means "there are many" or "are big," depending on context. Nui nā kāma'a, the shoes are big/there are many shoes. The meaning "there are many" is very common. This pattern is in constant use. Start using it over and over.

(3)	*Nui nā noho.*	(3)	*There are many chairs.*
	Nui nā Kepanī.		There are many Japanese.
	Nui nā ali'i.		There are many chiefs.
	Nui nā 'āina.		There are many lands.
	Nui nā hale *hou.		There are many new houses.

(4) Nui nā *ha'awina.
Nui nā noho 'olu'olu.

Nui nā *ōlelo.
Nui nā kāne.

Nui ka 'ai.

(4) There are many lessons.
There are many comfortable chairs.
There are many languages.
There are many men/males/ husbands.
There is a lot/plenty of food/poi.

C.   He kama'ilio 'ana.

Kumu. E Noelani, 'o 'oe 'o 'Ā.
E Lopaka, 'o 'oe 'o Pī.
Mahalo.
A.   'O wai lāua?
B.   'O Keoni, lāua 'o Pua.

A.   Noho lāua i Waikīkī?

B.   *'Ae. Noho lāua me ka makuahine o Pua.*

A.   *Pehea ka hana a Keoni?*
B.   He kumu kula 'oia.
A.   He kumu mākaukau?
B.   'Ae, mākaukau loa.
A.   *Hānau 'oia ma O'ahu?*
B.   'Ae, *he keiki hānau o ka 'āina.*
A.   Pehea ka wahine?
B.   Hānau 'oia ma Hilo.
A.   Pehea? Maika'i 'o Hilo?

B.   'A'ole loa. *Nui ka ua.*
A.   Pehea 'o Honolulu?
B.   'A'ole maika'i. Nui ka po'e.
Nui nā malihini. Nui nā keiki. Nui ka pilikia.

K.   Lawa ka ha'awina. Mahalo nui.

C.   A conversation.

Teacher. O Noelani, you become A. O Robert, you become B. Thank you.
A.   Who are they (2)?
B.   John and Pua (John they-2 Pua).

A.   Do they (2) live at Waikīkī?

B.   Yes. *They live with Pua's mother* (the mother of Pua).

A.   *What's John's work?*
B.   He's a school teacher.
A.   A competent teacher?
B.   Yes, very competent.
A.   *Was he born on O'ahu?*
B.   Yes, *a child born of the land.*
A.   What of the wife?
B.   She was born in Hilo.
A.   How about it? Is Hilo okay?

B.   Not at all. *Too much rain.*
A.   How about Honolulu?
B.   No good. Too many people. Too many tourists. Too many children. Too much trouble.

T.   Enough lesson. Thank you.

ʻEHIKU

A. Numbers (nā huahelu).

1 ʻekahi, hoʻokahi	3 ʻekolu	5 ʻelima	7 ʻehiku	9 ʻeiwa
2 ʻelua	4 ʻehā	6 ʻeono	8 ʻewalu	10 ʻumi

Use *ʻekahi* in counting in a series; otherwise use *hoʻokahi*. All these numbers begin with *ʻe-* except *ʻumi*. All begin with a glottal stop.

B. *Nā wāhine ʻelua.*

Lopikana wahine. Aloha kāua.

Pinamu wahine. Aloha.

L. *Helu kāua.*

P. Hiki nō.

L. Helu i nā noho, e ʻoluʻolu ʻoe.

(Helu ʻo P.)

L. Helu i nā *haumana, i nā penikala, i nā *puke, i nā kāmaʻa, i nā *pepa, i nā papaʻeleʻele.
(Helu ʻo P.)

L. *Mahalo nui *loa.*

P. E Lopikana wahine, *pehea *keia haʻawina?

L. Haʻawina ʻehiku.

P. Maopopo iāʻoe keia haʻawina?

L. Maopopo iaʻu. Mākaukau loa.

B. *Two ladies.* (Note macron on plural.)

Mrs. Robinson. Hello.

Mrs. Bingham. Hello.

R. *Let's count.*

B. Certainly.

R. Count the chairs, please. (*I* precedes the object of a verb.)
(B counts.)

R. Count the students, pencils, books, shoes, papers, blackboards.

(B counts.)

R. *Thank you very much.*

B. O Mrs. Robinson, what is this lesson?

R. Lesson seven.

B. Do you understand this lesson?

R. I understand. (I'm) well prepared.

23

C. Ke ana ʻehiku: counting (ka helu ʻana).

(1) *ʻEhā aliʻi/nā aliʻi ʻehā.*

      ʻEkolu papaʻeleʻele.
      ʻElua wahi.
      Hoʻokahi penikala.
      ʻEwalu puke.

(1) *Four chiefs.* (Either model is acceptable, but the first is more common.)
Three blackboards.
Two places.
One pencil.
Eight books.

(2) *ʻEiwa noho ʻoluʻolu.*
      ʻUmi kāmaʻa.
      ʻEono kumu.
      ʻEhā lole.
      ʻEkahi, ʻelua, ʻekolu.

(2) *Nine comfortable chairs.*
Ten shoes.
Six teachers.
Four dresses.
One, two, three.

(3) ʻElua haumana akamai.
      ʻEhiku poʻe Kepanī.
      ʻEkolu poʻe Pākē.
      ʻElima hale nui.
      ʻElima hale hou.

(3) *Two smart students.*
Seven Japanese people.
Three Chinese.
Five big houses.
Five new houses.

D. Review of pronouns.
Write the table in *haʻawina ʻeono* from memory.

(4) Hānau lāua *ma Molokaʻi.

      Noho mākou ma Honolulu.
      Hele kākou i Punaluʻu.
      Namu haole māua.
      *Hele ʻolua i *ke kula.*

(4) They (2) were born on Molokaʻi.
We (exc. 3) live in Honolulu.
Let's (inc. 3) go to Punaluʻu.
We (2) speak (mutter) English.
You (2) go to school.

(5) *Heluhelu ʻoukou.*
      Hula maikaʻi lākou.
      Kokoke lāua i ke kula.
      Maʻi loa kō kākou makuakāne.
      Maikaʻi kō mākou kula.

(5) *You (3) read.*
They (3) dance well.
They (2) are close to school.
Our (inc. 3) father is very sick.
Our (exc. 3) school is good.

(6) Akamai kō mākou makuahine.
      Hele lāua i ka hana.

(6) Our (exc. 3) mother is smart.

They (2) go to work.

Helu maika'i 'oe.   (You) count well.
Namu haole lākou.   They (3) speak (mutter)
                                       English.
Hula kāua.   Let's (inc. 2) dance.

E.   Substitution drill.

Nui nā puke hou.
hale   Nui nā hale hou.
kama'āina   Nui nā kama'āina hou.
maika'i   Nui nā kama'āina maika'i.
'olu'olu   Nui nā kama'āina 'olu'olu.

There are many   good   shoes.
                  cool
                  haole
                  large

One   new   dress.
       cool
       fine
       Chinese

ʻEWALU

A.	He kamaʻilio ʻana.		A.	A conversation.	

A.	Aloha kakahiaka.		A.	Good morning.
B.	Aloha nō!		B.	Hi!
A.	ʻIke anei ʻoe i ka *hula?		A.	Do you know the hula?
B.	*ʻAʻole ʻike loa. *Hemahema.* ʻAʻole *au ʻike i ka hula.		B.	(I) don't know well. (I'm) *awkward/unskilled/ incompetent/unprepared.* I don't know the dance.
A.	ʻIke anei ʻoe i ka helu?		A.	Do you know how to count?
B.	ʻIke loa.		B.	(I) sure do know.
A.	Helu ʻoe!		A.	Count! (B counts from one to ten.)
A.	Maikaʻi kēlā. ʻIke anei ʻoe i ka ʻōlelo Hawaiʻi?		A.	That's good. Do you know the Hawaiian language?
B.	ʻIke hemahema.		B.	(I) don't know well. (Know imperfectly.)
A.	ʻIke ʻoe i ka ʻōlelo *Pākē?		A.	Do you know the Chinese language?
B.	ʻAʻole ʻike pono.		B.	(I) don't know correctly.
A.	ʻIke ʻoe i keia puke?		A.	Do you see this book? (A holds up a book.)
B.	ʻIke.		B.	Sure. (Literally, see.)
A.	ʻIke ʻoe i keia penikala?		A.	Do you see this pencil? (A holds pencil behind his back.)
B.	ʻAʻole au ʻike i kēnā penikala.		B.	I don't see that (near) pencil.
A.	*ʻIke ʻoe i keia mea?*		A.	*Do you see this thing/person?* (A holds up anything or points to a person.)
B.	ʻAe.		B.	Yes.

A. 'Ike 'oe iā _____ ?

B. 'Ike loa.

A. 'Ike 'oe ia'u?

B. 'A'ole. *'O wai kou inoa?

A. 'O _____ .

A. Do you know _____ ?
   (A inserts the name of a fellow student.)

B. I know (him/her) well.

A. Do you know me?

B. No. What's your name?

   (A tells his name.)

B. Ke ana 'ewalu: *i/iā* marking direct and indirect objects. This is the most difficult lesson in the book, but difficult only because it is easy to forget the marker, or because some students confuse the object of a verb with a predicate nominative.

Models: 'Ike au i ka papa'ele'ele. I see the blackboard.
'Ike au iā lākou. I see them.
'Ike au iā Kalei. I see Kalei.

Comments: *Iā* replaces *i* before pronouns and names of people. It is customary to write *ia'u, iāia*, and *iā'oe* as single words. *I/iā* means "to/at" as in (4) below. Translation of *'ike* by "see" or "know" depends on context: *'Ike au i ka lei* has to mean "see." *'Ike au i ka ha'awina* probably means "know."

(1) Makemake mākou i ka hula.
Makemake lākou i ke kula.
Makemake lāua i kēlā keiki.
Makemake au iā'oe.
Makemake au iāia.

(1) We (exc. 3) like/want the hula.
They (3) like school.
They (2) like that child.
I like you (1).
I like him/her.

(2) *Aloha 'o Kū iāia.*
Aloha 'o Kū iā'oe.
Aloha au iā'oe.
'Ai māua i ka 'ai.
'Ai lāua i ka mea'ai.

(2) *Kū loves her.*
Kū loves you.
I love you (1)
We (exc. 2) eat poi.
They eat the food.

(3) 'Ike au iā Lei.
'Ike 'oe ia'u.
Aloha 'oe ia'u.
Makemake 'oe ia'u.
'Ike ka haole iāia.

(3) I see Lei.
You see me.
You love me.
You like me.
The haole sees her.

(4) *Kākau au iāia.*
Kākau 'oia iā Mele.
*Hele iā Luka.
Kākau i *nā wāhine ma'i.
Maopopo iā'oe?

(5) Pehea 'oe? *Hemahema?*

Pono kēlā kanaka.
Hau'oli kō mākou makua.
'Olu'olu keia Pokoliko.
Akamai nō 'oia.

(4) *I write to him/her.*
He writes to Mary.
Go to Ruth.
Write to the sick ladies.
Do you understand?

(5) How are you? *Awkward/
ignorant?*
That man is honest.
Our (exc. 3) *parent is happy.*
This Puerto Rican is polite.
He's quite smart.
(In this group there are no
object markers. Why?)

C.   Nā huahelu.

C.   Numbers.

(6) *'Umi-kūmā-kahi/'umi-
kumamā-kahi.*
'Umi-kūmā-lua.
'Umi-kūmā-kolu.
'Umi-kūmā-hā.

(6) *Eleven.*

Twelve.
Thirteen.
Fourteen. Numbers through
nineteen are formed in
the same way. Remember
macrons on *kūmā.* The
kumamā form is rare
Biblical usage.)

(7) 'Umi-kūmā-iwa,
'umi-kūmā-lua.
'Umi-kūmā-hā, 'umi-
kūmā-walu.
'Umi-kūmā-kahi, umi-
kūmā-kolu.
'Umi-kūmā-lima, 'umi-
kūmā-hiku.
'Umi-kūmā-ono, 'umi-
kūmā-lua.

(7)   19, 12.

14, 18.

11, 13.

15, 17.

16, 12.

Translate: 8, 12, 16, 19, 15, 11, 13, 18, 14, 17, 19, 18, 17, 16, and so on to 1;
1, 2, 3, and so on to 19.

D. Hawaiian children sang the multiplication tables, as the following (for reference). *'Alua* is a variant of *'elua.*

'Alua kahi, 'alua.
'Alua lua, 'ahā.
'Alua kolu, 'aono.
'Alua hā, 'awalu.
'Alua lima, 'umi.
'Alua ono, 'umi-kūmā-lua.

E. Particles learned thus far.

ke, ka	the (singular)	Intensifiers
nā	the (plural)	learned are
he	a	*nō* and *noho'i.*
'o	subject marker	
i/iā	object marker, to	
e	vocative	
i	to	
i, ma	at, in, on, to	
me	with	

ʻEIWA

A.	Ke kula.	A.	School.

Kumu. He kula Hawaiʻi keia. Komo mai. E nānā aku ʻoe i ka puke.

Teacher. This is a Hawaiian school. Come in. Look at the book.

Haumana. Hiki.

Student. All right.

K. *E nānā aku ʻoe i ka ʻaoʻao ʻumi-kūmā-hā.*

T. *(You) look at page 14.*

H. Ka ʻaoʻao ʻumi-kūmā-hā. Maopopo *iaʻu.

S. Page 14. I understand.

K. E heluhelu mai ʻoe i ka haʻawina ʻumi.

T. (You) read lesson 10.

H. Haʻawina ʻumi. *Eia.*

S. Lesson 10. *Here it is.*

K. *E heluhelu mai ʻoe i kekahi huaʻōlelo hou.*

T. *(You) read a/another new word.*

H. *Pukikī, he huaʻōlelo hou ia. Kōlea, he huaʻōlelo hou ia.*

S. *Portuguese, that's a new word. Korean, that's a new word.*

K. *He aha ka manaʻo o Pukikī?*

T. *What's the meaning of Pukikī?*

H. ʻAʻole au e ʻike. ʻAʻole *mākaukau.

S. I don't know. Unprepared.

K. ʻO Portuguese. He huaʻōlelo haole ia. Pehea ka manaʻo o Kōlea?

T. Portuguese. That's an English word. What's the meaning of Kōlea?

H. ʻIke. ʻO Korean.

S. (I) know. Korean.

K. ʻAe. *Pono nō ʻoe. Mākaukau.

T. Yes. You are quite right. Prepared.

B. Ke ana ʻeiwa: *e (verb) ʻoe*, imperative.

A command to one person is expressed by *e (verb) ʻoe*. The subject *ʻoe* is commonly expressed in Hawaiian. Form the habit of *e (verb) ʻoe*.

Hawaiian uses the same pattern for the third person, and this is a common way to translate English "should, ought, must." Practice the commands listed below. The intonation should show that they are commands. Note: they are still commands without the initial *e* if the intonation so indicates. Practice with and without *e*.

E hele aku ʻoe. E hele mai ʻoe.	*Go away. Come.*
E hele mai ʻoe e *ʻai.	Come and eat.
E ʻai ʻoe. E noho ʻoe.	Eat. Stay.
E ʻai ʻoe i keia hua.	*Eat this fruit.*
E ʻai ke Kōlea.	The Korean must eat.
E noho ʻoia i keia noho.	He ought to sit in this chair.

C. Delete the imperative marker *e* and the pronoun subjects in the following:

E nānā aku ʻoe i ka papaʻeleʻele.	Look at the blackboard.
E komo mai ʻoe.	Come in.
E heluhelu mai ʻoe i nā noho.	Count the chairs.
I ʻai ʻoukou i keia mea.	Eat this thing.
E aloha aku ʻoe i ke kumu hou.	Greet the new teacher.
E ʻai ʻolua.	Eat (to two people).

ʻUMI

A.	*He mele.*	A.	*A song.*

Pua.	Aloha *kāua.	Pua.	Hello (we 2 inc.).
Ke-kai-malu.	Aloha nō.	Ke-kai-malu.	Hello there.
P.	Pehea ʻoe?	P.	How are you?
K.	Maikaʻi nō.	K.	Fine.
P.	E Ke-kai-malu.	P.	O Ke-kai-malu.
K.	ʻAe.	K.	Yes.
P.	ʻIke ʻoe i nā mele?	P.	Do you know songs?
K.	Pehea?	K.	What about it?
P.	Nā mele Pukikī?	P.	Portuguese songs?
K.	ʻAʻole loa.	K.	Certainly not/(I) sure don't.
P.	Nā mele Pokoliko?	P.	Puerto Rican songs?
K.	ʻAʻole loa.	K.	(I) certainly don't.
P.	Nā mele Pilipino?	P.	Filipino songs?
K.	ʻAʻole loa.	K.	Certainly not.
P.	Nā mele Hawaiʻi?	P.	Hawaiian songs?
K.	ʻAe. ʻIke nō. Mākaukau.	K.	Yes. (I) do know (some). (I'm) clever.
P.	Ua ʻike ʻoe i ka mele *"Nā moku ʻehā"?*	P.	Do you know the song *"The Four Islands"?*
K.	ʻIke hemahema. Hilahila.	K.	(I) know (it) awkwardly. (I'm) bashful.
P.	Tsa! *E mele mai ʻoe!*	P.	O dear/shucks! (You) *go on and sing!*

B.	Nā Moku ʻEhā.	B.	The Four Islands.

Hanohano Hawaiʻi la.

Lei ka lehua la.
Kuahiwi nani la, ʻo Mauna-kea.

Glorious Hawaiʻi (la is for rhythm).

Lehua is the lei.
The beautiful mountain is Mauna-kea.

Kilakila ʻo Maui la, lei lokelani la.	*Majestic Maui,* rose the lei.
Kuahiwi nani la, ʻo Hale-a-ka-lā.	The beautiful mountain is Hale-a-ka-lā.
ʻOhuʻohu Oʻahu la, lei ka ʻilima la.	*Oʻahu is lei bedecked,* ʻilima is the lei.
Kuahiwi nani la, ʻo Kaʻala.	The beautiful mountain is Kaʻala.
Haʻaheo Kauaʻi la, lei mokihana la.	Kauaʻi cherishes the mokihana lei.
Kuahiwi nani la, Wai-ʻaleʻale.	The beautiful mountain is Wai-ʻaleʻale.
Haʻina ʻia mai ana ka puana la: Nā moku ʻehā o ka Pākīpika.	*Tell the refrain:* The four islands of the Pacific.

C. Ke ana ʻumi: ua hele au i Molokaʻi, *I went to Molokaʻi.* Ua maikaʻi au, *I am well. Ua* is a particle that introduces verbs. It marks completed action, and is translated into English by past tense and by present tense with the meaning "present state," as illustrated above.

(1) *Ua ʻike ʻoe i ka ʻōlelo Pilipino?*
    Ua ʻike **ʻoia i ka ʻōlelo Kōlea.
    Ua hele lāua i Kōlea.
    Ua makemake *lākou i kēlā mea.
    Ua aloha ka hapa haole i kou poʻe.

(1) *Do you know the Filipino language?*
    He knows the Korean language.
    They (2) went to Korea.
    They (3) like that thing/ person.
    The hapa haole loves your people.

(2) Ua nani ke keiki.
    Ua uʻi nā wāhine.

    Ua lapuwale lākou.

    Ua pupuka ka manaʻo o ka huaʻōlelo.
    Ua hemahema ka haumana.

(2) The child is pretty.
    The women are youthfully beautiful.
    They (3) are no good/ worthless.
    The meaning of the word is ugly.
    The student is awkward.

D. Abstract nouns in Hawaiian are preceded by the article or other *k*-word. Models: ke aloha, kona nani, kēlā hemahema, ka hilahila, ke Akua, ke akamai, ka hanohano. One also says *ke kula*. If the student is thinking in Hawaiian, rather than in English, he will say *ke/ka* or other *k*-word with such terms.

(3) Maika'i ke aloha.
Aloha au i ke Akua.
Pupuka ka hemahema.
U'i ka mana'o.
'A'ole maika'i ka hilahila.

(3) Love is good.
I love God/the ghost.
Lack of skill is ugly.
Thinking is beautiful.
Bashfulness/shame is no good.

(4) 'A'ole maika'i ka lapuwale.

Maika'i ka nani.
Makemake 'oia i ka u'i.

Ha'aheo lāua i ka lāhui.

'A'ole maika'i ke kula.
Me ke aloha.

(4) Being worthless/without value is no good.
Beauty is fine/good.
He likes beauty/youthful heroism.
They cherish the nation/race.
School is no good.
With aloha.

E. He kama'ilio 'ana.

A. 'O wai kēlā wahine u'i?

B. 'O wai la, *'a'ole au e 'ike i kona *inoa.*

A. He aha kona lāhui?

B. Ka lāhui Kōlea.

A. *Makemake au e 'ike iāia.* He u'i.

B. 'Ae, he nani loa.

A. Kōkua mai! Makemake au e 'ike iāia.

B. Tsa! He lapuwale 'oe!

A. *U'i na maka!*

B. Lapuwale!

E. A conversation.

A. Who is that beautiful woman?

B. How should I know who, *I don't know her name.*

A. What is her race?

B. The Korean race.

A. *I want to know her.* (She's) a beauty. (*E* introduces a subordinate verb of purpose.)

B. Yes, (she's) very pretty.

A. Help! I want to know her.

B. Goodness! You're no good!

A. *Beautiful eyes!*

B. (You) good-for-nothing!

A. Kōkua mai! Makemake au e 'ike iāia.	A. Help! I want to know her.
B. 'A'ole loa! Lapuwale!	B. I should say not! Good-for-nothing!
A. Kōkua mai!	A. Help!
B. 'A'ole loa! Hilahila au.	B. I should say not. I'm bashful.
A. *'A'ole aloha?*	A. *No pity/mercy/aloha?*
B. 'A'ole loa!	B. Not a bit.

F. *Hoe-wa'a* versus *hoe-i-ka-wa'a*. The common *hoe-wa'a* type of construction may be called a compound. See ha'awina 'umi-kūmā-kahi, A.

E 'ai-poi ana 'oe.	You are eating-poi.
E 'ai ana 'oe i ka poi.	You are eating the poi.
Heluhelu-puke *kākou.	Let's read-books.
Heluhelu kākou i ka puke.	Let's read the book.
Ua 'ōlelo-Pākē lāua.	They speak-Chinese.
Ua 'ōlelo lāua i ka 'ōlelo Pākē.	They speak the Chinese language.
Hoe-wa'a mākou.	*We paddle-canoe.*
Hoe mākou i ka wa'a.	We paddle the canoe.

G. Repeat the dialogue in ha'awina 'eiwa, A, but change the page numbers (as 16, 14, 12, 11), lesson numbers, and vocabulary.

ʻUMI-KŪMĀ-KAHI

A. E (verb) ana, progressive.

A.	*Pehea kā ʻoukou hana?*		A.	*What are you (3) doing?*
B.	E ʻai poi ana au.		B.	I'm eating-poi.
C.	E heluhelu puke ana au.		C.	I'm reading-a-book.
D.	*E kākau leka ana au.*		D.	*I'm writing-a-letter.*

A.	*Kēlā ʻapōpō*, pehea kā ʻoukou hana?		A.	*Tomorrow*, what will you (3) do?
B.	*E hoʻomaʻamaʻa ana au* i ka haʻawina Hawaiʻi.		B.	*I'll practice* the Hawaiian lesson.
C.	E hoe waʻa ana au.		C.	I'll canoe-paddle.
D.	*E holoholo ana au.*		D.	*I'll go-riding.*

A.	Pehea ka hana a nā keiki i *kēlā makahiki aku nei?*		A.	What did the children do *last year?*
B.	*E pāʻani ana lākou.*		B.	*They were playing.*
C.	E hele kula ana lākou.		C.	They were going to school.
D.	E hula ana lākou.		D.	They were dancing.

Note: *e (verb) ana* translates English present, future, and imperfect tenses. It denotes action continuing and unfinished.

B. Contrast of *e (verb)* and *e (verb) ana.*

(1)	E hele aku ʻoe.		(1)	Go away (you-1).
	E hele aku ana ʻoe.			You were/will be going away.
	E aloha ʻoia i ke *aliʻi.			He ought to love the chief.
	E aloha ana ʻoia i ke aliʻi.			He will love the chief.
	E kākau ʻoukou i ka haʻawina.			Write (you-all) the lesson.
	E kākau ana ʻoukou i ka puke.			You (3) were writing the book.

C.   Contrast of *ua* and *e (verb)*.

(No one will treat an utterance beginning with *ua* as a command. If you want someone to do something, begin speaking with *e!*)

(2)	Ua aloha aku ʻoe i ke Akua.	(2)	You love/loved God.
	E aloha aku ʻoe i ke Akua.		Love God.
	Ua hoʻomaʻamaʻa lākou i ka haʻawina.		They practiced the lesson.
	E hoʻomaʻamaʻa lākou i ka haʻawina.		They should practice the lesson.
	E mele mai ʻoe.		*Sing (you-1).*
	Ua mele mai ʻoe.		You (1) sang.

D.   Practice with object markers.

In the following sentences, note how the presence or absence of *i/iā* changes the meaning.

(3)	Nīnau ke Kōlea.	(3)	The Korean asks questions.
	Nīnau i ke Kōlea.		Ask the Korean.
	*Pane ke *kumu.*		*The teacher answers.*
	Pane i ke kumu.		Answer the teacher.
	*ʻIke ʻoia.		He knows.
	ʻIke iāia.		See him.
	Hele aku iā Kalani.		Go to Kalani.
	Hele aku ʻo Kalani.		Kalani goes.

E.   *He kiʻi.*   E.   *A picture.*

A.	E nānā aku ʻoe i ke kiʻi.	A.	Look at the picture.
B.	E nānā aku ana au i ke kiʻi.	B.	I am looking at the picture.
A.	*ʻEhia *poʻe ma ke kiʻi?*	A.	*How many people in the picture?*
B.	ʻEiwa.	B.	Nine.
A.	ʻEhia kāne?	A.	How many men?
B.	ʻElima kāne.	B.	Five men.
A.	ʻEhia wāhine?	A.	How many women? (Note macron in *wāhine* as plural marker.)
B.	ʻEhā wāhine.	B.	Four women.

A. ʻEhia haole?	A. How many haoles?
B. ʻElua. E noho ana *lāua.	B. Two. They are sitting down.
A. *ʻEhia kānaka e kū ana?*	A. *How many people are standing?* (Note macron in *kānaka* as plural marker.)
B. ʻElua.	B. Two.
A. ʻO wai ke aliʻi nui?	A. Who is the big chief?
B. ʻO Kamehameha ʻEkahi.	B. Kamehameha the First.
A. Ua kū ʻoia?	A. Is he standing?
B. ʻAʻole. Ua noho. E noho ana.	B. No. (He) is seated. (He) is sitting.
A. *ʻO wai ke aliʻi wahine?*	A. *Who is the chiefess?*
B. ʻO Ka-ʻahu-manu. Ua noho ka lani.	B. Ka-ʻahu-manu. The royalty is seated.
A. Ua makemake ʻoe i keia kiʻi?	A. Do you like this picture?
B. ʻAe. Ua nani loa.	B. Yes. (It) is very pretty.
A. *He aha ka haʻawina* o ke kiʻi?	A. *What is the lesson* of the picture?
(Pane ʻo B.)	(B answers.)
Pau nā nīnau. Ua lawa.	The questions are finished. Enough.

F.   Nā nīnau: Pehea. (For this drill the teacher may ask the students to sit in three separate groups of one, two, or three or more persons.)

A. Pehea ʻoe?	A. (To B.) How are you?
B. Maikaʻi *nō au. *ʻOia mau nō.*	B. I'm quite fine. *Same as usual.*
A. Pehea ʻolua?	A. (To B, C.) How are you?
B, C. Maikaʻi nō māua.	B, C. We're quite fine.
A. Pehea ʻoukou?	A. (To D, E, F.) How are you?
D, E, F. Maikaʻi nō *mākou.	D, E, F. We're quite fine.
A. ʻEhia ʻoukou?	A. (To G, H, I, J.) How many are you?
G, H, I, J. ʻEhā mākou.	G, H, I, J. We are four.

A points to several students, and B counts them. If A points to two students he says *lāua*.

G.   Translation: he moʻolelo no (story concerning) Kawelo.

ʻO wai ʻo Kawelo? He aliʻi ʻoia. He aliʻi nui. Hānau ʻoia ma Kauaʻi.
Ua ʻai nui ʻo Kawelo. Ua ʻai ʻoia i nā laulau kanahā (forty leaf packages
of food). Tsa! ʻAʻole lawa keia. ʻAi hou nō. Kanahā laulau. Auwē nohoʻi
e! He aha ke kumu o (reason for) keia ʻai nui? Pehea? Ua ʻike ʻoe? ʻAe,
ua ʻike. He akua ma-loko-o (within) Kawelo. ʻAi nō nā akua i keia
meaʻai, he nui loa.

*Kamehameha me Ka-ʻahu-manu me nā malihini haole, ʻo Kotzubue lāua
ʻo Choris. He mau Lukia. Mahope, kaha (draw) kiʻi ʻo Choris. Ka inoa o
ke kiʻi: "Kamehameha in a Red Vest." Aia keia kiʻi ma ka Hale Hōʻikeʻike
o Kamehameha (Bishop Museum).*

ʻUMI-KŪMĀ-LUA

A. Ke ana ʻumi-kūmā-lua: directionals.

> *mai: towards the speaker; come!
> aku: away from the speaker
> iho: down, downward; to come down

The directionals are commonly *not* translated into English:

> Nānā aku nā *wāhine: the women are looking (i.e., that way).
> Nānā mai nā wāhine: the women are looking (i.e., this way).

But note the differences in meaning with *hele aku* and *hele mai. Hele aku* is more definite than *hele.*

> hele: to go   hele aku: to go   hele mai: to come

Mai can be used as a verb in the imperative, but only alone, and *never* with the verb markers thus far studied, *e, e (verb) ana, ua. (Mai!* Come!) *Iho*, in contrast, can be used with the verb markers like most verbs.

Ua nānā aku ke kupuna i ke kuahiwi. *E piʻi aku ana* kekahi poʻe. *ʻŌlelo aku ʻo Tūtū:* "Ūi! *E iho hou mai!* Mai! Mai e ʻai!" *Hoʻi hou mai* ka poʻe. Ua ʻai lākou. Pau ka ʻai, hoʻi hou aku lākou a piʻi hou i ke kuahiwi.	*The grandmother looked up* at the mountain. Some people *were climbing up. Granny* said: "Hallo! *Come down again.* Come! Come and eat!" The people *came back again.* They ate. After eating, they went back again and climbed the mountain again.

B. Pehea. Note how many ways *pehea* is translated in the following:

1.	*Pehea ʻoe? ʻOia mau nō.*	1.	How are you? Same as usual.
2.	Pehea ʻoukou? Maikaʻi nō mākou.	2.	How are you (3)? We (exc. 3) are fine.

3. Pehea lākou? Maikaʻi nō
   lākou.
4. Pehea ka haʻawina?
   Maikaʻi nō ia.
5. Pehea ke kupuna? *Maikaʻi*
   nō ia.
6. *Pehea ka moʻolelo?* ʻAʻole
   ia e maikaʻi.
7. Pehea? ʻAʻole maopopo iaʻu.

3. How are they (3)? They
   (3) are fine.
4. What about the lesson?
   It's fine.
5. How is the grandparent?
   He/she is fine.
6. *What about the story?*
   It's no good.
7. What? I don't understand.

C. Change the following from *ua* sentences to *e* (verb) *ana* sentences.

Ua piʻi aku ʻoia.
Ua ʻai ʻoia.
Ua nānā aku ʻoia.
Ua iho mai ʻoia.
Ua hoʻomaʻamaʻa ʻoia.
Ua hoe-waʻa-mai ʻoia.
Ua pane mai ʻoia.

Repeat the sentences with *ua* and *e* (verb) *ana* using different subjects:
lākou, ke kumu, ke kupuna.

ʻUMI-KŪMĀ-KOLU

A. Ke ana ʻumi-kūmā-kolu: Locatives (words expressing location).

$$i \quad ma- \left\{ \begin{array}{l} luna \\ lalo \\ mua \\ waena \\ hope \\ loko \\ waho \\ kai \\ uka \end{array} \right\} o$$

Note carefully that *o* "of" connects each locative with a following noun: *i lalo o ka pepa,* under the paper. If you are thinking in Hawaiian you will add this *o* automatically. It is customary in writing to join *ma-* to the following locative, as *maluna, malalo, mauka, makai.* The particles *i* and *ma-* may ordinarily be used interchangeably, but see 14G. The locatives can be used also as nouns without *i/ma-* and *o,* as *ka luna* "the boss/the top" and *ke kai* "the sea."

(1) *Malalo o ka pepa.*
I luna o ke kāmaʻa.
I loko o ka lole.
Mawaho o ka hale. Maloko.
Makai o ka hale. Mauka o ka hale.

(1) *Under the paper.*
On/on top of the shoe.
In the dress.
Outside the house. Inside.
Seaward of the house. Inland/ mauka of the house.

(2) *Mahope o ka moʻolelo.*
(Mahape is a common colloquial variant.)
Mahope o ka haʻawina.
Hele aku ʻoe i kai.
Hele aku ʻoe i uka.
I mua. I hope.

(2) *After the story.*

After the lesson.
Go seaward.
Go inland.
Forward. Backward.

(3) *Waena.*
Mawaena o nā kuahiwi.
Mawaena o ke kuahiwi.
Mawaena o ka pepa.
Mawaena o nā pepa.
Mawaena o ka hula.
Mawaena o nā hula.

(3) *Middle, between, center.*
Between the mountains.
In the middle of the mountain.
In the middle of the paper.
Between the papers.
In the middle of the hula.
Between the hulas.

(4) Be careful to insert *o* where needed in the following sentences:

On top of the chair.   Outside the fruit.
Below/under the house.   Inside the book.
Before/in front of the chiefess.   On top of/on the mountain.
Between the pictures.   After the dance.
In the middle of the page.   Seaward of the school house.

B. He kamaʻilio ʻana.

Kumu.   *E ka papa, e *nānā
hou ʻoukou i ke kiʻi.

Haumana. *Mahea?*

K.   Ma ka haʻawina ʻumi-
kūmā-kahi.

H.   Hiki. Hiki nō.

K.   Mahea ʻo Kamehameha?

H.   Maloko o ke kiʻi.

K.   Pono nō ʻoe. Mahea
maloko o ke kiʻi?

H.   Mamua o ka hale.

K.   Maikaʻi nō ka pane.
Mahea ka pāpale haole?

H.   *Mahope o ka haole mua.*

K.   He haumana *akamai ʻoe.

H.   ʻAe. Akamai.

K.   He aha kēlā mea mahope
o ke aliʻi wahine.

H.   He kāhili. *He mea nui ia.*

K.   Pono nō ʻoe. ʻEhia haole
e noho ana ma ke kiʻi?

H.   ʻElua.

K.   Mahea ka puke?

H.   *Ma ka ʻaoʻao o ka haole.*

K.   Mahalo.

H.   ʻAʻole pilikia.

B. A conversation.

Teacher.   O class, look at the
picture again.

Student.   *Where?*

T.   In lesson 11.

S.   Okay, okay.

T.   Where is Kamehameha?

S.   In the picture.

T.   You are right. Where in the
picture?

S.   In front of the house.

T.   The answer is good/fine.
Where is the foreign hat?

S.   *Behind/in back of the first
haole.*

T.   You are a smart student.

S.   Yes, (I am) smart.

T.   What's that thing behind
the chiefess?

S.   A feather standard. *It's an
important thing.*

T.   You are right. How many
haoles are sitting in the
picture?

S.   Two.

T.   Where is the book?

S.   *At the side of/beside the
haole.*

T.   Thank you.

S.   It was no trouble.

C. Hoʻomaʻamaʻa.

    A. He aha nā lāhui ma Hawaiʻi?

    B. He Hawaiʻi, he Pilipino, he Pākē, he *Kepanī, he Pokoliko, he Kōlea, he haole, he Pukikī, he hapa haole.

    A. Maikaʻi loa ka pane. Pehea ka *moʻolelo no Kawelo?*

    B. He aliʻi ia. *Hānau ʻoia ma Kauaʻi. ʻAi nui ʻoia. ʻAi i ka poi. *Kanahā laulau.* ʻAʻole *lawa. ʻAi hou no.

    A. *He *kanaka hūpō paha?*

    B. ʻAʻole loa! He aliʻi nui. *Aia he akua.*

    A. Mahea?

    B. Maloko o Kawelo. ʻAi nō ke akua i keia meaʻai. He nui loa.

C. Practice.

    A. What are the races in Hawaiʻi?

    B. Hawaiian, Filipino, Chinese, Japanese, Puerto Rican, Korean, haole, Portuguese, hapa haole/half white.

    A. The answer is very good. What is the *story about/ concerning Kawelo?*

    B. He was a chief. He was born on Kauaʻi. He ate very much. (He) ate poi. *Forty leaf packages.* It wasn't enough. He just ate again.

    A. *Maybe he was a fool?*

    B. Certainly not! (He) was an important chief. *There was a god.*

    A. Where?

    B. Inside Kawelo. The god just ate this food. A great deal.

D. Nani ke Ao Nei, by Mary Kawena Pukui.

I luna la, i luna
Nā manu o ka lewa.

manu: bird; lewa: air

I lalo la, i lalo
Nā pua o ka honua.

pua: flower; honua: land

I uka la, i uka
Nā ulu lāʻau.

ulu lāʻau: forest

I kai la, i kai
Nā iʻa o ka moana.

iʻa: fish; moana: open sea

Haʻina mai ka puana:
A he nani ke ao nei.

ke ao nei: this earth

ʻUMI-KŪMĀ-HĀ

A. *O*-form possessives.

This table is important but it is not as difficult as the table in haʻawina ʻeono because there is little that is new in it. Some students confuse pronouns and possessives. The term "pronoun" in Hawaiian refers only to personal pronouns. If you have trouble distinguishing pronouns and possessives, ask your instructor for help.

Person	Singular	Dual	Plural
1	koʻu (my)	kō kāua (our, inc. 2)	kō kākou (our, inc. 3)
		kō māua (our, exc. 2)	kō mākou (our, exc. 3)
2	kou (your)	kō ʻolua (your, 2)	kō ʻoukou (your, 3)
3	kona (his, her)	kō lāua (their, 2)	kō lākou (their, 3)

Note that the dual and plural forms consist simply of *kō* before the dual and plural pronouns.

(1) *Nui koʻu pāpale.*   (1) *My hat is big.*
    Lohi kou waʻa.   *Your canoe is slow/late.*
    Nui koʻu hemahema.   I am most incompetent.
    Kokoke koʻu kula.   My school is near.
    ʻAʻole kokoke kou kula.   Your school is not near.

B. Ke ana ʻumi-kūmā-hā: He hale koʻu (I have a house).

There is no verb "to have" in Hawaiian. A common way to express "to have/own" is by this important pattern. Note that the Hawaiian possessives are here translated by English personal pronouns.

45

(2) He waʻa koʻu.   (2) I have a canoe.
He pāpale koʻu.   I have a hat.
He lei koʻu.   I have a lei.
He hale koʻu.   I have a house.
He pāʻū koʻu.   I have a sarong.

(3) The same as (2), but using *kou* and *kona*.

C. *Nui* again.

Thus far *nui* has meant "big, large" (haʻawina ʻekahi) and "there are many" (haʻawina ʻeono). *Nui* also may mean "much/very."

(4) Nui kona uʻi.   (4) She has much youthful beauty (much her beauty).

Nui kou hilahila.   *You have much shame.*
Nui kona naʻauao.   *He is very wise* (much his wisdom).

Nui kona naʻaupō.   *He is very ignorant* (much his ignorance).

Nui kona akamai.   He is very smart (much his smartness).

D. Hoʻomaʻamaʻa.   D. Practice.

(5) *Mahalo au i kou pāpale.*   (5) *I admire your hat.* (Since *kou* is a possessive and not a pronoun, the object marker is *i*, not *iā*. Nānā i ka haʻawina ʻewalu.)

Mahalo ʻoia i koʻu kupuna wahine.   He admires/thanks my grandmother.
*Makemake ʻoe i koʻu moʻolelo.   You like my story.
ʻO wai kou makuakāne?   Who is your father?
ʻO wai kona makuahine?   Who is his mother?

(6) He waʻa kona.   (6) He has a canoe.
He noho ʻoluʻolu kō lāua.   They (2) have a comfortable chair.

He pāpale ko'u.

He makuahine 'olu'olu kō
kākou.

He akua kō mākou.

(7) He mana'o hanohano kō
'oukou.

He moku kilakila kō lākou.

He lei nani kou.

He inoa hanohano kona.

He mele hou ko'u.

I have a hat.

We (inc. 3) have a kind
mother.

We (exc. 3) have a god.

(7) You (3) have a glorious
idea.

They (3) have a majestic
island.

You have a pretty lei.

He has a glorious name.

I have a new song.

E. He kama'ilio 'ana.

A. Aloha ahiahi.
B. Aloha. Pehea 'oe?
A. 'Oia mau nō. Pehea
'oe?
B. 'Oia mau nō.
A. Mahea kou hale?
B. Aia mauka loa.
A. *Mamao loa?*
B. 'Ae, mamao.
A. Mahea?
B. Mawaena *o nā kuahiwi.

A. *He lumi 'olu'olu kou?*
B. 'Ae, he lumi 'olu'olu
ko'u. Ma ka 'ao'ao.
A. Ka 'ao'ao makai?
B. 'A'ole. Ka 'ao'ao mauka.
A. *He ki'i maloko o kou
lumi?*
B. 'A'ole. He ki'i mawaho.
Ma Ka-lihi-waena ko'u
hale.
A. Mahea 'o Ka-lihi-waena?
B. *Aia mawaena o Ka-lihi-kai
ame Ka-lihi-uka.*

E. A conversation.

A. Good evening.
B. Hello. How are you?
A. Same as usual. How are
you?
B. Same as usual.
A. Where is your house?
B. There far inland.
A. *Very far?*
B. Yes, far.
A. Where?
B. In the midst of the
mountains.

A. *Do you have a cool room?*
B. Yes, I have a cool room.
On the side.
A. The sea side?
B. No. The mountain side.
A. *Is there a picture/statue/
doll inside of your room?*
B. No. There's a statue
outside. My house is at
Ka-lihi-waena.
A. Where is Ka-lihi-waena?
B. *There between Ka-lihi-kai
and Ka-lihi-uka.*

A.	Mahea ʻo Punaluʻu?	A.	Where is Punaluʻu?
B.	Ma ka ʻaoʻao Koʻolau o Oʻahu.	B.	On the Koʻolau side of Oʻahu.
A.	Mahea ʻo Honolulu?	A.	Where is Honolulu?
B.	Ma ka ʻaoʻao Kona o Oʻahu.	B.	On the Kona side of Oʻahu.
A.	Mahea ʻo Maui?	A.	Where is Maui?
B.	Mawaena o Hawaiʻi ame Molokaʻi.	B.	Between Hawaiʻi and Molokaʻi.

F. Object markers again. Translate the following:

Nānā ke aliʻi. Nānā i ke aliʻi.
Aloha ka wahine. Aloha i ka wahine.
Hele i ka Pilipino. Hele ka Pilipino.
Pane ke Kepanī. Pane i ke Kepanī.
ʻAi ka pōpoki. ʻAi i ka pōpoki.
Mahalo ʻoe. Mahalo iāʻoe.

G. The prepositions *i* and *ma*. The meaning of *i* is slightly more precise than that of *ma*. *I uka* is "in the uplands" and *mauka* is "in the general direction of the mountains, mountainward." *Ua noho au i Waikīkī ma Honolulu,* "I live in Waikīkī in Honolulu." One need not worry about which preposition to use unless there is a contrast in the size of two areas, as in the preceding sentence. *I* then precedes the smaller area, and *ma* the larger one.

Insert *i* or *ma* in the following.

Aia (there is) koʻu kula _____ Mānoa _____ Honolulu.
ʻO kona hale, aia _____ Hilo _____ Hawaiʻi.
Ua noho lākou _____ Tokyo _____ ka ʻāina Kepanī.

ʻUMI-KŪMĀ-LIMA

A. Ke ana ʻumi-kūmā-lima: He hale *kō ka Pokoliko (the Puerto Rican has a house).

This is a variation of *ke ana ʻumi-kūmā-hā*. A literal translation of the example: a house belonging-to the Puerto Rican.

(1) He waʻa hou kō ka poʻe.

    (1) The people have a new canoe (a canoe new belonging-to the people).

He waʻa hou koʻu.
He kaʻa kō ka malihini.
He kula hauʻoli kō ke *Kōlea.
He moʻolelo kō kēlā kanaka makapō.
*He kupuna kō nā *keiki.*

I have a new canoe.
The visitor/stranger/ malihini has a car.
The Korean has a happy school.
That blind man has a story.

The children have a grandparent.

(2) He kaʻa pupuka kou.
He makua kō lāua.
He hale kula kō ka poʻe naʻauao.
He wahi pupuka kō ka poʻe naʻaupō.
He ua nui kō ka ʻāina.

(2) You have an ugly car.
They (2) have a parent.
The wise people have a school house.
The ignorant people have an ugly place.
The land has heavy rain.

B. He kamaʻilio ʻana.

B. A conversation.

Kamaʻāina.   Aloha kakahiaka.
Malihini.   *Aloha nō. Pehea keia ʻāina?
K.   He ua nui kō keia ʻāina.
M.   Noho ʻoe ma Waikīkī?

Resident/kamaʻāina.   Good morning.
Visitor.   Hello. How is this land?
K.   This land has much rain.
V.   Do you live at Waikīkī?

K.   'Ae, noho au ma
     Waikīkī.

K.   Yes, I live at Waikīkī.

M.   'Ike 'oe i ka 'ōlelo
     Hawai'i?

V.   Do you know the Hawaiian
     language?

K.   'A'ole 'ike loa. 'Ike
     hemahema.

K.   (I) don't know very well.
     (I) know poorly.

M.   *Hiki *iā 'oe <u>ke</u> he'e
     nalu?

V.   *Can you surf?* (Note that
     hiki behaves like *maopopo*
     and is followed by *ke*.)

K.   Hiki nō. *He papa he'e
     nalu ko'u.*

K.   Sure. I have a surfboard.

M.   *Hiki iā 'oe <u>ke</u> kinipōpō?*

V.   *Can you play ball?*

K.   Hiki nō. He kinipōpō ka'u.

K.   Sure. I have a ball.

M.   *Hiki iā 'oe <u>ke</u> kalaiwa ka'a?*

V.   *Can you drive a car?*
     (Kalaiwa is from English
     "drive.")

K.   Hiki nō. He ka'a maika'i
     ko'u.

K.   Sure. I have a good car.

M.   Hiki iā 'oe *ke* hula 'apōpō?

V.   Can you hula tomorrow?

K.   'A'ole. Hilahila.

K.   No. (I'm) bashful.

M.   E hele hou aku ana au.
     A hui hou aku.

V.   I'm going again.
     Good-by (until meet again.)

K.   A hui hou aku.

K.   Good-by.

C.   He kama'ilio hou 'ana.

C.   Another conversation.

Nīnau. Mahea ka *penikala?
Pane 1. Malalo o ka pepa.
     2. Maluna o ka puke.
     3. Maloko o ka puke.
     4. Mawaena o nā *'ao'ao
        o ka puke.
     5. Mamua o ka lumi.
     6. Mawaho o ka lumi.
     7. Kokoke i ka
        papa'ele'ele.

Question. Where is the pencil?
Answer 1. Under the paper.
     2. On top of the book.
     3. In the book.
     4. Between the pages of
        the book.
     5. Front of the room.
     6. Outside of the room.
     7. Near the blackboard.

The students should improvise on this theme. A places an object in
various places and asks where it is. B answers appropriately.

D. He mele: Maika'i Kaua'i.

D. A song: Beautiful Kaua'i.

Maika'i wale nō Kaua'i
†Hemolele wale i ka mālie,
Kuahiwi *nani, Wai-'ale'ale,
Lei ana i ka mokihana.

So very beautiful is Kaua'i
So perfect in the calm,
Pretty mountain, Wai-'ale'ale,
The lei is the mokihana.

Hanohano wale 'o Hanalei
I ka ua nui hō'eha 'ili

So glorious is Hanalei
With the great rain that pains
the skin

I ka wai o 'u'inakolo
I ka poli o Nāmolokama.

In the rustling water
In the bosom/heart of Nāmolokama (name of a famous waterfall).

Maika'i nō Kaua'i
Hemolele i ka mālie,
Kuahiwi Wai-'ale'ale,
Lei ana i ka mokihana.

So beautiful is Kaua'i
Perfect in the calm,
Mount Wai-'ale'ale,
The lei is the mokihana.

†New words not in italics are for reference and need not be memorized at this point.

ʻUMI-KŪMĀ-ONO

A. Possessives.

This is one of the most exciting pages in the book. The Hawaiians divide the universe into two parts, and everything in the world belongs to one part or the other. These parts or classes may be called *o*-class and *a*-class. The *o*-class includes one's birthright: God, chief, grandparents, parents, siblings, name, body parts, clothes, house, land, canoe, automobile, emotion, aloha. The *a*-class includes objects that one himself acquires in life: spouse, sweetheart, most of one's possessions, most of one's actions. Some words *(hele)* are used with either *o* or *a*.

Note the two drawings. In one the man looks up to the *o* or *dominating* objects, and in the other the man points down to the *a* or *subordinate* objects. These terms (dominating, subordinate) are applied to Maori possessives by Bruce Biggs.

	O-words	*A*-words
	(koʻu, kou, kona, etc.)	(kaʻu, kāu, kāna, etc.)
People	akua aliʻi kupuna, tūtū makuakāne, makuahine poʻe, lāhui	kāne, wahine, ipo keiki, kaikamahine, keiki kāne moʻopuna kumu, haumana
Body parts	kino, lima, poli, poʻo	
Clothes	kāmaʻa, lole, pāpale, pāʻū	
Actions	hele	hana, hele, helu, heluhelu, namu, nīnau, ʻōlelo, pane

	O-words (cont'd)	*A*-words (cont'd)
Emotions and personal attributes	akamai, aloha, 'eha, hanohano, hau'oli, hemahema, hilahila, maka'u, ma'i, mana'o, maopopo, na'auao, na'aupō, nani, pupule, u'i	
Conveyances	ka'a, papa he'e nalu, wa'a	
Other objects	'āina, hale, inoa, kula, lani, lei, lumi, mo'olelo, moku, noho (chair), wahi	'ai, hua, huahelu, hua'ōlelo, kinipōpō, mea'ai, papa'ele'ele, penikala, papa (class), pepa, puke, wai

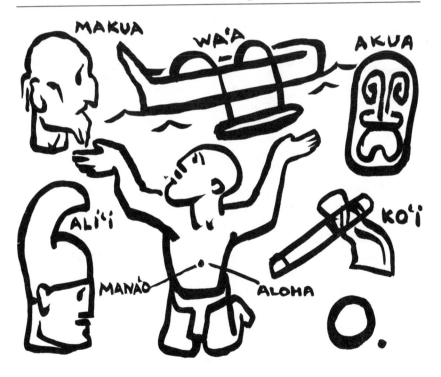

O-words are one's birthright

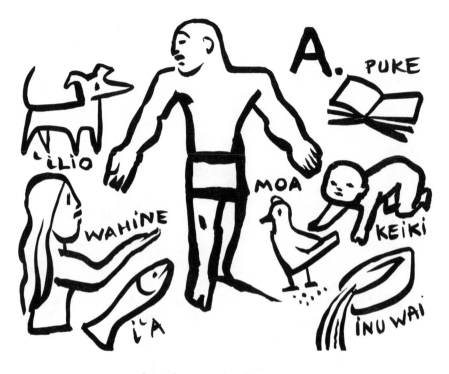

A-words are one's achievements

No philosophy of life is completely logical. A few exceptions to the general classification will be discussed later.

The *o*-possessives are listed at the beginning of ha'awina 'umi-kūmā-hā. The *a*-possessives are just the same except that *-a* and *-ā* replace every *-o* and *-ō* after initial *k-*, as *ka'u, kāu, kāna, kā kāua*, etc. Note macrons on kāu and kāna. Pronounce aloud all words in the lists on the previous page using (1) *ko'u*, my: *ko'u Akua, ko'u ali'i*, etc., and (2) *ka'u*, my: *ka'u kāne, ka'u wahine*, etc.

(1) *Aloha ko'u tūtū, i kāna*
    mo'opuna.
    Aloha ke keiki kāne, i
    kāna ipo.
    Aloha ka wahine, i kāna kāne.

(1) *My grandmother loves*
    her grandson.
    The boy loves his sweet-
    heart.
    The woman loves her
    husband.

Aloha ka *makuahine, i kāna kaikamahine hope loa. (*Kaikamahine* is often pronounced *keikamahine*.)	*The mother loves her youngest daughter.*
Aloha ka moʻopuna, i kona kupuna.	The grandchild loves his grandparent.

(2) Contrast: he kumu au, he kumu kaʻu.

He haumana ʻoia.	He is a student.
He haumana kāna.	He has a student.
He aliʻi ʻoe.	You are a chief.
He aliʻi kou.	You have a chief.
He kāne kā Lei.	Lei has a husband.
He kāne ʻo Lei.	Lei is a man.
He moʻopuna kāna.	She has a grandchild.
He moʻopuna ʻoia.	She is a grandchild.
He keiki kā Pua.	Pua has a child.
He keiki ʻo Pua.	Pua is a child.
He wahine kāna.	He has a wife.
He wahine ʻoia.	She is a woman.

(3) Insert *o*, *a*, or *ā* in the following blanks. Translate.

Māhalo wau i k __u kupuna.	Makemake au *e ʻike i k __u keiki.
Akamai loa k __na moʻopuna.	
Mamao loa k __ lākou waʻa.	Mahalo au i ke kiʻi __ Kamehameha.
ʻEha loa k __ʻu lima.	

B.	He kamaʻilio ʻana.	B.	A conversation.
	Keawe Wahine. *Pōmaikaʻi kaʻu mau moʻopuna.*		Mrs. Keawe. *My grandchildren are lucky.*
	Nālei Wahine. ʻAe. Pōmaikaʻi nō.		Mrs. Nālei. Yes. Very lucky.
K.	He waʻa kō Kū. He puke kā Kale. He *papaʻeleʻele kā Mele. He lole hou kō Makaleka. He ipo kā Pila.	K.	Kū has a canoe. Charles has a book. Mary has a blackboard. Margaret has a new dress. Bill has a sweetheart.

N. Auwē! Pōmaika'i lākou.
K. Pehea kāu mo'opuna?

N. Pohō loa. *'Eha kona
lima.* Pupuka kona pāpale.
Pau kāna 'ai. Lōlō kāna ipo.
*Ma'i kona makuakāne.
Hele *aku kona makuahine
i loko.

N. Say, they are lucky.
K. What about your grand-
child?

N. Out of luck. *Her hand
hurts.* Her hat is ugly. Her
food is gone. Her sweet-
heart is crazy. Her father
is sick. Her mother has
gone to the mainland
(to inside).
(K interjects *aloha 'ino* or
auwē noho'i after every
statement.)

C. Kekahi kama'ilio 'ana.

Keoni. *Pehea kāu wahine?*
Lopaka. *Pehea la.* Huhū
loa. He lole hou kona,
huhū nō. He kāma'a hou
kona, huhū nō.

K. Aloha 'ino. *Pēlā nō
ke 'ano o nā wāhine.*
L. He ka'a hou kou?
K. 'Ae, he ka'a hou ko'u.
L. He aha ke 'ano?
K. He Cadillac.
L. Auwē noho'i e. Hau'oli
kāu ipo?
K. *Pēlā paha!* Makemake au
e holoholo. Makemake
'oia e *heluhelu puke.
'A'ole makemake e
holoholo. Hūpō paha?
'Ōlelo mai 'oia, he
lapuwale ke ka'a.
L. Aloha 'ino. Pēlā nō ke
'ano o nā wāhine.

C. Another conversation.

John. *How's your wife?*
Bob. *How should I know.*
Very cranky. She has a new
dress (but) she's still cranky.
She's got new shoes, (but)
still cranky.

J. That's sure bad. *That's the
way women are.*
B. Have you a new car?
J. Yes, I have a new car.
B. What kind?
J. A Cadillac.
B. Boy! Is your sweetheart
glad?
J. *Maybe so!* I want to go
riding. She wants to read a
book. Doesn't want to go
riding. Dumb maybe?
She says the car's
worthless.

B. That's sure bad. That's
the way women are.

D. Ke ana 'umi-kūmā-ono: *o* and *a* possessives.
O and *a*, each meaning "of," follow the same classification as that just listed.

(4) *'A'ole maika'i ka wahine a Kale.*

(4) *Charles' wife is not well* (not well the wife of Charles).

U'i ke kāne a Pua.
Nani ka mo'opuna a Mele.
Aloha kākou i ke ali'i o ka **'āina.
Mahea ka penikala a ke kumu?

Pua's husband is handsome.
Mele's grandchild is cute.
We greet the chief of the land.
Where's the pencil of the teacher?
Where's the teacher's pencil?

(5) Ke kāne a Pua.
Ka makuahine o Kale.
Mahea *ka wa'a o ka mahi'ai?*
Mahea ka puke a ka mahi'ai?
Mahea ke keiki a Keawe?

(5) Pua's husband.
Charles' mother.
Where is *the farmer's canoe?*
Where is the farmer's book?
Where is Keawe's child?

E. Nā huahelu.

E. Numbers.

Kū. E helu mai 'oukou. *Eia nā huahelu haole:* 19, 17, 14, 18, 12, 16. (Helu A, B, C.) Maika'i. Na'auao. Mākaukau. E, A, he aha ka huahelu mawaena o 'ehiku ame 'eiwa?

Kū. Count (you-3). *Here are English numbers:* 19, 17, 14, 18, 12, 16. (A, B, C count.) Good. Wise. Prepared. Say, A, what is the number between 7 and 9?

A. **Ehā.

A. Four.

K. Tsa! Hūpō noho'i. E, Pī, he aha ka huahelu mawaena o 'ehiku ame 'eiwa?

K. Man! Surely dumb. Say, B, what's the number between 7 and 9?

B. 'Umi-kūmā-lua.

B. Twelve.

K. (Huhū.) 'A'ole loa. Lōlō ka pane. Pupule. E, C, he aha ka huahelu mawaena o 'elima ame 'ehiku?

K. (Angry.) Certainly not. The answer is stupid. Crazy. Say, C, what's the number between 5 and 7?

C.   'Ewalu.

C.   Eight.

K.   Na'aupō keia papa!
     Lapuwale! *E hele aku
     *ana au i Pīkī e noho ai.

K.   This class is ignorant!
     Worthless! I'm going to
     Fiji and stay (i Piki e
     noho ai).

F.   The two types of possessives.

(1) Ke ka'a o Pua, Pua's *car*.
(2) Kō Pua ka'a, *Pua's* car.

In Hawaiian, emphatic words or phrases tend to come at the beginning
of the sentence. The emphatic words in the English above are italicized.
In (1) the possessed object is in focus. In (2) the possessor is in focus.
Both types are common.

Change the following type (1) to type (2), that is, emphasize the
possessor rather than the possessed object.

Ka wa'a o Pua.
Ka penikala a Mele.
Ke kupuna o ke keiki. (Kō ke keiki kupuna.)
Ka puke a ka-haumana. (Kā ka haumana puke.)
Ka lei o Pua.

(*Kō* and *kā* seem to be fusions of the definite article *ka/ke* and the
possessives *ō* and *ā*.)

ʻUMI-KŪMĀ-HIKU

A. Neutral possessives.

Two possessive forms are neutral: *kuʻu* (my/mine) and *kō* (your/yours)
One can say *kō makuahine* (your mother) and *kō keiki* (your child).
When in doubt it is always safe to use *kuʻu* and *kō*. Kuʻu is sometimes
affectionate *(kuʻu ipo)*.

(1) *Kuʻu ipo kēlā.* Kaʻu ipo
     kēlā.
     Kuʻu papa heʻe nalu kēlā.
     Koʻu papa heʻe nalu kēlā.
     Kō wai kēlā. Kāu wai kēlā.
     Kō ʻai *kēnā. Kāu ʻai kēnā.

     He wahine uʻi kō wahine.

(1) *That is my sweetheart*
     (two ways).
     That is my surfboard.

     That is your water.
     That (near you) is your
     food.
     Your wife is a beautiful
     woman.

(2) *Ua ʻeha kō kino.*
     ʻAe, ʻeha koʻu lima.
     Holoholo *ʻolua me kō ipo?

     ʻAe, holoholo nō *māua,
     akā, maʻi ʻoia.

(2) *Your body aches.*
     Yes, my hand hurts.
     Are you and your sweet-
     heart going riding (ride
     you-2 with your sweet-
     heart)?
     Yes, we (exc. 2) are going
     riding, but she is sick.

B. Use of *o* or *a* possessive may change the meaning of some possessed
    objects.

    koʻu lei: my personal lei that I wear
    kaʻu lei: my lei to sell or give away, or made by me

    koʻu *kiʻi: my picture or statue, of me
    kaʻu kiʻi: my picture or statue, by me or owned by me

    kona *mele: his song, composed in his honor
    kāna mele: his song, composed by him

(3) Nani kāna ki'i.

Nani nā mele a Kale Kini.

Mahalo au i ke ki'i o
Kamehameha 'Ekahi.
Nani nā ki'i a Jean Charlot
i loko o keia puke.

'Eha ka iwi o ko'u lima.

E 'ai ana au i ka'u iwi moa.

(3) His picture (painted by
him) is pretty.
The songs by Charles King
are pretty.
I admire the statue of
Kamehameha I.
The pictures by Jean
Charlot in this book
are pretty.

*The bone of my hand
hurts.*

*I'm eating my chicken
bone.*

C.   Ke ana 'umi-kūmā-hiku: causatives.

Many words may be preceded by *ho'o-, hō-, ho'-,* or *ho-,* as *nani*
(beautiful) and *ho'onani* (to make beautiful, glorify).

(4) *Ho'oponopono i nā hewa
a ka haumana.*
Ho'onani i kou lumi.
*Ho'opau i ka *pilikia.*
Ua ho'oponopono 'oia i
ka'u hewa.

(4) *Correct the mistakes of
the student.*
Beautify your room.
Put an end to the trouble.
He corrected my mistake.

D.   Do not confuse pronouns and possessives *as used in Hawaiian.* This use
does not correspond to English usage. Note that the object marker *iā*
precedes pronouns, and that *i* precedes possessives.

Pronoun patterns

(5) 'Ike wau iā'oe.
Ho'oponopono mai iā
lākou.
Aloha wau iāia.
Namu *haole māua.
E 'ai ana kāua.
*Hau'oli 'o lāua.
E he'e nalu kākou.

I see you.
Correct them.

I greet him.
We speak (mutter) English.
We (2) are eating.
They (2) are happy.
Let's (3) surf.

Possessive patterns

(6) 'Ike wau i kāu keiki.   I see your child.
    Ho'oponopono mai i kā   Correct their mistake.
      lākou hewa.
    Aloha wau i ka'u kumu.   I greet my teacher.
    Namu haole i kā lāua keiki.   Speak English to their
                                                     child.

    He ka'a pupuka ko'u.   I have an ugly car.
    Hau'oli nā mo'opuna a   Their (2) grandchildren are
      lāua.   happy.
    Ma'i kō kākou tūtū.   Our (3 inc.) granny is sick.

E. Review of *k*-words (compare *ha'awina 'elua*).
    The *k*-words include the following:

ka/ke)   The *k*-words have similar distri-
nā   ) articles   butions; that is, most of them
                                             occur in the same positions in
keia)   the sentence. The two most
kēlā) demonstratives   common patterns are:
kēnā)
                                             k-word plus noun: ka hale, keia
ko'u, ka'u, ku'u)   hale, ko'u hale
kou, kāu, kō   )   *he* plus noun plus *k*-word: he
kona, kāna   ) possessives   hale keia, he hale ko'u
kō kāua, kā kāua)
kō māua, kā māua)
  and so forth

F. Review of patterns.

    (7) Ha'awina 1: he Pokoliko   HE
          'oia.
        She is a teacher.   That is an opinion.
        I am a male.   That is an honorable person.
        Lani is a farmer.   That (near) is a fool.

    (8) Ha'awina 2: nani ke   VERB + SUBJECT
          ki'i.
        The bone is ugly.   The chicken bone is good.
        The pain is great.   The paddle is new.
        My song is new.   The student is worthless.

    (9) Ha'awina 8: nānā lākou   I/IĀ OBJECT MARKERS
        i ke keiki.

Thank your teacher.
Answer his question.
Look at Pualani.

I love you.
The chief loves her.
They admire their teacher.

(10) Haʻawina 9: e hele
aku ʻoe.

E (VERB) ʻOE

Speak to your teacher.
Speak Portuguese.
Paddle-a-canoe.

Thank your teacher.
Come and eat.
Drive-a-car. Play-ball.

(11) Haʻawina 9, 10, 11:
Use a verb marker in
each of these:
Surf! Sing! Speak! COME!
The man will tell-a-story.
The boy loves his sweetheart.

E (VERB), UA, E (VERB) ANA

Sit on that side.
His grandchild was foolish.
Mele's mother is pretty.

(12) Haʻawina 12:
Use a directional in
each of these:
Come again.
They (2) looked at the
canoe.
Look at me.

MAI, AKU, IHO

They went down.
They told-a-story.

We (2 exc.) admire your hat.

(13) Haʻawina 13: maloko o
ke kiʻi.
Under the hat.
After the class.
Forward, Kamehameha.

LOCATIVES

Between the mountains.
In the middle of the lesson.
Before the house.

(14) Haʻawina 14, 16: he kaʻa
koʻu.
I have a child.
I have a teacher.
I have a mother.

O, A

He has a handsome canoe.
He has a sick wife.
She has a sarong.

(15) Haʻawina 15: he ua nui
kō Hilo.
The chief has a new house.
The child has a father.
Anuhea has a large canoe.

KŌ, KĀ

The chief has a car.
Kū has a surfboard.
My wife has a new ʻukulele.

G. Echelon drill. Practice until you can say (5) accurately and *fast*.

1.	Mahalo tūtū.	1.	Granny admires.
2.	(Mahalo tūtū) i koʻu hale.	2.	(Granny admires) my house.
3.	(Mahalo tūtū i koʻu hale) mawaena o Ka-lihi-uka.	3.	(Granny admires my house) in the middle of Ka-lihi-uka.
4.	(Mahalo tūtū i koʻu hale mawaena o Ka-lihi-uka) ame Ka-lihi-kai.	4.	(Granny admires my house between Ka-lihi-uka) and Ka-lihi-kai.
5.	(Mahalo tūtū i koʻu hale mawaena o Ka-lihi-uka ame Ka-lihi-kai) mauka loa.	5.	(Granny admires my house between Ka-lihi-uka and Ka-lihi-kai) far mauka.

H. Repeat the scene in haʻawina ʻumi-kūmā-ono, E, but let A, B, and C give correct answers. Kū tells them they are well prepared, smart, wise. Not unprepared, stupid, worthless, crazy.

I. A technical note about causatives.

hoʻo-: before bases beginning with *i-* or *u-* and all consonants except the glottal stop: *ikaika, hoʻoikaika*, strong, to strengthen. See also C.

hō-: before bases beginning with glottal stops followed by short vowels: *ʻeha, hōʻeha*, pain, to hurt.

hoʻ-: before bases beginning with short vowels other than *i-* or *u-*, with lengthening of that vowel: *ola, hoʻōla*, alive, to save.

ho-: before bases beginning with a glottal stop followed by a long vowel: *ʻāpuka, hoʻāpuka*, fraudulent, to cheat.

J. Practice the following until you can say them without stopping to think:

	a-words	*o*-words
I have a	child	house
	teacher	land
	picture	chief

	a-words (cont'd)	*o*-words (cont'd)
I have a	water	image *(akua)*
	chicken	father

Then replace "I" with other pronouns.

K.   Substitution drill.

Nani loa *kona waʻa.*

keiki	Nani loa kāna keiki.
pupuka	Pupuka loa kāna keiki.
pohō	Pohō loa kāna keiki.
kaʻu	Pohō loa kaʻu keiki.
makuakāne	Pohō loa kaʻu makuakāne.
ʻeha	ʻEha loa kaʻu makuakāne.
ka	ʻEha loa ka makuakāne.
mahiʻai	ʻEha loa ka mahiʻai.
holoholo	Holoholo loa ka mahiʻai.
pōmaikaʻi	Pōmaikaʻi loa ka mahiʻai.

ʻUMI-KŪMĀ-WALU

A. Ke ana ʻumi-kūmā-walu: *Hiki iaʻu ke hele (I can go).*

This common word has the same distribution as *maopopo: maopopo iaʻu ka haʻawina*, clear to me the lesson. Nānā hou i ke kamaʻilio ʻana ma ka haʻawina ʻumi-kūmā-lima. *Ke* (never *ka*) always introduces the verb following *hiki.*

(1) Hiki iaʻu *ke* hoe waʻa.   (1) I can paddle a canoe.
Hiki iāʻoe *ke* hoe waʻa.   You (1) can paddle a canoe.

Hiki iā kāua *ke* hoe waʻa.   We (inc. 2) can paddle a canoe.

Hiki i ke aliʻi *ke* hoe waʻa.   The chief can paddle a canoe.

Hiki i *koʻu kupuna *ke* hele.   My grandmother can go.

(2) Hiki iā lākou *ke* hoʻoponopono.   (2) They (3) can correct/administer.
Hiki i ke aliʻi wahine *ke* hoʻonani i ka lumi.   The chiefess can beautify the room.
Hiki iā Lei *ke pāʻani kinipōpō.*   Lei can *play ball.*
Hiki i *kaʻu moʻopuna *ke* heʻe nalu.   My grandson can surf.
Hiki iāʻoe *ke* kalaiwa kaʻa.   You (1) can drive a car.
Hiki ia kākou ke hoʻonani iāia.   *We (inc. 3) can glorify him.*

B. He kamaʻilio ʻana.   B. A conversation.

Moʻopuna.   E tūtū. E hele aku ana au, i ke kula. (Pronounce: eheleakuanau.)   Grandchild.   O grandmother. Iʻm going to school.

Tūtū.   E hele.   Grandmother.   Go (ahead).

65

M. Pau ke kula, hiki iaʻu *ke* pāʻani kinipōpō?

C. After school, can I play ball?

T. ʻIke ʻoe i ka haʻawina?

M. (Somewhat angry.) Do you know the lesson?

M. ʻAe, ʻike loa. Mākaukau nō.

C. Yes, (I) sure do know (it). Really prepared.

T. He keiki akamai ʻoe?

M. Are you a smart child?

M. ʻAe, akamai loa.

C. Yes, very smart.

T. Hiki nō iāʻoe ke pāʻani kinipōpō.

M. You can play ball.

M. *Maikaʻi maoli.* Mahalo. Pau kuʻu kinipōpō, hiki iaʻu ke hula me kuʻu ipo?

C. *Very/truly good.* Thank you. After my ball (playing), can I dance with my sweetheart?

T. (Huhū.) Tsa! Hoʻi mai i ka hale, e heluhelu puke!

M. (Angry.) Goodness! Come back to the house and read books!

M. Makemake māua e hula!

C. (Pleading.) We want to dance!

T. ʻO wai ka inoa o kāu ipo?

M. What's the name of your sweetheart?

M. ʻO Hiʻiaka-i-ka-poli-o-Pele, kona inoa.

C. Hiʻiaka-in-the-bosom-of-Pele is her name.

T. *A laila, hiki nō ke hula.* He kaikamahine pono kēlā.

M. *Then, (you) can dance.* That's an honest girl.

C. Practice with *i* and *iā*.

(3) Nānā mai iā Ke-kai-malu.
Nānā mai i *ke kai malu*.
Mahalo lāua iā Kaʻuhane.
Mahalo lāua i ka ʻuhane.
Hoʻi ʻoia i ka lani.

(3) Look at Ke-kai-malu.
Look at *the peaceful sea*.
They (2) admire Kaʻuhane.
They (2) admire the soul.
She went back to the chief/heaven.

(4) They (3) see me.
I love you.
Look at him.

(5) Watch Ka-lani.
Watch the sky.
Go to them (3).

(6) What is the thing?
Sing to them.

D.   Echelon drill. Add each new element in its proper place.

1. Ua ho'i 'oia.	1. He went-back.
2. (Ua ho'i 'oia) mai.	2. (He came-back) this way.
3. (Ua ho'i mai 'oia) hou.	3. (He came-back this-way) again.
4. (Ua ho'i hou mai 'oia) a laila.	4. (He came-back again this-way) then.
5. (A laila, ua ho'i hou mai 'oia.)	5. (Then he came-back again this-way).

ʻUMI-KŪMĀ-IWA

A. Ke ana ʻumi-kūmā-iwa: aia ka haku, aia he haku (there is the master, there is a master).

Aia has a limited distribution and occurs only after a pause, and never with the verb markers (e, e . . . ana, ua).

Aia ka haku maoli.	*There's the real master.*
	There's the true lord.
Aia ka ʻeha.	There's the pain.
Aia he mahiʻai.	There's a farmer. ˙
Aia ka hewa. Nānā aku ʻoe.	There the mistake is. Look!
Aia maluna o ke *kuahiwi.	There on top of the mountain.
Aia ke keiki kāne.	There's the boy.

B. He kamaʻilio ʻana i ke kula.

B. A conversation in school.

Kumu. E nā haumana, *e hoʻomaka kākou i ka haʻawina.* E Lei-lani, nānā i ka puke ma ka haʻawina *ʻumi-kūmā-kahi.

Teacher. O students, *let's begin the lesson.* O Lei-lani, look at the book at lesson eleven.

Lei-lani. Hiki.

Lei-lani. Okay.

K. E Lei-lani. Pehea nā mea o loko o ke kiʻi?

T. O Lei-lani. What are the things inside the picture (of inside of the picture)?

L. *Kēlā mea keia mea.*

L. *This and that* (that thing this thing).

K. ʻO wai ka wahine *mawaena o ke kiʻi?

T. Who is the lady in the middle of the picture?

L. ʻO Ka-ʻahu-manu.

L. Ka-ʻahu-manu.

K. He haumana akamai ʻoe. ʻO wai ke kaikamahine ma ka ʻaoʻao o ka wahine?

T. You are a smart student. Who is the girl at the side of the woman?

L. ʻO kā lāua keiki paha.

L. Perhaps their child.

K.	Pēlā paha. Ua lawa. Mahalo. E Waʻa-lani, *mahea ʻo Kamehameha?		T.	Maybe so. (That's) enough. Thanks. O Waʻa-lani, where is Kamehameha?

K. Pēlā paha. Ua lawa. Mahalo. E Waʻa-lani, *mahea ʻo Kamehameha?

Waʻa-lani. Ma ke kiʻi.

K. Mahea ma ke kiʻi?

W. Mawaena.

K. Ua kū ʻoia?

W. ʻAʻole loa. Ua noho.

K. Pehea kēlā *mea mahope o nā aliʻi?

W. He kāhili. *ʻElua.

K. Lawa ke kula. *Pau ka haʻawina. A hui hou aku kākou.

T. Maybe so. (That's) enough. Thanks. O Waʻa-lani, where is Kamehameha?

Waʻa-lani. In the picture.

T. Where in the picture?

W. In the middle.

T. Is he standing?

W. Of course not. (He's) sitting.

T. What is that thing behind the chiefs?

W. Kāhilis. Two.

T. Enough school. The lesson is finished. Good-by.

Nā pea ʻekolu, Goldilocks, me ʻekolu ʻiole makapō

C. *He moʻolelo nō ʻekolu pea (bears)* a Kawena Johnson a me Palani Charlot.

He moʻolelo keia nō ʻekolu pea. ʻAʻole keia he moʻolelo Hawaiʻi. He moʻolelo hou a ke kumu. Ua maikaʻi ʻoia.

Ua noho ʻekolu pea ma ka moku o Kauaʻi. Nui loa ka makuakāne. ʻAʻole nui ka makuahine. *Liʻiliʻi (small) ke keiki.* Ua makemake lākou e ʻai i ka poi. Ua noho ka *makuakāne ma *kona noho. He noho nui loa ia. Ua noho ka makuahine ma kona noho. ʻAʻole nui kona noho. Ua noho ke keiki ma kona noho. Ua liʻiliʻi kēlā noho.

Ua ʻai nui ka makuakāne. ʻAʻole ʻai nui ka makuahine. ʻAʻole makemake ke keiki e ʻai i ka poi. Ua makemake ʻoia e hele aku i ke kai e heʻe nalu. Ua ʻae ka makuakāne ame ka makuahine. Ua ʻōlelo ka makuakāne: " ʻAe. E hele kākou."

Ua hele mai ke kaikamahine, ʻo Goldilocks. He maikaʻi ke nānā aku. Pali ke kua (back), mahina ke alo (front a moon). Ua makemake ʻoia e ʻai. Ua makemake ʻoia e noho ma nā noho. Ua makemake ʻoia e nānā i ka hale.

Ua hoʻi mai nā pea ʻekolu. Ua nānā ka makuakāne i ka ʻai. ʻAʻole ʻai. Ua nānā ka makuahine i kona noho. Ua ʻōlelo ʻoia: " ʻAʻole maikaʻi ka noho." Ua nānā ke keiki i kēlā mea keia mea i loko o ka hale. He kaikamahine maloko o ka hale!

Ua ʻōlelo ka makuakāne: " ʻO wai ʻoe?" " ʻO Goldilocks koʻu inoa. Aloha kākou."

ʻŌlelo ke keiki: "E mele kākou."

Ua mele lākou i keia mele:

ʻEkolu ʻiole makapō.	*Three blind mice.*
ʻEkolu ʻiole makapō.	
ʻIke i ka holo o lākou.	*See them run.*
ʻIke i ka holo o lākou.	
Holo aku mahope o ka	
wahine mahiʻai.	
ʻOki ʻia ka huelo me ka	The tail was cut with the
pahi kālai.	carving knife.
ʻIke ʻoe (i) kekahi mea i	
like me neia,	(neia: this)
ʻEkolu ʻiole makapō.	

Nui ke aloha o Goldilocks i ka pea liʻiliʻi. Pau kēlā makahiki, male (marry) lāua. He lau (many many) a lau kā lāua keiki. He mau keiki hapa haole a hapa pea.

Nā nīnau: He moʻolelo Hawaiʻi keia? Ua nui anei ke keiki? Ua nui anei ka makuakāne? ʻO wai ke kaikamahine i hele mai i ka hale? Ua ʻai ke kaikamahine? ʻAi i ke aha? Ua makemake ke keiki e heʻe nalu? Ua mele lākou i ka mele, "Nā moku ʻehā"? He aha ka mele a lākou? Maikaʻi keia moʻolelo?

D. Change these possessives to the pattern with *kō* or *kā*.

Unuhi.

Ke keiki a ka mahiʻai, aia hoʻokahi wale nō.

Ka ʻāina o ka uʻi.

Ka hoe a ka waʻa lohi.

Ka moku o ke aliʻi wahine.

Ka ipo a Goldilocks.

Change these possessives to the pattern with *o* or *a*.

Unuhi.

Kō ʻUmi pāpale.

Kā ke kupuna wahine moʻopuna.

Kā Pua wai.

Kā Mahi hoe.

Kō kaʻu keiki lumi.

IWAKĀLUA

A. Nā huahelu.

20	iwakālua	30	kanakolu	40	kanahā
21	iwakālua-kūmā-kahi	31	kanakolu-kūmā-kahi	50	kanalima
22	iwakālua-kūmā-lua	32	kanakolu-kūmā-lua	60	kanaono
			etc.		etc.

B. Possessive *o* and possessive *a*.

1. *My* canoe is big.　　　　　　Nui *koʻu* waʻa.
   My child is big.　　　　　　 Nui *kaʻu* keiki.

2. *I* (*he* has) have a mother.　　 He makuahine *koʻu* (*kona*).
   I (*he* has) have a sweetheart.　He ipo *kaʻu* (*kāna*).

3. I (you) see *my* chair.　　　　 ʻIke au (ʻoe) i *koʻu* noho.
   I (you) see *my* teacher.　　　 ʻIke au (ʻoe) i *kaʻu* kumu.

4. *My* father's canoe is big.　　 Nui ka waʻa *o koʻu* makuakāne.
   My father's class is big.　　 Nui ka papa *a koʻu* makuakāne.

5. *My* grandchild's canoe is big.　Nui ka waʻa *o kaʻu* moʻopuna.
   My grandmother's dress is　　Nani ka lole *o koʻu* tūtū.
   　pretty.

6. John's canoe is slow.　　　　Lohi ka waʻa *o* Keoni.
   John's book is pretty.　　　　Nani ka puke *a* Keoni.

7. *His* grandmother took *my*　　Ua lawe *kona* tūtū i *kaʻu* ipo.
   　girl.
   His girl took *my* father.　　Ua lawe *kāna* ipo i *koʻu*
   　　　　　　　　　　　　　 makuakāne.

8. We took *his* hat and (*his*)　　Ua lawe kāua i *kona* pāpale a
   　book.　　　　　　　　　 me *kāna* puke.
   We took *her* hat and (*her*)　 Ua lawe kāua i *kona* pāpale a
   　sarong.　　　　　　　　　me *kona* pāʻū.

9. *Your* father took *your* child.

Ua lawe *kou* makuakāne i *kāu* keiki.

Your teacher took *my* children.

Ua lawe *kāu* kumu i *ka'u* mau keiki.

10. That distinguished chief is *mine* (*hers*).

Ko'u (*kona*) kēlā ali'i hanohano.

This pretty woman is *mine* (*his*).

Ka'u (*kāna*) keia wahine u'i.

11. The teacher'*s* pencil is good.

Maika'i ka penikala *a* ke kumu.

The teacher'*s* shoes are large.

Nui nā kāma'a o ke kumu.

12. *Our* class is not big.

'A'ole nui *kā kākou* papa.

Our house is big.

Nui *kō kākou* hale.

C. He mo'olelo keia. E unuhi mai 'oe. 'O Wahi-a-wā ka makuakāne. 'O Kū-kani-loko ka makuahine. 'O Ka-uka-ali'i ka makuahine o Kū. 'O Halemano e pili la me (next to) Līhu'e ka 'āina, i Wai-'anae. 'O O'ahu ka moku. Ma ka noho 'ana (marriage) o Wahi me kāna wahine 'o Kū, ua hānau kā lāua keiki 'eono, 'ehā kāne, 'elua wāhine. [Fornander, vol. 5, p. 229]

D. Ka helu 'ana.

Kumu. E nā haumana, ho'omaka kākou.
Haumana. Hiki.
Kumu. E Kalani. E helu mai 'oe *mai 'ekahi ā 'elima.*
(Helu Kalani mai 'ekahi a 'elima.)
Kumu. Maika'i kāu *hana. Mākaukau nō. E Pua. E helu mai 'oe mai 'eono a 'umi.
(Helu Pua mai 'eono a 'umi.)

Kumu. *Pololei 'oe.* E Leo-lani, e helu 'oe mai 'umi-kūmā-kahi a 'umi-kūmā-lima.

D. Counting.

Teacher. Students, let's begin.
Students. Okay.
T. O Kalani. Count *from one to five.*
(Kalani counts from one to five.)
T. You have done well (good your performance). (You are) certainly prepared. O Pua. Count from six to ten.
(Pua counts from six to ten.)

T. *You are correct/right.* O Leo-lani, count from 11 to 15.

(Helu Leo-lani mai 11 a 15.)

(Leo-lani counts from 11 to 15.)

K. He hana maika'i kāu.
E Keoki, e helu 'oe mai
'umi-kūmā-lima a
iwakālua. (Helu Keoki.)

T. You've done a good job.
O George, count from 15
to *20.* (George counts.)

K. Pololei nō. E Keawe, e
helu 'oe mai iwaKĀlua
a *kanakolu.* (Helu Keawe.)

T. Very correct. O Keawe,
count from 20 to *30.*
(Keawe counts.)

K. Maika'i loa! Mahalo nui
loa. Ua lawa ka ha'awina.
A hui hou aku kākou. Ke
aloha nō!

T. Very good! Thank you
very much. This is enough
lesson. Good-by. Aloha!

E. He mea pā'ani. Hiki iā'oe ke unuhi? Mai ka 'ōlelo haole keia.

Mōkē, mōkē, alapia,
Hauna mōkē alahia?
Wana kū, kalī (one, two, three),
Au, kō, kī!

F. Double possessives.

(Awkward English is used in the translation in order to help the student remember the *two* Hawaiian patterns.)

A. Ua ma'i kā ka'u kumu
keiki.

A. My teacher's child is sick.

B. Ma'i ke keiki a kāu kumu?
Aloha 'ino!

B. The child of your teacher
is sick? What a shame!

A. 'Ae, akā, maika'i kō ka'u
kāne makuahine.

A. Yes, but my husband's
mother is fine.

B. Maika'i ka makuahine o
kāu kāne? Pōmaika'i
nō 'oia.
Pehea ke *ka'a o kāu
haumana?

B. The mother of your
husband is fine? She's
lucky.
How's the car of your
student?

A. Maika'i loa kō ka'u
haumana ka'a. Kēlā
makahiki aku nei, pohō.
'A'ole ka'a. *Keia manawa,*
pōmaika'i ka'u haumana.

A. My student's car is just
fine. Last year, out-of-
luck. No car. *Now,* my
student's lucky.

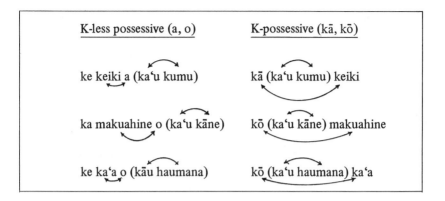

The possessives (o, a, kō, kā) refer to the *possessed object*.

IWAKĀLUA-KŪMĀ-KAHI

A.	Nā ʻano *hale-pule.*	**A.**	Kinds of *churches.*

Nīnau. He aha nā ʻano hale ma Honolulu?

Question. What kinds of buildings are there in Honolulu?

Pane. Nui nā ʻano hale ma Honolulu. *He kūlanakauhale nui ia.*

Answer. There are many kinds of buildings in Honolulu. *It's a big city.*

N. He aha nā ʻano?

Q. What are the kinds?

P. *He hale-leka, he hale-kūʻai, he hale-maʻi,* he hale-pule.

A. *Post office, store, hospital,* church.

N. Nui nā ʻano hale-pule?

Q. Many kinds of churches?

P. ʻAe, nui nā ʻano hale-pule.

A. Yes, many kinds of churches.

N. *Mahea ka hale-pule Kakolika?*

Q. *Where is the Catholic church?*

P. *Ma ke alanui* Pāpū.

A. *On* Fort *Street.*

N. *Aia i hea ka hale-pule Kalawina?*

Q. *Where is the Protestant (Calvinist) church?*

P. Aia he hale-pule Kalawina haole, ma ke alanui Belekania.

A. There is a haole Protestant church on Beretania Street.

N. He hale-pule Kalawina Hawaiʻi?

Q. Is there a Hawaiian Protestant church?

P. ʻAe.

A. Yes.

N. ʻEhia?

Q. How many?

P. ʻElua. Hoʻokahi *ma ke alanui Mōʻī.* Kekahi ma Ka-pā-lama.

A. Two. *One on King Street.* Another at Ka-pā-lama.

N. He hale-pule Molemona?

Q. Is there a Mormon church?

P. Aia ʻelua. Hoʻokahi ma ke alanui Belekania. Aia kekahi ma ke kūlanakauhale o Lāʻie.

A. There are two. One on Beretania Street. There is another in the town of Lāʻie.

N. Aia i hea ʻo Lāʻie?

P. Ma ka ʻaoʻao Koʻolau
o ka *mokupuni o Oʻahu*.
Mawaena o Hauʻula a me
Kahuku. A, kala mai iaʻu.
He hana kaʻu. E hoʻi ana au.

N. Hiki. Nui nā ʻano nīnau.
A nui nā ʻano pane. He
mau pane naʻauao *kāu.
I kēlā ʻapōpō, e hele aku
ana au i Lāʻie. Makemake
au e ʻike i kēlā kūlanakauhale
uʻi me ke kula hou o kēlā
wahi.

Q. Where is Lāʻie?

A. On the Koʻolau side of the
island of Oʻahu. Between
Hauʻula and Kahuku. Ah,
excuse me. I have work.
I'm leaving.

A. Okay. There are many
kinds of questions. Many
kinds of answers. Yours
were clever answers.
Tomorrow, I'm going to
Lāʻie. I want to see that
beautiful town and the
new school of that place.

B. Ka Lama Hawaiʻi.

(This is a story from a Hawaiian newspaper. Glottal stops and macrons
have been added. Aia nā huaʻōlelo hou malalo o ka moʻolelo. Aʻo mai i
nā huaʻōlelo *in italics*.)

Makahiki 1. Lahainaluna, Maui, Pepeluali 14, 1834. Helu 1.

Nō ka ʻelepani

ʻO ka ʻelepani ka mea nui o nā mea *wāwae* ʻehā *apau. Inā* e kū kekahi
kanaka maluna o ke poʻo o kekahi, a laila, like kō lāua *kiʻekiʻe* *me kō
ka ʻelepani. ʻEwalu kapuaʻi ke kiʻekiʻe o kekahi a he ʻumi-kumamā-lima
kō kekahi.

ʻAʻole i like ke ʻano o ka ʻelepani me kō kekahi *ʻīlio* ʻē. *Ua kiʻekiʻe
kona kua, a ua kuapuʻu; ʻaʻole hoʻi i like me ke kamelo. Ua nui loa kona
kino; ua *pōkole* kona *ʻā*ʻī, a ua nui hoʻi; ua pālahalaha kona mau *pepeiao*
ʻaʻole naʻe i kū i luna; ua pili nō i ke poʻo; ua *ʻuʻuku* (liʻiliʻi) loa kona
mau maka, e like paha me kō ke kao; ua nui loa kona mau wāwae, a ua
lōʻihi, a ua manamana hoʻi, *ʻelima nō mana, ua pōkole naʻe. He ʻano
ʻē wale kona *ihu*, ua lōʻihi loa mehe *lāʻau* la, a hiki (hele) loa ka nuku
(ihu) i lalo i ka lepo; a ma kēlā ʻaoʻao, keia ʻaoʻao o ka ihu, he *niho* nui
loa, ʻoia ka mea i ʻōlelo ʻia he niho ʻelepani.

Nā huaʻōlelo hou a me nā manaʻo

lama	torch	pālahalaha	flat, broad
makahiki	*year*	*pepeiao*	*ear*
Pepeluali	February	naʻe	still
ʻelepani	elephant	pili	close
wāwae	*foot, leg*	kao	goat
apau	*all*	lōʻihi	tall, long
inā	*if*	manamana	to have toes
kiʻekiʻe	*height, high*	ʻano ʻē	strange, unusual
kapuaʻi	foot (12 inches)	*ihu*	*nose*
ʻīlio	*dog*	mana	toe
ʻē	other, different	mehe	like
kua	back	*lāʻau*	*tree, stick*
kuapuʻu	humped	la	there
hoʻi	indeed	*lepo*	*dirt, ground*
kamelo	camel	*niho*	*tooth*
pōkole	*short*	ʻōlelo ʻia	is called, is said
ʻāʻī	neck		

IWAKĀLUA-KŪMĀ-LUA

A. Ka makuahine ʻoluʻolu.

Ka makuahine. *Mai holo!*
Ke keiki. *Auwē!
M. *Mai uwē!*
K. Makemake au e hele
i ka hula!
M. Mai hele ʻoe. *ʻŌpiopio
loa ʻoe.*
K. Makemake au e kalaiwa
kaʻa.
M. Mai kalaiwa kaʻa ʻoe.
Mai holoholo. E hana
wale.
K. Makemake au e pāʻani
kinipōpō.
M. Mai pāʻani kinipōpō.
Pono e hoʻomaʻamaʻa
i ka haʻawina.
K. ʻAʻole ʻoe aloha iaʻu?
M. Mai ʻōlelo pēlā. Hūpō!
Aloha au iāʻoe.
K. Auwē! E hele aku ana
au i Kahiki.
M. Mai hele ʻoe. Keiki
lapuwale!

A. The pleasant mother.

Mother. *Don't run!*
Child. Oh!
M *Don't cry!*
C. I want to go to the dance!

M. Don't go. *You are too
young.*
C. I want to drive a car.

M. Don't you go driving. *Don't
go riding.* Just work.

C. I want to play ball.

M. Don't play ball. (You)
should study the lesson.

C. Don't you love me?
M. Don't talk like that.
Stupid! I love you.
C. Oh! I'm going away to
Tahiti.
M. Don't go. Wretched child!

B. Ke ana iwaKĀlua-kūmā-lua: mai hele ʻoe (don't go; *negative command*).
In English the word "don't" has two meanings: (1) Simple negative. I
don't like poi (ʻaʻole au makemake i ka ʻai). (2) Negative command.
Don't go (mai hele aku).

C. Ma ke alanui.

Nohea. *E ʻoluʻolu ʻoe.*
He malihini au. *Mahea*
*kekahi hale-ʻaina?
Lani. *(ʻĀwīwī.)* *Aia kekahi
hale-ʻaina, *ma ke kihi mua*
loa, Ka-lā-kaua, **a me*
Ka-piʻo-lani. **Maopopo iaʻu.*
He kamaʻāina au.
N. ʻAʻole maopopo pono iaʻu.
Mai ʻōlelo ʻāwīwī ʻoe. Namu
*hou mai. ʻŌlelo lohi.

L. (Lohi.) Ma ke kihi mua loa.
Ka-lā-kaua. A me Ka-piʻo-
lani. Maopopo?
N. ʻAe. Mahalo nui loa.
L. *He mea iki.* Mahea ʻoe i
aʻo ai i ka ʻōlelo Hawaiʻi?

N. Ma ka papa Hawaiʻi *ma ke*
kula-nui. Tsa! *Hemahema
maoli au.
L. Akamai loa! *Naʻauao!
N. ʻAʻole! Hūpō! Naʻaupō!
L. *Pono ke hoʻomaʻamaʻa!*
Pono ke hoʻomanawanui.
Mai hilahila!
N. Pono nō ʻoe. ʻAʻole
maikaʻi ka hilahila. He
hūpō! *Hoʻopaumanawa!*

D. Ma ka hale-ʻaina.

Kuene. Aloha ʻoe.
Nohea. Aloha kakahiaka.
Hiki nō ke hoʻoluhi iāʻoe?
Makemake au e ʻai.
Pōloli au.

C. On the street.

Nohea. *Please.* I'm a stranger.
Where is a/any restaurant?

Lani. *(Fast.)* There is a restaurant *on the first corner,* Ka-
lā-kaua, and Ka-piʻo-lani.
I understand. I'm a native.

N. I don't understand exactly.
Don't speak fast. Speak
(mutter) again. Speak
slowly.

L. (Slowly.) On the first
corner. Ka-lā-kaua. And
Ka-piʻo-lani. Understand?
N. Yes. Thanks very much.
L. *You are welcome/it's just*
a trifle. Where did you
learn the Hawaiian
language?

N. At the Hawaiian class *at*
the University. Gosh! I'm
real stupid!
L. Very smart! Wise!
N. No! Dumb! Ignorant!
L. (You) *must practice.*
(You) *must be patient.*
Don't be bashful!
N. You are so right. No good
to be bashful. Dumb!
Waste time!

D. At the restaurant.

Waiter. Hello.
Nohea. Good morning. *May (I)*
bother you? I want to eat.
I'm hungry.

K. He aha kō makemake?

W. What would you like (what your desire)?

N. 'O ka *poi, palaoa, i'a.

N. Poi, bread, fish.

K. Hiki. Makemake 'oe i wai?

W. Okay. Do you want water?

N. Tsa! Mamake au i lama!
Lawe mai i lama!

N. Heavens no! I want rum! (*Mamake* is commonly heard instead of *make-make*.) *Bring rum!*

K. Hiki. *Eia ka poi,* palaoa hou, i'a, a me ka lama. Ua lawa? *Piha? Mā'ona* 'oe?

W. Okay. *Here is the poi,* fresh bread, fish, and rum. Enough? *Full?* Satisfied? (*Mā'ona,* commonly pronounced but never written *mā'ana,* refers only to food.)

N. 'Ae. Mahalo nui. *'Ehia kālā?*

N. Yes. Thank you. *How much money/dollars?*

K. 'Elua kālā.

W. Two dollars.

N. Eia. A hui hou aku.

N. Here. Good-by.

K. Aloha.

W. Aloha.

N. Aloha. 'Ono loa kēlā 'ai! Piha maika'i. E ho'i hou mai ana au i keia hale-'aina.

N. Aloha. That food was delicious. So well filled! I'm coming back again to this restaurant.

IWAKĀLUA-KŪMĀ-KOLU

A. Ke ana iwakālua-kūmā-kolu: mau (plural).

Mau (sometimes pronounced mou) replaces nā as a sign of the plural after the following k-words:

demonstratives: keia mau lio, these horses (keia lio, this horse);

possessives: koʻu mau lio, my horses (koʻu lio, my horse);

kekahi: kekahi mau lio, some horses/some other horses;

and also after:

he: he mau lio kona, he has horses (he lio kona, he has a horse);

numbers: ʻehiku mau lio, seven horses.

Mau always precedes nouns!

Mau is in constant use, but never in the same position as nā.

This is one of the most important lessons in the book.

(1) Note carefully the new meanings for the demonstratives, kekahi, and he when preceding mau.

Keia mau kuene wāhine.	(1) These waitresses.
Kēlā mau koa hope loa.	*Those youngest/last soldiers.*
Kekahi mau leka *naʻaupō.	Some ignorant letters.
He mau *waʻa ʻelima kona.	He has five canoes.

(2) *Kō mākou mau makaʻu.*	(2) *Our (exc. 3) fears.*
Kā ke aliʻi wahine mau kaua.	*The chiefess' wars.*
Nani kēlā mau *lumi.	Those rooms are pretty.
Aʻo ʻoe i *kekahi mau pule lōʻihi.*	Learn *some long prayers.*
Kēnā mau wahi *pupuka.	Those (near you) ugly places.

B. The following words have long vowels in the plural: kānaka, wāhine, kaikamāhine, kāhuna, kūpuna, mākua.

(3) *Nui nā kāhuna.*	(3) *There are many kahuna/ priests.*
Auwē! Maʻi koʻu mau mākua!	Alas! My parents are sick!
*Uʻi nā wāhine.	The women are beautiful!
*Pāʻani nā kānaka apau.	All the people play.

Lapuwale nā kaikamāhine!
Makapō kēlā mau kūpuna!
He hana lapuwale kā kekahi
mau kāhuna.

The girls are worthless!
Those grandparents are blind!
Some magicians have wicked
ways/some magicians do
foolish deeds.

He niho nui loa kō ka
ʻelepani.
ʻElua pepeiao o ka lio.

The elephant has a very big
tusk.
The horse has two ears.

C. E ka haumana. E kākau mai ʻoe i keia mau mea o lalo nei: this horse, my canoe, this fear, some wars, this blind waiter, that university, a dollar, a restaurant, a soldier; these horses, my canoes, these fears, these blind waiters, those universities, some restaurants, some soldiers.

Are-a versus *have-a*. He mau kumu mākou; he mau kumu kā mākou. He kumu ʻoia, he kumu kāna. I'm a student; I have a student. We are students, we have students. He's a rat; he has a rat. You are a mother, you have a mother.

Double possessives. Ka wai a koʻu kupuna. Kō kō mākou mau kūpuna hale. His wife's hand. His wife's car. Pua's food. Pua's opinion. His mother's bread. This father's student. My grandchild's chicken.

D. Ka makaʻu.

D. Fear.

Keiki. *Makaʻu au i ka pō.*

Child. *I fear/am afraid of the night.*

Makuakāne. *Pono e koa!*
K. Nui nā lapu i ka pō!
   Makaʻu au i nā lapu.
M. Pono e hoʻomanawanui.
K. *Makaʻu au i ka mākaʻi!*
M. Mai makaʻu *iāia.
K. Makaʻu ʻo Keoki iā Mele.
M. ʻO wai ʻo Mele?
K. He lio wahine *ia. ʻAʻole
   au e makaʻu iāia.
M. *ʻĀʻoia.* He keiki koa ʻoe.

Father. (You) *must be brave!*
C. There are many ghosts at
   night. I fear ghosts.
F. Better be patient.
C. *I fear the policeman!*
F. Don't fear him.
C. George fears Mary.
F. Who's Mary?
C. She's a mare. I don't fear
   her.
F. *That's right.* You are a
   brave child.

K. Makaʻu ʻo *Tūtū iā Pele!
    Makaʻu ka luna i ka hana
    lima. Makaʻu ka haumana
    i nā hewa. Makaʻu ka mea
    maʻi i ka make.
M. Aloha ʻino!

C. Granny fears Pele. The
    boss fears manual (hand)
    work. The student fears
    mistakes. The sick person
    fears death.
F. Woe, woe!
    Remember: *makaʻu* takes object
    markers!

E. ʻUkulele.

Ka moʻopuna. *Hūi!*
Ke kupuna. Mai! Mai mai
  mai mai! Mai mai mai mai!

Grandchild. *Hello!*
Grandmother. Come! Come,
  come, come, come! Come,
  come, come, come!

M. E Tūtū. Hiki nō ke
    hoʻoluhi iāʻoe?
K. Pehea?
M. ʻIke nō ʻoe i ka moʻolelo
    o ka ʻukulele?
K. ʻIke loa.
M. *Mai hea mai ka ʻukulele?*
    He mea Hawaiʻi maoli?

C. Say, Granny. May (I)
    bother you?
M. What is it?
C. Do you know the story
    about the ʻukulele?
M. (I) know (it) well.
C. *Where is the ʻukulele from?*
    (Is it) a real Hawaiian
    thing?

K. ʻAʻole. Lawe mai ka poʻe
    Pukikī i keia mea.
M. *ʻOia?*
K. *I kēlā manawa* aia ma ke
    alo (court) o ka mōʻī
    he haole Pelekane. ʻO
    Edward Purvis kona inoa.
    He kanaka liʻiliʻi. Liʻiliʻi
    ke kino. ʻEleu (spry) ke
    kino. Kona inoa kapakapa
    (nickname), *ʻoia hoʻi ʻo
    ʻUkulele.* Nō kona liʻiliʻi,
    a no kona ʻeleu.

M. ʻO wai ka mōʻī ia manawa?

M. No. The Portuguese people
    brought this thing.
C. *Is that so?*
M. *At that time* there was at
    the court (alo) of the king
    an English haole. His name
    was Edward Purvis. A little
    man. Small body. Spry
    (ʻeleu) of body. His nick-
    name (inoa kapakapa),
    was *namely leaping flea.*
    Because of his smallness,
    and because of his
    spryness.
C. Who was the king at that
    time?

K. ʻO Ka-lā-kaua. Nui ka makemake o ʻUkulele i keia mea Pukikī. *Hoʻokani ʻoia* i ke alo o Ka-lā-kaua.

M. Ka-lā-kaua. ʻUkulele liked this Portuguese thing very much. *He played* at Ka-lā-kaua's court.

M. Huhū anei ʻo Ka-lā-kaua?

C. Was Ka-lā-kaua angry?

K. **ʻAʻole loa! Piha hauʻoli! Mahope mai *hāʻawi ka poʻe i ka inoa* ʻukulele i keia mea hoʻokani.

M. Not at all! (He was) full of joy! Afterwards *the people gave the name* ʻukulele to this musical instrument (playing thing).

M. Maikaʻi ka moʻolelo. Mahalo nui loa. He ʻukulele kaʻu. Hiki nō iaʻu ke hoʻokani. I keia manawa, ʻike nō au i ka moʻolelo o ka ʻukulele.

C. What a fine story. Thanks so much. I have an ʻukulele. I can play. Now (at this time) I know the story about the ʻukulele.

F. Hoʻomaʻamaʻa: the daughters of the farmer, the farmer's daughters; the ʻukulele of Purvis, Purvis' ʻukulele; the king of Hawaiʻi, Hawaiʻi's king; the ghosts of the night, the night's ghosts; the war of the soldiers, the soldiers' war.

HAʻAWINA

IWAKĀLUA-KŪMĀ-HĀ

A. Ke kula.

Kumu. E hoʻomaka kāua.
Lei-aloha. Hiki. *Pehea ke kumuhana?*
K. Nānā aku ʻoe i ke kiʻi ma ka haʻawina mamua o ka haʻawina ʻumi-kūmā-lua.
L. Hiki.
K. Pehea nā mea o loko o ke kiʻi?
L. Pehea la? ʻAʻole au ʻike.

K. E ʻoluʻolu ʻoe e nānā pono! He poʻe Hawaiʻi *anei?
L. ʻAe.
K. He poʻe haole kekahi?
L. Eia ʻelua haole.

K. Kū lāua i luna?
L. ʻAʻole. Ua noho.
K. Pehea kēlā mea mahope o ke kanaka e kū ana?
L. He hale ia.
K. He aha kekahi mea mahope?
L. He mau kāhili *paha.
K. ʻO wai ka wahine ma ka ʻaoʻao o Kamehameha?
L. ʻO kāna wahine kēlā.
K. Ua lawa. Maikaʻi kāu hana. E Helena, ua mākaukau ʻoe? Hiki iaʻu ke hoʻoluhi iāʻoe?

A. School.

Teacher. Let's begin.
Lei-aloha. Okay. *What subject?*
T. Look at the picture in the lesson before lesson 12.
L. Okay.
T. What are the things in the picture?
L. What are they? I don't know.
T. Please look carefully! Are there Hawaiian people?
L. Yes.
T. Are there haoles too?
L. (Pointing.) Here are two haoles.
T. Are they (2) standing?
L. No. Sitting.
T. What is that thing behind the man standing?
L. It's a house.
T. What else is in back?
L. Maybe some kāhilis.
T. Who is the woman at Kamehameha's side?
L. That's his wife.
T. (That's) enough. Your work has been fine. O Helen, are you prepared?

'Ike 'oe i *nā hua'ōlelo
pa'akikī?*

May I bother you? Do you
know *the hard/difficult
words?*

Helena. *Pehea? E like me
ke aha?*

Helen. *What about them?
Like what?*

K. Nā 'ano hale, 'oia ho'i, ka
hale-ma'i, ka hale-'aina,
ka hale-leka, ka hale-pule.

T. Kinds of houses, namely,
hospital, restaurant, post
office, church.

H. 'Ike.

H. Know (them).

K. Nā 'ano kānaka, 'oia ho'i,
Pelekane, Kōlea, Pukikī,
Pilipino, *hapa haole,
kupuna wahine, mahi'ai.

T. Kinds of people, namely,
Englishman, Korean, Portuguese, Filipino, hapa haole,
grandmother, farmer.

H. Ua 'ike nō.

H. Surely know.

K. Lawa ka pā'ani, kua, kino,
'ohu'ohu i nā *lei, kēlā
mea keia mea.

T. Enough play, back, body,
decked with leis, this and
that.

H. Maopopo ia'u. *Loa'a.*

H. I understand. *Got.*

K. He keiki na'auao 'oe.

T. You are a wise young
person.

H. Pololei 'oe. Akamai loa.
Mākaukau no *ka hō'ike.*

H. You are right. Sure smart.
Prepared for *the test.*

K. E Pili-aloha, 'ōlelo mai 'oe
i ka mo'olelo o ka 'ukulele.

T. O Pili-aloha, tell me the
story of the 'ukulele.

Pili-aloha. Hiki nō. Aia kekahi
haole Pelekane. He kino li'ili'i
kona. He kino 'eleu kona. 'O
'Ukulele kona inoa kapakapa.
Noho 'oia i ka hale o Ka-LĀ-
kaua. He mea ho'okani kāna.
Mai ka 'āina Pukikī mai.
Ho'okani. Ho'okani. Hau'oli
ka mō'ī. Hā'awi ka po'e i
keia inoa 'ukulele i ka mea
ho'okani.

Pili-aloha. Okay. There was a
British haole. He had a small
body. He had an active body.
'Ukulele was his nickname.
He stayed in Ka-LĀ-kaua's
house. He had a musical
instrument. From the Portuguese land. (He) played.
The king was happy. The
people gave this name 'ukulele to the musical instrument.

B. A common way to form the plural is: ka po'e wāhine, the women. In
such cases do not translate *po'e* by "people." *Po'e* is sometimes used
with inanimate objects, as *ka po'e hale*, the houses.

Maka'u noho'i ka po'e koa.	*The soldiers are certainly/surely afraid.*
Na'auao ka po'e wāhine.	The women are wise.
Koa loa ka po'e kama'āina.	*The natives are very brave.*
*Hilahila ka po'e haku.	The masters are ashamed.
Na'aupō ka po'e *malihini.	The tourists are ignorant.
He niho nui kō ka pōpoki.	The cat has a large tooth.
He hō'ike pa'akikī noho'i!	What a difficult examination!

C.   Insertion of directionals in inseparable *hoe-wa'a* constructions.

Ho'olohe pololei mai ia'u.	*Listen carefully to me.*
E ho'okani-'ukulele mai ana 'o Purvis.	Purvis was playing the 'ukulele.
Ua he'e-nalu aku ka po'e koa.	The soldiers surfed.
Ua ho'oponopono-ha'awina mai nō ke kumu.	The teacher indeed corrected lessons.
Holo-lio 'āwīwī mai nā koa.	The soldiers rode horseback fast.

HAʻAWINA

IWAKĀLUA-KŪMĀ-LIMA

A. Ke ana iwakālua-kūmā-lima: paha (maybe/perhaps/might). *Paha* is not said alone. *Paha* is in constant use, and renders speech less abrupt and commanding. It is polite and corresponds roughly to English "should, would, might" which softens speech.

A.	Hele paha kāua i ke kula-nui?	A.	Should we go to the University?
B.	Maikaʻi paha, akā, *paʻa hana nō au.*	B.	That would probably be all right, but *I'm busy.*
A.	ʻAʻole pilikia. Kala mai iaʻu. Hele paha kāua *mahope o ka hana.	A.	(It) doesn't matter. Excuse me. Maybe we'll go after work.
B.	Maikaʻi paha.	B.	(That's) probably okay.
A.	Mahea ke kula-nui?	A.	Where is the University?
B.	Aia paha ma ke alanui Kula-nui.	B.	It's probably on University Avenue.
A.	ʻĀʻoia. Pono nō ʻoe. Hūpō nō au.	A.	That's right. You are sure right. I'm dumb.
B.	Pēlā paha! Naʻaupō wale paha.	B.	Maybe so! Maybe just/only ignorant.
A.	Tsa! *Kulikuli!*	A.	Darn it! *Keep still/shut up!*

B. Hoʻomaʻamaʻa: hiki ke.   B. Practice: can.

Keawe.	E Ululani, *hiki iāʻoe ke holo lio?*	Keawe.	O Ululani, *can you ride horseback?*
Ululani.	Hiki paha.	Ululani.	Suppose (I) can.
K.	Hiki iāʻoe ke *hoe waʻa?	K.	Can you paddle a canoe?
U.	ʻAʻole loa, akā, hiki *iā Pua.	U.	Not at all, but Pua can.
K.	Hiki i kou *kupuna ke hula?	K.	Can your grandmother hula?
U.	ʻAe. Hiki nō iā Tūtū ke hula.	U.	Yes. Granny can hula.
K.	Hiki iāia ke kalaiwa kaʻa?	K.	Can she drive a car?

U. 'A'ole. Maka'u.

K. Hiki i kēlā keiki li'ili'i ke *kākau leka?

U. Hiki nō. Lawa nā nīnau. *Nīele 'oe.*

K. 'A'ole nīele. *'Imi na'auao nō!* He aha ka mana'o o kou inoa, 'oia ho'i, 'o Ululani? He hua 'ai?

U. 'A'ole loa. 'O heavenly inspiration!

U. No. (She's) afraid.

K. Can that little/small child write a letter?

U. Surely. Enough questions. *You are too curious/inquisitive/busybody.*

K. Not curious. *Just seeking knowledge!* What's the meaning of your name, that is, Ululani? A fruit?

U. No indeed. Heavenly/divine inspiration!

C. *Nā waiho'olu'u like 'ole.*

Kealoha. He aha ka waiho'olu'u o *ke koko?*
Pua. *He 'ula.*
K. He aha ka waiho'olu'u o ko'u pāpale?
P. *He ke'oke'o paha.*
K. Pehea ka waiho'olu'u o keia puke?
P. *He 'ula.*
K. Pehea ka waiho'olu'u o ka papa'ele'ele?
P. 'Elua nō 'ano. *Ke 'ano mamua, he 'ele'ele; ke 'ano hou, he 'ōma'oma'o paha.*
K. He aha ka waiho'olu'u o ka lani?
P. *He uliuli.*

K. He aha ka waiho'olu'u o kō Lei-lani *lole?
P. *He melemele.*
K. Pehea ka waiho'olu'u o kō *Kimo pālule?*

C. *The different/various colors.*

Kealoha. What's the color of *blood?*
Pua. *Red.*
K. What's the color of my hat?
P. *Probably white.*
K. What's the color of this book?
P. Red.
K. What's the color of the blackboard?
P. There are two kinds. *The old kind, black; the new kind, green.*
K. What's the color of the sky?
P. *Blue.* (*Uliuli* is also the color of the green of vegetation and the blackness of clouds.)
K. What's the color of Leilani's dress?
P. *Yellow.*
K. What's the color of *James' shirt?*

P.	He 'ōma'oma'o.	P.	Green.
K.	Pehea ka waiho'olu'u o kō moa?	K.	What's the color of your chicken?
P.	He ke'oke'o.	P.	White.

D. Ho'oma'ama'a: don't.

Negative declaration: They (2) don't sing well. They (3) don't fear war. I don't like that color. We don't like blue. You don't surf well.
Negative command: Don't sing. Don't speak like that. Don't be afraid. Don't paddle (a) canoe. Don't surf.

E. Reduplications.

Some bases may be repeated partially or wholly. The resulting forms are called *reduplications.* Colors are frequently reduplications, as in C above. A few examples of reduplications follow. Note that the meanings of bases and derived reduplications are not always the same.

Base	Reduplication
helu, count	heluhelu, read
holo, run	holoholo, go for a walk or ride
lau, leaf	laulau, leaf food package
li'i, small	li'ili'i, small
make, desire (rare)	makemake, mamake (colloquial), want, like
mu'u, cut off	mu'umu'u, gown without a train
'olu, pleasant	'olu'olu, pleasant, cool

The above are complete reduplications except for colloquial *mamake,* a partial reduplication (only the first syllable is repeated). Another partial reduplication is *'u'uku,* small from *'uku,* flea.
The repeated first syllable is not lengthened. *Kākau,* to write, tattoo, is composed of the rare causative prefix *kā-* + *kau,* to place. The same *kā-* prefix occurs also:

hili, to hit, smite	kāhili, feather standard
lepa, flag	kālepa, merchant (Merchants hoisted tapa flags.)
lua, pit	kālua, cook in the ground oven
pulu, mulch	kāpulu, messy

The prefixes *ho'o-* and *ma-* are not reduplicated:

luhi, tired, burden	māluhiluhi, tired
	ho'omāluhiluhi, to burden
pono, right	ho'oponopono, to correct

F.   Ho'oma'ama'a.

I have a green shirt, hat.
I have a red shirt, hat.
I have a blue shirt, hat.
I have a white shirt, hat.
I have a black shirt, hat.
I have a yellow shirt, hat.
She has a _____ dress.
You have a _____ horse.

IWAKĀLUA-KŪMĀ-ONO

A. Ke ana iwakālua-kūmā-ono: *k*-less possessives.
After *ʻehia, ʻaʻole, ʻaʻohe,* and numbers, *k*- is omitted from possessives.

A.	**ʻEhia ou mau lima?*	A.	*How many hands have you you?*
B.	*ʻElua oʻu lima.*	B.	*I have two hands.*
A.	*ʻEhia ou kuli?*	A.	*How many knees have you?*
B.	ʻElua oʻu kuli.	B.	I have two knees.
A.	*ʻEhia ona waha?*	A.	*How many mouths has he/she?*
B.	Hoʻokahi ona waha. Hoʻokahi *wale nō.	B.	He/she has one mouth. Only one.
A.	*ʻEhia āna kālā?*	A.	*How much money has he?*
B.	**ʻUmi-kūmā-lua āna mau kālā.*	B.	He has twelve dollars.
A.	*ʻEhia ihu o ka mahiʻai?*	A.	*How many noses has the farmer?*
B.	Hoʻokahi wale nō ona ihu.	B.	He has only one nose.
A.	ʻEhia maka o ka Pokoliko?	A.	How many eyes/faces has the Puerto Rican?
B.	ʻElua ona maka.	B.	He has two eyes.
A.	ʻEhia ou kaʻa?	A.	How many cars have you?
B.	ʻEhiku oʻu kaʻa. *Waiwai au.*	B.	I have seven cars. *I'm rich.*
A.	ʻEhia ou lio? *Āu moa?*	A.	How many horses have you? *Your chickens?*
B.	ʻEhā oʻu lio. *ʻAʻohe aʻu mau moa.*	B.	I have four horses. *I have no chickens. (ʻAʻohe: to have none/to be none; ʻaʻole plus he equals ʻaʻohe.)*

B. *Nā māhele *kino like ʻole.*   B. *Different parts of the body.*

A. He aha keia mea?   A. What is this thing?
(Points to his hand.)

B. Kou lima.   B. Your hand.

(A points in succession to nose, mouth, ear, eye, knee, leg/foot, *shoulder (poʻohiwi),* body, bone, *cheek (papālina),* bosom, back, *stomach (ʻōpū).* B answers.

C. Ma ka hale-maʻi.   C. At the hospital.

Kauka. Komo mai. Komo mai.   *Doctor.* Come in. Come in.

Mea maʻi. Aloha ahiahi, e ke kauka.   Sick person. Good evening, doctor.

K. Pehea? Leo nui! *ʻAʻole au lohe pono!*   D. What? Speak loud! *I don't hear well!*

M. ʻAʻole au maikaʻi. ʻEha koʻu ʻōpū. *I ka ʻai nui paha.*   S. I'm not well. My stomach hurts. *From eating too much maybe (i: because of, from).*

K. Pehea ke poʻo?   D. What about the head?

M. Nui ka ʻeha. *I ka inu lama paha.*   S. Hurts a lot. *From drinking liquor maybe.*

K. Pehea kou leo?   D. What of your voice?

M. Nui ka ʻeha. *I ke kamaʻilio nui paha.*   S. Hurts a lot. *From chatting too much maybe.*

K. *Pehea ka puʻuwai?*   D. *What about the heart?*

M. ʻEha i ke aloha!   S. Love-sick!

K. Pehea kāu *ipo?   D. What about your sweetheart?

M. E pāʻani kinipōpō ana. Loaʻa he pilikia. ʻEha ka wāwae. ʻAʻohe āna kālā. Kōkua mai!   S. Playing ball. Got an accident. Hurt his foot. He has no money. Help!

D. Nā māhele kino (for reference).

Adam's apple	puʻu	armpit	pōʻaeʻae
ankle	puʻupuʻu wāwae	artery (vein, nerve)	aʻa

beard	ʻumiʻumi	hair (body)	huluhulu
buttocks	ʻōkole, lemu	kidneys	puʻupaʻa
chest	umauma	lip	lehelehe
chin	ʻauwae	liver	ake
crown	piko	lung	akemāmā
(of head)		mustache	ʻumiʻumi
elbow	kuʻekuʻe lima	nail (of finger	maiʻao,
eyebrow	kuʻekuʻe maka	or toe)	mikiʻao,
eyelash	lihilihi		māiʻuʻu
face	maka	navel	piko
features	helehelena	neck	ʻāʻī
finger	manamana	throat	puʻu
	lima	thumb	manamana
forehead	lae		lima nui
genitals	maʻi, piko	toe	manamana
			wāwae

E. Nā mea Hawaiʻi.

Hina. E Keoki. He
hoʻoluhi keia. Nānā aku
ʻoe i ke kiʻi ma ka
haʻawina **ʻumi-kūmā-
kahi.
Keoki. Hiki.
H. ʻO wai ke aliʻi?
K. ʻO Kamehameha
**ʻEkahi.
H. ʻĀʻoia. Pololei. ʻO
wai ka mea i kona
ʻaoʻao?
K. ʻO kāna wahine, ʻoia
hoʻi, ʻo Ka-ʻahu-manu.
H. Pehea ka lole o Ka-ʻahu-
manu?
K. He pāʻū. *He lei palaoa.*
He mea waiwai loa.
He mea nui ia.

E. Hawaiian things.

Hina. O George. This is a
bother. Look at the picture
in lesson 11.

George. Okay.
H. Who's the chief?
G. Kamehameha I.

H. That's right. Correct.
Who is the person at his
side?
G. His wife, namely/to wit,
Ka-ʻahu-manu.
H. What's the dress of
Ka-ʻahu-manu?
G. A sarong. *A whaletooth
pendant.* A very valuable
thing. It's an important
thing.

H. Pehea ka lāhui o nā haole 'elua?	H. What is the nationality of the two haoles?
K. Pehea la? *He Lukia paha.*	G. How should I know? *Maybe Russian.*
H. Pehea ka mea *maluna o ke po'o o ka Lukia mua?	H. What's the thing over the head of the first Russian?
K. *He mai'a ia.*	G. *It's a banana.*

(H and K finish their conversation either very politely or rudely. The student should be equipped with both types of salutation.)

F. Practice the dialogue in ha'awina iwakālua-kūmā-lua. But this time do some improvisation and do not follow literally the dialogue given in that lesson.

(1) Kanahele greets Noe-lani on the street and asks where he can find a restaurant. N answers but speaks too fast. K asks her to repeat, which she does. She asks where he learned Hawaiian and he says at the University but that he's dumb. She encourages him.

(2) At the restaurant K is greeted by the waiter. He orders. W brings his order and asks if he wants water. He either says yes or asks for liquor. He asks for the bill.

HAʻAWINA

IWAKĀLUA-KŪMĀ-HIKU

A. Ke ana iwakālua-kūmā-hiku: ʻumi-kūmā-iwa, kanaono-kūmā-lua (1962).

A. He aha ka makahiki o ke kaua hope loa?	A. What was the year of the last war?
B. Hoʻomaka i ka makahiki ʻumi-kūmā-iwa, kanahā-kūmā-kahi. Pau i ka makahiki ʻumi-kūmā-iwa, kanahā-kūmā-lima. ʻAʻole anei?	B. Began in the year 1941. Finished in the year 1945. Isn't that so?
A. ʻĀʻoia. Pehea nā makahiki o ke kaua mua?	A. That's right. What are the years of the first war?
B. Mai ʻumi-kūmā-iwa, ʻumi-kūmā-hā, a ʻumi-kūmā-iwa, ʻumi-kūmā-walu. ʻAʻole anei?	B. From 1914 to 1918. Isn't that so?
A. ʻĀʻoia. E kākau ana au i nā makahiki like ʻole ma ka papa-ʻeleʻele. Nānā mai ʻoe.	A. That's right. I'm going to write various years on the blackboard. You look. (A goes to the blackboard and writes various years, as 1776, 1816, 1492, 1820.)
	Say B, please read these years. (B reads.) What was *last year?* (B answers.)
E B, ʻoluʻolu ʻoe. Heluhelu mai ʻoe i keia *mau makahiki. (Heluhelu ʻo B.) Pehea *kēlā makahiki aku nei?* (Pane ʻo B.)	
B. Hana nui! *Māluhiluhi au.* Auwē nohoʻi e! Nīele! *Kou manawa keia.*	B. Hard work. *I'm tired/exhausted.* Boy, oh boy! Too inquisitive! *Your turn/time* now. (B goes to the blackboard and writes other dates.)

	He aha keia mau makahiki?		What are these years?
A.	*ʻUmi-kūmā-iwa hanele.*	A.	*1900.* 1806.
	ʻUmi-kūmā-walu me ʻeono.		
B.	ʻEhia ou mau makahiki?	B.	How old are you?
A.	Iwakālua oʻu makahiki wale nō.	A.	I'm just 20.
B.	ʻŌpiopio loa ʻoe!	B.	You are so young!
A.	ʻAʻole. *Luahine (aiʻole) ʻelemakule.* Luahine loa (aiʻole) ʻelemakule loa.	A.	No. *Old woman (or) old man.* Too old!

B.   Word order.

Verb + verb	± *wale*	± directional	± *ana*	± *nō, la,*
marker		*(hoe-waʻa*		*(mai, aku,*		*anei,*
	construction*)*	*iho)*		*paha*

Insert *mai, aku,* or *iho* in the following. A laila, unuhi mai.

Ua hoʻoponopono hou ʻoia i nā hewa. Hanele!

Piʻi wale i ke kuahiwi.

E *kalaiwa kaʻa ana lāua i *nā lā* apau (all *days,* every day).

A hui hou nō kāua.

E heluhelu puke ana nō ka poʻe wāhine.

E mele paha ʻoe i keia manawa.

E nānā ʻoe i ka hale mua aiʻole i ka hale hope loa?

ʻImi naʻauao nō ka poʻe haumana.

C.   Restatement: shift from indirect to direct discourse.

Indirect	Direct
ʻŌlelo mai ʻoia, ua māluhiluhi.	ʻŌlelo mai ʻoia: "Māluhiluhi au."
ʻŌlelo ka ʻelemakule, ua māʻona ʻoia.	ʻŌlelo ka ʻelemakule: "Ua māʻona au."
ʻŌlelo ʻoia pono au e hele.	ʻŌlelo ʻoia: "Pono ʻoe e hele."
He said (he) was tired.	He said: "I'm tired."
The old man said he was full.	The old man said: "I'm full."
He said that I must go.	He said: "You must go."

D. He inoa nō Kīna'u.

E Kīna'u e, noho nani mai.
Kō kino e, ki'i milimili.
Kō maka e, noweo wale.
Kō papālina, e kukū ana.
Kō ihu e, e hanu *onaona.*

Kō waha e, e māpu ana.
Kō po'ohiwi, kau mai i luna.
Kō *lima e, ani pe'ahi.
Kō poli e, nahenahe wale.
Kō 'ōpū, *pahu* wai lana.

Kō kuli e, nuku moi oe.
Kō wāwae, ki'i palanehe.
Ha'ina 'ia mai ana ka puana:
Kīna'u e, noho nani mai.
He inoa nō Kīna'u.

D. A name song for Kīna'u.

O Kīna'u, sit in pretty fashion.
Your body, a doll to play with.
Your eyes, so bright.
Your cheeks, standing.
Your nose, shall breathe *soft fragrance.*

Your mouth, wafting perfume.
Your shoulders, placed high.
Your hand, swings fan-like.
Your bosom, so soft.
Your stomach, *a keg/box* of floating water.

Your knee, just a moi fish beak.
Your feet, dainty fetching.
Tell the refrain:
O Kīna'u, sit in pretty fashion.
A name song for Kīna'u.

IWAKĀLUA-KŪMĀ-WALU

A. Nānākuli.

Malihini.	He aha ʻo Nānākuli?	Stranger.	What is Nānākuli?
*Kamaʻāina.	He kūlanakauhale ia.	Native.	Itʻs a town.
M.	Mahea keia kūlanakauhale?	S.	Where is this town?
K.	ʻAʻole ʻoe ʻike?	N.	You donʻt know?
M.	ʻAʻole.	S.	No.
K.	Nīele paha ʻoe? Aia ma- waena o ʻEwa a me Waiʻanae.	N.	You are too curious maybe? Itʻs between ʻEwa and Waiʻanae.
M.	Pehea ka *manaʻo o kēlā inoa?	S.	Whatʻs the meaning of that name?
K.	*Penei hoʻokahi manaʻo.* ʻOia hoʻi, ka nānā ʻana i kekahi mea, i ka hale paha, i ka lio paha, i ke kaikamahine paha.	N.	*One meaning goes like this.* Namely, looking at some- thing, at a house maybe, at a girl maybe.
M.	Pehea ka manaʻo o "kuli"?	S.	Whatʻs the meaning of "kuli"?
K.	ʻElua paha manaʻo. Hoʻokahi, ʻoia kekahi o nā māhele o ke kino. ʻO ka manaʻo o Nānākuli, *e pili ana i nā kānaka* e nānā ana i nā kuli o ke kanaka.	N.	Probably two meanings. One is one of the parts of the body. The meaning of Nānākuli *refers to people* looking at peoplesʻ knees.
M.	Pupule kēlā manaʻo. Pehea kekahi manaʻo o "kuli"?	S.	That meaning is crazy. Whatʻs another meaning of "kuli"?
K.	Penei nō:	N.	(It goes) like this:

" ʻO kekahi manaʻo o ʻkuli,ʻ e pili ana i kekahi kanaka ʻaʻole maikaʻi kona lohe ʻana. ʻO Nānākuli, he ʻāina maloʻo (dry) *i ka wā kahiko* (an- cient times). ʻAʻohe *wai. He ʻāina nani, *akā, ʻaʻole momona (fertile) loa. Ua lawe mai ka poʻe i ka wai mai kekahi wahi mamao mai. Ka poʻe o Nānākuli i ka wā kahiko, ʻaʻole lākou e *walaʻau (speak/shout)* i nā kānaka e hele ana ma ke alanui. ʻAʻole walaʻau aku: ʻHele mai e ʻai. Mai! Mai ʻoukou e ʻai! Mai! Mai! Mai! Mai!ʼ ʻAʻole nui o kā lākou ʻai a me kā lākou wai. Ua like pū lākou me nā kānaka kuli. ʻAʻole lākou *pane mai. Hoʻokuli (pretend to be deaf) lākou. ʻAʻole walaʻau, ʻaʻole kamaʻilio. ʻO ka noho wale ʻana mai nō.ʼ (Mai iā Simeon K. Nawaa.) Pololei *keia wehewehe ʻana (explanation)*, ʻaʻole paha.

He aha ka manaʻo o Nānākuli?

B.   Ke ana iwakālua-kūmā-walu: ʻana, noun-maker.

New pattern without directional:
kona lohe ʻana	his hearing
ka noho wale ʻana	the sitting, living
keia wehewehe ʻana	this explanation

New pattern with directional:
ka hele ʻana aku	the departure

kona hele ʻana mai	his arrival
ka noho wale ʻana mai	just sitting, just living

Do not confuse with *old* pattern:

e hele aku ana au	I am going away
e hele mai ana au	I am coming
e wehewehe mai ana ʻoia	he is explaining

If X represents a noun or verb, and Dir a directional (mai, aku, iho), the two patterns may be shown thus:

	New pattern	Old pattern
Without directional:	k-word X ʻana (ka hele ʻana)	e X ana (e hele ana)
With directional:	k-word X ʻana Dir (ka hele ʻana aku)	e X Dir ana (e hele aku ana)

C. *Hoʻomaʻamaʻa i nā *huaʻōlelo ʻekolu: mai.

Mai Lukia kēlā *ʻano maʻi.	That type of sickness is *from* Russia.
Mai hoe waʻa ʻoe pēlā.	*Don't* paddle a canoe that way.
Maikaʻi ʻole kēlā ʻano moku.	That kind of island is *no good*.
ʻAʻole lākou i ohuʻohu i kēlā manawa.	They weren't lei bedecked at that time.
*Holo mai nā waʻa ʻekolu.	Three canoes sailed *here*.
Hele mai! Mai! Komo mai!	Come here! Come! Come in!
Mai ʻimi i kēlā pōpoki.	Don't look for that cat.

D. Restatement: substitute the proper pronouns for the noun phrases in italics: Hele mai *ka poʻe haumana* me *ke kumu* e ʻike i *ka ʻelemakule*. ʻAʻole i walaʻau *ka poʻe o Nānākuli* (put the pronoun before the verb marker). ʻAʻole e pili keia inoa i *ka poʻe pī. ʻAi maiʻa nā Lukia*.

IWAKĀLUA-KŪMĀ-IWA

A. Ka mea waiwai.

Lono. ʻIke ʻoe iā Keawe?
Haulani. ʻAe, he kanaka
waiwai loa. ʻElua ona
kaʻa, *ʻekolu ona lio,
ʻehā ona papa heʻe nalu,
ʻeono āna puaʻa.
L. ʻEhia āna keiki?
H. ʻAʻohe āna keiki. ʻAʻohe
āna wahine.
L. He hale nani anei kona?
H. Nani loa, akā ʻaʻole ʻoia
noho paʻa i kēlā hale.
*Holoholo nō. ʻAʻole
hauʻoli kona puʻuwai.

L. ʻOia! Nui ke kālā,
kaumaha ka naʻau!

B. Ke kiʻiʻoniʻoni.

A. E B, *haʻi mai,* mahea
ka hale kiʻiʻoniʻoni?
B. Aia, ma ke kihi.
A. Mahea? ʻAʻole wau e ʻike.
B. *Ma ʻō aku.* Mauka aku.
(Pronounce: maʻōwaku,
maukaku.)

A. He aha ka inoa o ke kiʻi?

B. *Ke koko ame ke one*
(aiʻole: Ke kino ame ka
ʻuhane; Ke keiki kāne a
Kakana).

A. The rich man.

Lono. Do you know Keawe?
Haulani. Yes, a very rich man.
He has two cars, three horses,
four surfboards, *six pigs.*

L. How many children has he?
H. He has no children. He has
no wife.
L. Has he a beautiful house?
H. Very beautiful, but he
doesn't *stay permanently*
in that house. Just keeps
running around. His heart
is not happy.
L. Is that so! Much money, a
sad heart.

B. The moving picture.

A. O B, *tell me,* where is the
moving picture theater?
B. There, on the corner.
A. Where? I don't see (it).
B. *Over there.* Inland.

A. What's the name of the
picture?
B. *Blood and Sand* (or: Body
and Soul; The Son of
Tarzan).

A. *Pehea la? He ki'i'oni'oni maika'i paha? Maika'i 'ole paha?

A. What about it? Maybe it's a good movie? No good maybe?

B. Auwē noho'i e! He maika'i loa. Nui ka maika'i. Maika'i maoli.

B. Boy, oh boy! Very good. Wonderful. Real good.

A. E hele paha kāua i loko e nānā ai?

A. Should we go in and look at it?

B. Hiki nō!

B. Okay!

A. He ki'i'oni'oni me nā waiho'olu'u like 'ole?

A. Is it a moving picture with different colors?

B. Pēlā paha.

B. Maybe so.

A. 'Ehia kālā?

A. How much money?

B. 'A'ole pilikia. Aloha wau iā'oe. He kālā ka'u. Hele kāua i loko e nānā i ke ki'i'oni'oni.

B. Never mind. I have aloha for you. I have money. Let's go inside and look at the movie.

C. Eia nā *nīnau like 'ole. Aia nā pane i waena o nā hua'ōlelo malalo iho o nā nīnau.

1. *Kaha i *ho'okahi lālani malalo o (draw a line under)* nā inoa o na waiho'olu'u like 'ole.

2. Kaha i 'elua lālani malalo o nā 'ano hale.

3. Kaha i 'ekolu lālani malalo o nā māhele kino.

4. Kaha i nā hua palapala (letters) "lā" malalo o nā 'ano lāhui.

5. Kākau i nā hua palapala "lo" malalo o nā 'ano lole.

6. Kākau i ka hua'ōlelo e pili ana i ke kanaka e hana ana i ka hale-'aina.

7. Kākau i ka hua'ōlelo e pili ana i ke kanaka penei kona 'ano: 'a'ole nui ona *makahiki.

8. He aha paha ka hana a ke kanaka 'a'ole 'oia i pa'a hana?

'ele'ele, hale-leka, hale-pule, holoholo, holo lio, kālā, kalaiwa ka'a, *kāma'a, ke'oke'o, koko, kuene, kula-nui, leo, Lukia, mai'a, maka, kēlā makahiki aku nei, malo, māluhiluhi, manawa, melemele, moa, mokupuni, 'ōma'oma'o, 'ōpiopio, pa'a hana, pālule, *Pokoliko, pu'uwai, uliuli, uwē, waha.

Inā nīnau 'āwīwī ke kumu, maopopo iā'oe nā nīnau like 'ole?

D. Ha'i mai i ka mo'olelo o nā pea 'ekolu. *Inā poina 'oe (if you have forgotten)* nānā hou i ka ha'awina 'umi-kūmā-iwa.

KANAKOLU

A. *Nā lā o ka pule.*

Sunday	lāpule	Thursday	pōʻahā
Monday	pōʻakahi	Friday	pōʻalima
Tuesday	pōʻalua	Saturday	pōʻaono
Wednesday	pōʻakolu		

Days of the week, like abstract nouns (haʻawina ʻumi), are preceded by *k*-words. Hawaiian names need not be capitalized.

Keawe. ʻEhia lā o ka pule hoʻokahi?

Keawe. How many days in (of) one week?

Hina. *ʻEhiku. *ʻOia hoʻi . . . (haʻi aku ʻoia i nā inoa *like ʻole).

Hina. Seven. Namely . . . (she names the various days).

K. He aha ka lā *mua loa o ka pule?

D. What is the first day of the week?

H. *Ka lāpule.*

H. *Sunday.*

K. He aha ka lā hope loa o ka pule?

K. What is the last day of the week?

H. *Ka pōʻaono.*

H. *Saturday.*

K. He aha nā lā ʻelua hope loa o ka pule?

K. What are the two last days of the week?

H. *Ka pōʻalima a me ka pōʻaono.*

H. *Friday and Saturday.*

K. He aha keia lā?

K. What's today?

H. *Ka pōʻakolu.*

H. *Wednesday.*

K. *He aha nehinei?*

K. *What was yesterday?*

H. *Ka pōʻalua.*

H. *Tuesday.*

K. He aha kēlā ʻapōpō?

K. What's tomorrow?

H. Ka pōʻalima. ʻAʻole anei?

H. Friday. Isn't it?

K. ʻAʻole loa. Ua *hewa ʻoe. *Hoʻaʻo hou mai.*

K. Certainly not. You're wrong. *Try again.*

H. Ka lāpule?

H. Sunday?

K. ʻAʻole. Pōʻakolu keia lā. ʻApōpō, *pōʻahā.*

K. No. Today, Wednesday. Tomorrow, *Thursday.*

H.	'Oia? A laila, he *papa Hawai'i ka'u. Holo au. Inā 'a'ole hele i ka papa, huhū wela loa ke kumu.	H.	Is that so? Then I have a Hawaiian class. I'm running. If (I) don't go to the class, the teacher is red-hot angry.
K.	'Oia? A laila, holo nō. Pau ka papa, ho'i hou mai! Mai poina!	K.	Is that so? Then run. After class, come back again! Don't forget!

B. Ho'oma'ama'a i nā māhele kino, nā 'ano hale, ame nā waiho'olu'u like 'ole. Unuhi i keia mau hua'ōlelo.

(1) Body parts: mouth, nose, cheeks, ear, eyes, head, knee, bone, shoulder, arm, blood, belly, voice, bosom. A'o i keia mau mahele kino hou: *'ili (skin), lauoho (hair).*

(2) Kinds of houses: church, restaurant, hospital, post office, store.

(3) Different colors: red, black, white, green, yellow, blue (of sky). A'o i keia waiho'olu'u hou: *polū (blue).*

C. Ho'oma'ama'a i nā ana like 'ole. E kākau 'oe *malalo iho i nā *huahelu o nā ana like 'ole.

(4) Ke ana _____ . He *ho'oluhi kēlā. That is a big rain. That is a green dress. This is a deaf Korean. That is beautiful hair.

(5) Ke ana _____ . Ho'opaumanawa kēlā mea. The rooms are new. The body parts are different. There are many kinds of churches. That help is good. This island is big. Her hat is very new. Your daughter is busy.

(6) Ke ana _____ . Ho'okahi a'u kumu. He has no car. How many children has she? They have many children.

(7) Ke ana _____ . Nānā mai ia'u. The farmer likes food. The girl likes Keawe. I like you.

(8) Ke ana _____ . Waiwai ko'u hale. Your husband is not busy. His wife does not speak much. Their store is not magnificent.

D. He unuhi. Eia ka ho'omaka 'ana o kekahi mo'olelo. He wahine maika'i loa 'o Hoa-make-i-ke-kula, a he nani loa kona mau helehelena (features) ke (when) nānā aku. 'O kona 'ili, ua like me ka 'ili o ka 'ōpu'u (bud) mai'a o ka hua hou 'ana iho. 'O kona *maka, ua like me ka pua o ka weleweka (velvet), a 'o kona kino, ua pololei (straight) a kīnā 'ole (without a blemish). [Fornander, vol. 4, ka 'ao'ao 533]

KANAKOLU-KŪMĀ-KAHI

A. Ke ana: nō, nā (for/belonging to/by). *N*-words.

nō	nā
no'u	na'u
nou	nāu
nona	nāna
nō kāua	nā kāua
nō māua	nā māua
etc.	etc.

Nō and *nā* are used like *o* and *a*, with the added meanings "for/by." *N*- may replace every initial *k*- in the possessives (ha'awina 'umi-kūmā-hā a me 'umi-kūmā-ono). These are called *n*-words. Nānā pono! 'A'ole like ka hua'ōlelo *nānā* "to see" a me *nānā*, "by him/her." Nānā pono mai 'oe i nā mana'o like 'ole malalo iho:

Kumu. *Nā wai keia māmala'ōlelo?*
Noe-lani. Nā Pua.
K. Nāna?
N. 'Ae, nāna.
K. (Iā Pua.) Nāu?
Pua. *Na'u.*
K. *Eia he mau hewa *li'ili'i. E ho'oponopono mai 'oe penei:
Nō wai kēlā ka'a ma 'ō aku?
Nā wai kēlā puke 'ula?
Nā wai ka wai?
*No'u kēlā *lio.*

He inoa nō Lili'u.
He mele nā Kale Kini.

Teacher. *Whose sentence is this* (by whom this sentence)?
Noe-lani. Pua's (by Pua).
T. Hers (by her)?
N. Yes, hers.
T. (To Pua.) Yours (by you)?
Pua. *Mine.*
T. Here are some small mistakes. Make corrections as follows:
Whose car is that over there?
Whose red book is that?
Whose water is that?
Give me that horse/that horse is for me.
A name song for Lili'u.
A song by Charles King.

B. Nānā hou i ke kama'ilio 'ana e pili ana i ke ki'i'oni'oni. Aia ma ka ha'awina iwakālua-kūmā-iwa. Practice this dialogue again, taking all parts, but follow the outline below. Improvising is fine if you use tried and true idioms and patterns.

A asks B if he speaks Hawaiian. B says "yes" and A asks where a
movie is. B says the movie is near, at the corner, towards the mountains.
A thanks him. He asks the name of the movie. B says "Blood and Sand"
or "War and Peace" or "Red and White." A asks if it's a good and if it's
in technicolor. B answers. B asks what it costs. A says two dollars and B
says that's too much. B says that it's no trouble, that he has money, and
that the two should go to the movie.

C.   Hoʻomaʻamaʻa ʻoe i nā ana like ʻole. E kākau ʻoe malao *iho i nā huahelu
     o nā ana.

   (1) Ke ana _____ . E haʻi mai ʻoe i kou inoa. Go to that ugly
        store. Let's sing. Come here and eat! The farmer should go down
        below. Stand up! Sit down!
   (2) Ke ana _____ . Nui nā lālani. There are many kinds of rooms
        over there. There are many blind people. There is much trouble
        and pain.
   (3) Ke ana _____ . Makaʻu ʻoia i nā lapu. He admires the statue of
        the king. The student corrects his mistakes. What's the answer?
   (4) Use e, e . . . ana, or ua in the following:
        Paddle the canoe slowly. They should play ball. He ate chicken.
        They (2) were eating in the restaurant. I will practice.

D.   Review for final examination.

Nā ana like ʻole:

   1-3.   He puke pupuka kēlā.
   4-6.   He Lukia akamai ʻoia.
   7-10. Kulikuli kēlā mea *hūpō.
   11-13. Uʻi anei kona leo?
   14-16. ʻAʻole nīele *kāna keiki.
   17-22. *Mahalo au i kāna kumu.
          Mahea ke kūlanakauhale?
   23-25. Ua waiwai ka *mahiʻai.
          E hoʻolohe pono mai ʻoe.
   26-29. Ua māluhiluhi ka poʻe
             lapuwale.
          Eʻai i ka palaoa keʻokeʻo.
          E holoholo ana lākou.

30-36. Aloha ke akua iā kākou.
37-42   Hoʻonani aku lākou i ke
           Akua.
        Uʻi ka lākou hoʻonani
           ʻana aku.

Nā unuhi:

   1. This is a new sarong.
   2. That is a new meaning.
   3. That is a red loincloth.
   4. You are a good teacher.
   5. He is a polite person.
   6. I am a fat soldier.

7. That help is good.
8. This land is fertile.
9. My hat is new.
10. Your child is good.

(Supply *anei* in the following.)

11. Is the moving picture new?
12. Is the meaning difficult?
13. Is the hungry person polite?

14. Your husband does not sit.
15. His wife does not speak much.
16. His house is not big.

(In sentences 17-22, supply markers only before *objects* of verbs; not before *subjects* of verbs, nor in verbless sentences.)

17. The teacher explained the lesson.
18. The student corrected my mistakes.
19. His name is Kekai.
20. Where is the movie?
21. Is the horse near?
22. How about the subject?

(Use *ua* or *e* in the following.)

23. Paddle the canoe.
24. They should play ball.
25. He ate the poi.

(Use *ua, e,* or *e . . . ana* in the following.)

26. They were eating in the restaurant.

27. Eat the fruit.
28. The visitor danced over there.
29. The university is big.

(Supply *ke* or *ka* when desirable in the following.)

30. O chief, is your child sick?
31. They want water.
32. Teacher, stand up please.
33. Wife, don't be afraid of work.
34. Come on Tuesday.
35. God is glorious.
36. Fear is no good.

(Rewrite the following with *mai* or *aku* inserted in the proper place. Note on pages 35 and 88 that parts of a *hoe-waʻa* construction are not separated by insertion of directionals or particles.)

37. Ua holo lio ka poʻe Lukia.
38. ʻĀwīwī ka lākou holo lio ʻana.
39. E ʻōlelo lohi ʻoe.
40. E haʻi moʻolelo ana ʻoia.
41. Lōʻihi kona haʻi moʻolelo ʻana.
42. Hele hou lāua i ke kūlanakauhale.

E. Hoʻomaʻamaʻa i ka huaʻōlelo "hiki" penei: Hiki iā Pua ke noho. I can help. His chief can farm. Kale can play ball. He can come down.

F. Possessives. Tell a student to admire your automobile, to take care of his mother, to inspect your (plural) university, to be careful of his books, to love his country, to go with you to the movie, to correct your mistakes, to come to the house of you and your wife.

G. The sentences in A beginning with *n*-words are VERBLESS sentences, as are the following:

He kanaka maikaʻi	ke kumu.	The teacher is a good person.
ʻO Kini	ke kumu.	Jean is the teacher.
Nā Kini	ka haʻawina.	The lesson is by Jean.
Nō ka lani	ka inoa.	The name chant honors the royal chief.

Nā- phrases also occur in sentences containing verbs, but the verb phrase is subordinate and follows the *na-* phrase. The use of *e* (non-past) and *i* (past) suggests the use of these particles in the pattern *ʻaʻole lākou* (*e* + verb, haʻawina ʻehā, B):

Nā wai e kalaiwa i ke kaʻa?	Who should drive the car?
Nā wai i kaha i ke kiʻi?	Who drew the picture?

Unuhi:

Nāna i hoʻoponopono i ka haʻawina.
Nā lākou i lawe mai ka meaʻai.
Nā ke aliʻi e lawe mai i ke kāhili.
I corrected the lesson. I will correct the lesson.
Jean saw the house. Jean will see the house.

Note the object marker after the verb following the *nā-* phrases above. This *i* object marker is often omitted, especially in old texts. In such constructions, a verb after *nā-* may be considered *passive*. The noun phrase following is the *subject*.

Nā Pua i kākau ka haʻawina.	The lesson was written by Pua.

Remember these contrasts:

nā	the (plural)
nā	for/by
nō	intensifier
nō	for

H.   Practice *can.*

I can paddle.
I can paddle-canoe.
I can drive.
I can drive-car.
I can draw.
I can draw-picture.
I can learn.
I can learn the lesson.
I can learn that lesson.
I can learn my lesson.

Can you _____ (same phrases)?
He can't _____ .
We couldn't _____ .

KANAKOLU-KŪMĀ-LUA

A. Ke ana 32: Makemake au e hoʻaʻo (I want to try).
    E introduces subordinate verbs, often with the idea of purpose.

(1) *Makemake ʻoia e ʻai ʻuala.*	(1) *He likes to eat sweet potatoes.*
Makemake ke kumu e *wehewehe i ka moʻolelo.*	The teacher wants to *explain the story.*
Pono e kōkua iā lāua.	It's necessary to help them (2).
Makemake au e hoʻaʻo e holo lio.	I want to try to ride horseback.
Hoʻaʻo e hoʻopaʻanaʻau!	*Try to memorize!*

B. Hoʻomaʻamaʻa i nā ana like ʻole. Nō ka hōʻike keia.

   (1) Ke ana _____. ʻAʻohe a lākou ʻuala. How many shoes have you? They have no leis. How much money has he? You have six horses and three dogs. George has no sons. Yes, we have no bananas.

   (2) Ke ana _____. Hiki i kaʻu mau *moʻopuna ke hoʻokani. He can understand. The farmer can play fairly. Robert can't ride horseback. My son can sing well. Can you?

   (3) Ke ana _____. Mai *lohi mai ʻoe. Don't be afraid of a long war. Don't eat that banana. They don't learn fast.

   (4) Ke ana _____. Naʻu kēlā mea. Give me that banana. Whose fault is that? His. Mine. The new car is for you.

   (5) Ke ana _____. *Mauka o ka hale-kūʻai. In the room. Outside the university. In the middle of the time. There.

   (6) Ke ana _____. He ʻīlio kāna. The rat has bread. The land has rain. She has a red dress. I have black shoes.

   (7) Ke ana _____. *Lapuwale kēlā mau ʻiole. Those errors are shameful. The blue sarongs are pretty. Fresh fruits.

   (8) Ke ana _____. Ka iʻa a kaʻu kumu. The man's sweetheart is sick. My grandchild's bread. His wife's father. The girl's back hurts. His student's story.

(9) Ke ana _____ . *ʻUmi-kūmā-iwa kanaono-kūmā-lua. 1352.
1948. 1066. 1766. 1932. 1829. 58. 76. 29. 30.

C. ʻIke pono nō ʻoe i keia mau huaʻōlelo paʻakīkī, ʻoia hoʻi, naʻau, poli,
pōʻakolu, ʻili, polū, lauoho melemele, mōʻī, hale-maʻi Kakolika, mokupuni, *alanui pololei, poʻohiwi, papālina, wāwae māluhiluhi, pahu lama,
hale-kūʻai palaoa, *kua pololei.

D. Review for final examination.

1-7. Aia ʻoia *mamua o ka
papa.

8-11. Aloha au iāʻoe.

12-14. Ke kua o kāna wahine.
Kō kāna wahine kua.

15-17. He ʻiole kā ke keiki.

18-20. Nui nā ʻano hale-leka.

21-24. Keia mau ʻuala.
Kona mau mākua.

25-28. Nui ka *nīele o ke keiki
ʻuʻuku.

29-32. Hiki i kaʻu wahine KE
holo lio.
Hiki iāia KE hoe waʻa.
Hiki iā Pua KE *heʻe
nalu.

1. There the doctor is in front
of his house.

2. Inside the chiefʻs box.

3. Outside their school.

4. Inland of your grandchild.

5. Between the pages.

6. In the middle of the city.

7. After Saturday.

8. Tell Lipoa.

9. Look at him.

10. Are you afraid of us?

11. Did you buy the bread?

(Write the following in two
ways.)

12. My sweetheart's pain.

13. His teacher's grandmother.

14. Mahealani's car.

15. The Englishman has red
blood.

16. The child has a feather
cloak.

17. The priest has a pencil.

18. There are many kinds of
fish.

19. There are many kinds of
green shirts.

20. There are many visitors.

21. Several years.

22. Some good girls.

23. My hats.

24. Those yellow dresses.

(Begin the following with
nui ka.)

25. The lesson is very hard.

26. The song is very pretty.

27. The doctor is very near.

28. This town is very good.

29. The Portuguese can eat
bananas.

30. I can hear well.
31. My farmer son can try.

32. Ku'ulei can bother you.

E. More review.

1-3. Makemake lāua e heluhelu puke.
Makemake lāua e heluhelu i nā puke.
4-9. 'Ehia ou wa'a? 'Ehia āna kālā? 'A'ohe o'u hale.
10-12. Maika'i kō kākou noho 'ana.
13-16. Hele i ka pō'alua.
17-19. Nānā ke keiki.
21-24. *Mai kū aku.
Mai Kahiki mai ka malihini.

Write the following twice, once in the *hoe-wa'a* construction, and then in the *hoe-i-ka-wa'a* construction.

1. I like to ride horseback.
2. He paddles a canoe.
3. They (2) eat poi on Friday.
4. How many fish bones have you?
5. How many automobiles has he?
6. He has no students.
7. I have eight books.
8. I have no money.
9. John has no hat.
10. Our conversation is ignorant.
11. Their going is foolish. (Use *o*-form.)
12. Your reading is correct.

13. Help on Thursday.
14. Pray on Sunday.
15. Go to the movie on Monday.
16. Blue, red, yellow, green.
17. Give me that car. (Use *n*-word.)
18. Give him that surfboard.
19. Give us that test.
20. Name fourteen *māhele kino*.
21. Don't listen to him.
22. They don't play fairly.
23. This doesn't refer to that.
24. He is from Maui.
25. 78, 83, 92, 47, 25, 34, 27. (Exclusive or inclusive?)
26. How are you (2)? We are fine.
27. How are you (3)? We are sick.
28. Give us a famous plant.
29. We don't like the lesson, teacher.
30. Hawaiian is hard.
31. Speak slowly.
32. I don't understand.
33. I'm awkward, dumb, ignorant, prepared.
34. Please speak again.
35. What?
36. What's the meaning of that?
37. I want to learn.

KANAKOLU-KŪMĀ-KOLU

A. Ma ka hale-ʻaina.

Luka. He mau hua
manakō kā ʻoukou?
*Haku hale. Ua ʻai ʻia
nā manakō.*
L. Nā wai?
H. *Ua ʻai ʻia e ke kuene
kāne.*
L. Aia he lama?
H. ʻAʻole loa. *Ua inu ʻia e
ke kuene wahine.*
L. Lawe mai he pipi.
H. ʻAʻole. *Ua kūʻai ʻia aku
ka pipi e kuʻu wahine.*
L. *Auwē nohoʻi e! Pōloli
au. Make wai au. I kēlā
ʻapōpō, e lawe ʻia mai ana
he pipi hou. ʻAʻole anei?
H. *Pēlā paha. E lawe ʻia
mai ana paha.
(*Komo mai ke keiki a
Luka.)
Keiki. Ūi!
L. Aloha kāua. E kuʻu
keiki, eia ka haku hale,
ʻo ʻŌlapa-ka-uila-kuʻi-
ka-hekili.
K. Aloha, ʻŌlapa-ka-uila-
kuʻi-ka-hekili.
H. Ua lawa Ka-uila. *Hauʻoli
nō au i kō kāua hui ʻana.*
K. *Hauʻoli pū nō au i kō
kāua hui ʻana.*

A. At the restaurant.

Ruth. Have you any mango
fruits?
*Owner. The mangoes were
eaten.*
R. By whom?
O. *Eaten by the waiter.*
R. Is there rum?
O. Not a bit. (It's been) *drunk
up by the waitress.*
R. Bring me a steak.
O. No. *The steak was sold by
my wife.*
R. Goodness! I'm hungry. I'm
thirsty. Tomorrow some
fresh steak will be brought
in. Won't it?
O. Maybe so. Maybe (some)
will be brought.
(Ruth's child comes in.)

Child. Hi!
R. Hello. My child, here is the
owner, Lightning-flashes-
thunder-roars.
C. Hello, Lightning-flashes-
thunder-roars.
O. Lightning's enough. *I'm
happy that we have met.*
C. *I'm happy too that we
have met.*

L. Ua pau ke kula?

R. Is school over?

K. ʻAe, ua pau. Akā, ʻaʻole i maopopo maikaʻi ka haʻawina. *ʻA ʻole i wehewehe pono ʻia mai ka haʻawina e ke kumu.*

C. Yes, pau. But (I) didn't understand the lesson well. *The lesson was not explained well* by the teacher.

B. *ʻIa* marks the passive voice.

ʻAi ʻia ka pipi e ka wahine
eaten the beef by the woman
Verb   Subject   Agent

ʻia: marker of passive voice
e: marker of agent

The *passive voice* is not to be confused with the *past tense*. In the story above note that the passive voice is used for future time (*i kēlā ʻapōpō e lawe ʻia mai ana*).

C. One way to tell the active voice and passive voice apart in English is this: If you can ask "by whom?" the statement is in the passive voice. If you cannot ask "by whom?" the statement is in the active voice. Unuhi: The poi was eaten. The man was reading. The man will be reading. The poi will be eaten. The letter was written.

D.   E aʻu.   By me.

Unuhi ʻia ka mele e aʻu.   The song was translated by me.
Wehewehe ʻia ka pepa e aʻu.   The paper was explained by me.
Kākau ʻia ka leka e ka mahiʻai.   The letter was written by the
                                  farmer.

Aloha ʻia nō ʻo Maui.   Maui was indeed loved.

Retranslate the English sentences, but substitute when appropriate *by them, by the chief, by the farmer, by us* (2, inc.).

E. The passive voice is expressed in two ways.

1. Kākau ʻia ka leka e Pua.   Pua wrote the letter.
2. Nā Pua i kākau ka leka.   *Pua* wrote the letter.

In 2 the focus is on *Nā Pua*. The translations are in the active voice. Hawaiian favors passive constructions.

F.   Review of prepositions.

The prepositions introduce noun phrases. The order of the elements making up noun phrases is as follows:

Preposition ± Determiner + Noun ± Postnoun elements

The determiners are

> *k*-words
>> *ka, ke,* definite article (singular)
>> *k*-demonstratives ± *mau*
>> *k*-possessives ± *mau*
>> *kekahi* ± *mau*
> *ia,* indefinite demonstrative
> *nā,* definite article (plural)
> *he,* indefinite article + *mau*
> numbers

The postnoun elements include qualifying content words, *pū, wale, ʻia,* directionals, *k*-less directionals, *ai,* and qualifiers (see page 246).

The following prepositions have been studied thus far (some of the case names are new):

> Nominative: ʻo
> Objective: i, iā
> Vocative: e
> Agentive: e
> Locatives:
>> Definite: i, iā
>> Indefinite: ma
>> Distance as far as: a
> Commitative/instrumental: me
> Ablative: mai
> Focus markers:
>> Dominate benefactive/causative: nō
>> Subordinate benefactive/agentive: nā

G.   Insert the proper prepositions in the following. Unuhi.

ʻAi _____ ia _____ ka poi.
ʻAi ʻia ka ʻuwala _____ ia.
Hele _____ ia _____ ka hale leka.

Nānā _____ ia _____ lāua.

ʻIke lākou _____ ia.

Makaʻu _____ Pua _____ nā ʻiole apau.

Hoʻopaʻanaʻau nā huaʻōlelo _____ ka mele _____ ka *Lukia.

_____ wai i kalaiwa kaʻa?

_____ wai ke keiki?

_____ wai ka hale.

_____ Aberahama _____ Isaaka (Matao 1:2).

Hele mai lāua _____ ka makuakāne.

_____ ke aliʻi, hele mai nō.

Noho nā kumu _____ Hilo _____ Hawaiʻi.

Kākau ʻoe _____ keia penikala.

Holo lio lākou _____ Nuʻu-anu.

_____ ka makapō i wehewehe ka haʻawina.

_____ ke Akua i hana ka lani.

_____ ke aliʻi, ka inoa.

_____ Pua, _____ wai ka inoa _____ kāu moʻopuna.

KANAKOLU-KŪMĀ-HĀ

A. Ke ana kanakolu-kūmā-hā: a/a hiki i (until/as far as). *Hiki* has a second meaning: to go, come, arrive. This *hiki* must not be confused with *hiki* meaning "can." Idiomatic uses of *a hiki i* and *a* are listed below. *A* is commonly prolonged for emphasis. This may be shown by a macron.

Ua hana ā *māluhiluhi.	*Worked until exhausted.*
Mahalo ā nui loa.	Thanks very very very much.
Aloha ā nui loa.	With much love/affection.
Ua hiki aku ka *moʻopuna *i ka *hale-leka.*	*The grandchild arrived at the post office.*
Hiki mai ka ʻelemakule.	The old man came.
Hiki i ka manu ke lele.	*The bird can fly.*
Hiki i ke kuene ke lawe mai i *lama.	The waiter can bring rum.
Ua hele aku a hiki i Oʻahu.	*(He) went as far as Oʻahu.*

B. He moʻolelo nō ʻOlomana.

B. A story about ʻOlomana.

1. *I ka wā kahiko,* ua noho kekahi koa, ma Kauaʻi.
1. *In ancient times,* a certain warrior lived on Kauaʻi.

2. ʻO Palila, kona inoa.
2. His name was Palila.

3. *He kanaka, ikaika loa,* i ke kaua. (*Ikaika* is commonly pronounced *ikeika.*)
3. (He was) *a man very strong* in war.

4. *He lāʻau, pālau,* kāna.
4. He had a *war club/stick.*

5. *Hiki iāia, ke lele,* me keia lāʻau.
5. *He could leap/fly* with this club.

6. Ua lele mai kekahi moku-puni, a hiki i kekahi mokupuni.
6. (He) jumped from one island to/as far as another island.

7. Ua lele, mai Kauaʻi, a hiki i Oʻahu.
7. (He) jumped from Kauaʻi to/as far as Oʻahu.

8. *Ua lele, a kau,* ma ka
poʻohiwi o kekahi koa,
lōʻihi loa.

8. (He) *jumped and landed*
on the shoulders of a
very tall warrior.

9. ʻO ʻOlomana, ka inoa, o
keia koa, lōʻihi loa.

9. ʻOlomana was the name of
this very tall warrior.

10. He koa ikaika loa, a
kaulana loa ia.

10. He was a warrior very
strong and *very famous.*

11. He ʻumi-kūmā-lua, kahakū,
ka lōʻihi, o ʻOlomana.

11. Twelve kahakū (96 feet)
was the height of
ʻOlomana.

12. Ua kau, ʻo Palila, ma ka
poʻohiwi o ʻOlomana.

12. Palila landed on the
shoulders of ʻOlomana.

13. Makaʻu ʻo ʻOlomana iā
Palila.

13. ʻOlomana was afraid of
Palila.

Ua kau ma ka poʻohiwi

14. Walaʻau aku, ʻo ʻOlomana,
    iā Palila: " ʻO wai kou
    inoa? ʻO wai ʻoe?"
15. Pane mai ʻo Palila: " ʻO
    Palila, kuʻu inoa."
16. Ua papaʻi, ʻo Palila iā
    ʻOlomana.
17. Wāhi ʻia, ʻo ʻOlomana.
18. Ua lele aku hoʻokahi
    ʻaoʻao o ʻOlomana.
19. *ʻOia ka mauna,* Mahi-nui.

20. Aia ma ka ʻaoʻao o
    ʻOlomana, *a hiki i
    keia lā.*
21. *Ua lilo iā lāua, i mau
    mauna ʻelua.*

14. ʻOlomana cried out to
    Palila: "What's your
    name? Who are you?"
15. Palila answered: "Palila's
    my name."
16. Palila slapped ʻOlomana.
17. ʻOlomana was split.
18. One side of ʻOlomana
    flew off.
19. *It is the mountain,*
    Mahi-nui.
20. It is on the side of ʻOlo-
    mana, *to this day.*
21. *The two turned into/be-
    came two mountains.*

C. Change from active to passive voice. Many sentences can be stated in
either active or passive voice. In English the active voice is favored; in
Hawaiian the passive voice is very common. Change the following from
active to passive voice. Unuhi. Model: Ua heluhelu ke kumu i ka leka/ua
heluhelu ʻia ka leka e ke kumu, the letter was read by the teacher.

Ua aloha ke keiki i ka makapō.
Ua wehewehe ʻoia i ka
 haʻawina.
Ua haʻaheo lākou i ka ʻāina.
Ua ʻai ka Lukia i ka ʻuala.

E *hoʻomaikaʻi (congratulate,
 thank, bless)* ana ka hapa
 haole i ka haumana.
E *hoʻomaka ana au i ke
 kumuhana.
Aloha ke kuene i ka wahine.

D. Word order.

ua	+	verb ± ʻia	±	mai ± ana ± ai ± nō
e				
k-word + noun ± ʻia ± ʻana ± mai			±	ai ± nō

Change the following passive-voice constructions from *ua* to *e (verb)
ana* forms. *Unuhi.

Ua hoʻomaikaʻi ʻia ka mahiʻai e ke kahuna (e hoʻomaikaʻi ʻia ana).
Ua *hoʻoponopono ʻia mai nā hewa e ke *kaikamahine. (*Mai* goes after
ʻia but before *ana.)

Ua wehewehe ʻia ka hana e ka haku.
Ua *aʻo ʻia nā māmalaʻōlelo *apau e ka poʻe wāhine.
Ua hoʻopaʻanaʻau ʻia nā inoa o nā ʻano hale e nā koa.

E. Rewrite the māmalaʻōlelo in D in active voice, with both *ua* and *e*
    (verb) ana forms. Ua hoʻomaikaʻi ke kahuna i ka mahiʻai. E hoʻomaikaʻi
    ana ke kahuna i ka mahiʻai.

F. In the following, "it" is understood and should be supplied in English
    as the subject of the verb. Unuhi. Ua ʻōlelo ʻia, he *mōʻī kaulana loa. Ua
    manaʻo ʻia, paʻa hana lākou. Ua wehewehe ʻia, he kiʻiʻoniʻoni ma ʻō aku.
    Manaʻo ʻia, holoholo wale nō lāua.

G. Unuhi. Practice over and over until you can go through the list fast, as a
    habit, without thinking of the rules. (Aloha ʻia ke kauka.)

The doctor was loved.   The book was read.
The lesson was explained.   The book will be read.
The child will be loved.   The work was helped.
The lesson will be explained.   The work will be helped.

KANAKOLU-KŪMĀ-LIMA

A. Ke ana kanakolu-kūmā-lima: e (verb) ai, i (verb) ai (linking *ai*). Both *e (verb) ai* and *i (verb) ai* link the medial verb to a previous word. *Ai* is usually not translated into English, and in Hawaiian can be omitted without change of meaning. It is, however, extremely common in written Hawaiian and in the speech of many fluent speakers of Hawaiian. Care must be exercised not to confuse it with *ʻai*, to eat. The preceding *e* indicates incompleted or future action. The preceding *i* indicates completed or past action.

```
                    refers  back

    ka      lā      i     hele mai      ai      ka makua
    ka      poi     i     ʻai ʻia       ai      e lākou
       Pehea        i     hana ʻia      ai?
    ka      pule    e     hoe waʻa mai  ai      au
```

Ka lā i hele mai ai ʻoia.	*The day she came.*
Ka lā e hele mai ai ʻoia.	*The day she is coming/will come.*
Ka pahu i hana ʻia ai e Kale.	The box which was made by
(*ʻia ai* is pronounced *ʻiai.*)	Charles.
Ke kupuna wahine i aloha ʻia	The grandmother loved by
ai e Keoki.	George.
Pehea ʻoia i maʻi ai?	How did he get sick?
Pēlā lāua i *kaua ai.	*Thus/like that did the two make war.*
Ka mea e *ʻeha ai ke poʻo.	The thing that causes a headache.
(*ʻeha ai* is pronounced *ʻehai.*)	
Ke kahu i makaʻu ʻia ai.	*The minister/attendant/guardian* who was feared.
Pēlā i molowā ai ka ʻelemakule momona.	*Thus the fat old man was lazy.*

B. *Ka poʻe pī.*

Kalaiwa kaʻa hoʻolimalima.
E ʻAkamu, eia kāua i
Kahana.

ʻAkamu.   Uʻi *maoli keia
ʻāina! He moʻolelo e pili
ana i keia ʻāina?

K.   ʻAe.

A.   E haʻi mai ʻoe.

K.   Hilahila nō au. Pēlā nō
ke ʻano o nā kalaiwa kaʻa.
Hilahila wale.

A.   E ʻoluʻolu ʻoe, e haʻi mai.
*Waiho i ka hilahila i ka
hale.*

K.   Pili keia moʻolelo i ka wai.
I ka wā kahiko, hiki mai
ʻelua *akua. Pōloli lāua.
*Noi lāua i wai inu a i *wahi
moe.* ʻAʻole ʻae nā kamaʻāina
o ka ʻāina. ʻAʻole hāʻawi aku
i wai. Mahope, lilo ka wai i
wai ʻawaʻawa.

A.   Maikaʻi nō ka moʻolelo.
Koe keia, pōkole loa. Haʻi
mai mai ka hoʻomaka ʻana
a pau. Mai hilahila. Waiho i
ka hilahila i ka hale.

K.   Hiki nō. Penei:

B. *The stingy people.*

Taxi driver.   Say Mr. Adams,
here we are at Kahana.

Mr. Adams.   This land is certainly beautiful. Is there a
legend about this land?

T.   Yes.

A.   Tell me.

T.   I'm shy. That's the way
(taxi) drivers are. Shy for
no reason.

A.   Please tell me. *Leave shyness at home.*

T.   This story is about water.
In ancient times, two gods
arrived. They were hungry.
*They asked for water to
drink and a place to sleep.*
The natives of the land did
not agree. Did not give
water. Afterwards, the water became brackish water.
(Nīnau: to ask a question;
noi: to ask for something.)

A.   The story is fine. *But/how-
ever/except that* (it's) very
short. Tell me from the
beginning until finished.
Don't be shy. Leave shy-
ness at home.

T.   All right. (It goes) like this:

I ka hele ʻana a kekahi mau akua ma Oʻahu, ua hele aku lāua i
Kahana. Ua ʻike aku lāua i kekahi hale. Ua noi lāua i wai inu a i wahi e
moe ai. ʻAʻole i ʻae mai nā kamaʻāina. Ua pane aku: " ʻAʻole hiki iā
mākou. ʻAʻole lawa ka wai nā mākou. ʻAʻole hiki iā mākou ke hāʻawi
aku i wai nā ʻolua."

Manaʻo nō nā akua: "He poʻe pī loa keia! Tsa!"

Iho aku keia mau akua i kai. Ua nānā aku i kekahi hale 'u'uku loa (li'ili'i loa). 'O ka po'e o ka hale, ua aloha mai iā lāua: "Mai! Mai e 'ai! Mai! Mai! Mai! Mai!"

*A laila, ua hā'awi aku lākou i kēlā mea keia mea, 'oia ho'i nā mea'ai apau a i wahi moe. 'A'ole he nui o kā lākou wai, a he wai 'awa'awa wale nō.

I kekahi lā mahope iho, ua lilo ka wai a ka po'e pu'uwai aloha i wai maika'i, a ua lilo ka wai a ka po'e na'au aloha 'ole i wai 'awa'awa.

Aia nō keia mau wai 'elua a hike i keia lā.

Pa'a i ka hana

KANAKOLU-KŪMĀ-ONO

A. Ke ana kanakolu-kūmā-ono: ʻAʻole ʻoia i hele aku (he did not go).
I after *ʻaʻole* or other word, and preceding a verb, indicates completed or past action.

(1) *ʻAʻole i kulikuli ke kālepa.*

    ʻAʻole ʻoia i minamina i ke ola.
    ʻAʻole lākou i lohe i ke kahu.
    He aupuni i aloha *ʻia ai e ka poʻe makaʻāinana.

    He mōʻī wahine i makaʻu ʻia ai.

(1) *The merchant was not noisy.*
He did not prize/set value on/feel sorry about life.
They did not listen to/hear the minister.
A government/nation loved by the citizens/ commoners.
A queen feared.

(2) ʻAʻole i hiki iāia ke lele.
ʻAʻole i hiki iaʻu ke noho paʻa.
*Pēlā i kaua ai nā koa a *lōʻihi ka *manawa.
ʻAʻole i hiki iā Mele ke moe.

ʻAʻole i ua nui. ʻOia mau nō.

(2) He could not fly.
I could not stay permanently.
Thus the soldiers fought until the time was long.
Mary could not lie down/ sleep.
It didn't rain much. Same as usual.

B. He kiʻi.

B. A picture.

(Teacher tells students to look at the picture on such and such a page. He tells the students to memorize the dialogue, and then asks A to take the part of Maluhia, and B that of Kealiʻi.)

Maluhia. ʻEhia makaʻāinana ma ke kiʻi?
Kealiʻi. ʻEkolu *kānaka.

Maluhia. How many commoners in the picture?
Kealiʻi. Three people.

M. ʻEhia *kāne? ʻEhia poʻe
wāhine?
K. ʻEkolu kāne. *ʻAʻohe
wahine.
M. ʻEhia ʻelemakule?
K. Hoʻokahi wale nō.
M. He aha kāna hana? *E
kuʻi ʻai ana?* ... He aha
ka mea i kona lima ʻākau?
He pōhaku kuʻi ʻai?
... ʻEhia poʻe ʻōpiopio
ma ke kiʻi?

K. ʻElua wale nō kāne
ʻōpiopio.
M. He aha kā lāua hana?
K. E *lawe puaʻa* ana lāua.
M. *Ua make anei ka puaʻa?*
K. Pēlā paha. Ola paha.
M. *Aia kekahi holoholona
ma ke kiʻi?*
K. *He mau ʻīlio ʻekolu.* Ua
ola nohoʻi lākou. Hauʻoli
nō lākou. E ʻai aku ana
paha lākou i nā iwi puaʻa.
M. He aha kēlā mea, mahope,
o ka ʻelemakule?
K. *He wāilele ia.* Aia ma ka
mauna.
M. *He aha ka lāʻau, ma ka
ʻaoʻao hema,* o ke kiʻi?
K. *He pū hala.*
M. Nā wai ke kiʻi? Nāu?

K. ʻAʻole loa. ʻAʻole naʻu.
Hūpō au. Nā Jean Charlot.
M. ʻĀ ʻoia.

M. How many men? How
many women?
K. Three men. No women.
M. How many old men?
K. Only one.
M. What is he doing? *Pounding
poi?* (K raises his eyebrows
in assent.) What is the thing
in his right hand? *A poi
pounder?* (K raises eye-
brows.) How many young
people in the picture?
K. Only two young men.

M. What are they doing?
K. They are carrying *pig.*
M. *Is the pig dead?*
K. Maybe so. Maybe alive.
M. *Are there other animals* in
the picture?
K. *There are three dogs.* They
are certainly alive. They
are happy. Maybe they
will eat pig bones.
M. What is that thing behind
the old man?
K. *It's a waterfall.* There on
the mountain.
M. *What is the tree on the left
side* of the picture?
K. *A pandanus tree.*
M. Who is the picture by?
You?
K. Certainly not. Not by me.
I'm dumb. By Jean Charlot.
M. That's right.

C. Note about *ʻia*. *ʻIa*, the passive voice marker, has a second function that is not much used today except in song and legend: it replaces *e* as an imperative marker. (No object marker can be used with *ʻia* for either function.)

Haʻina ʻia mai ka puana.   Tell the refrain.
Moe ʻia! ʻAi ʻia.   Lie down! Eat!

D. The linking *ai* again (see haʻawina kanakolu-kūmā-lima, A). This common particle is traditionally callled a *relative particle*, probably because English relative pronouns are sometimes translated into Hawaiian by *e* (verb) *ai* and *i* (verb) *ai*.

Ka lā e hele mai ana ʻoia.   The day on *which* she will come.
Ka manawa i hele mai ai ke aliʻi. The time *that* the chief came.
Ke aliʻi wahine i aloha ʻia ai e ka   The chiefess *who* was beloved by
  makaʻāinana.   the populace.

KANAKOLU-KŪMĀ-HIKU

A. Nā nīnau like ʻole e *pili ana i ka moʻolelo nō ʻOlomana. Pane mai i keia poʻe nīnau ma ka ʻōlelo Hawaiʻi.

A. Various questions concerning the story of ʻOlomana. Answer these questions in Hawaiian.

1. ʻO wai ke *koa i noho ma Kauaʻi?
2. He aha kona ʻano?
3. He aha ke ʻano o kāna lāʻau pālau?
4. Mahea ʻoia i lele ai?
5. Ua kau i hea?
6. He aha ke ʻano o ʻOlomana?
7. He aha kona lōʻihi?
8. He aha ka nīnau a ʻOlomana?
9. Pehea ka hana a ʻOlomana?
10. I keia *lā, *ehia mauna e koe?*

1. Who was the warrior who lived on Kauaʻi?
2. What was his character?
3. What was his war club like?
4. Where did he jump?
5. Where did he land?
6. What was ʻOlomana like?
7. What was his height?
8. What was ʻOlomana's question?
9. What did ʻOlomana do?
10. Today, *how many mountains are left?*

B. Ke ana kanakolu-kūmā-hiku: Ua lilo ʻoia i mākaʻi (he became a policeman).

Kaua. Makaʻu ʻoe iā Pele?
Leolani. ʻAʻole. He hana pono au. He puʻuwai aloha koʻu. ʻO ka poʻe lapuwale, makaʻu nō lākou.
K. ʻOia?
L. Pololei. Hoʻokahi manawa, lilo ʻo Pele, i wahine uʻi. Noi ʻoia, i wai, a i wahi moe. ʻAʻole i ʻae ka poʻe.

War. Are you afraid of Pele?
Royal Voice. No. I behave myself. I have a loving heart. Good-for-nothings, they are sure afraid.
W. Is that so?
R.V. Right. One time, Pele became a beautiful young woman. She asked for water and a place to sleep.

*Huhū 'o Pele. A laila,
lilo ke keiki lapuwale, i
pōhaku; lilo ka'u mo'opuna
i pua'a; lilo ka 'uku, i
manu; a *lilo ke kahaki'i,
i 'uhane lapu.*

K. *Aloha 'ino. Keia manawa
lilo au i kumu kula.

L. *Kōkua mai! Maka'u au.

K. E ka haumana, *ha'i mai
i nā *māhele kino.

K. Maika'i maoli. E 'olu'olu
'oe, ha'i mai i *nā 'ano 'a'ahu.*

L. He pālule polū kō Kimo.
He lole melemele kō
Kahekili. He *pāpale
ke'oke'o kō Wiliama. He
kāma'a 'ula kō Ipolani.
He malo 'ele'ele? 'A'ole
loa! He pā'ū 'ōma'oma'o?
He 'ahu'ula? 'A'ole! Ua
pau.

K. *He aha la nā 'ano 'oihana?*

L. *Penei, *kuene, kālepa,
mahi'ai, mō'ī, kahuna,
kahu, *wilikī, paniolo,*
kauka.

K. 'O ka lā hea la keia?

L. Pō'akolu. He papa Hawai'i
'ekolu manawa o ka pule
ho'okahi. 'Oia ho'i, ka
pō'akahi, ka pō'akolu,
a me ka pō'alima.

K. He aha ka 'ai maika'i a
'ono?

L. 'O ka i'a, poi, mai'a, 'uala,
kalo, īlio, pua'a, hua, lio,
*moa, *palaoa.

The people did not agree.
Pele became angry. Then
the no-good child turned
into stone, my grandchild
turned into a pig, a flea
turned into a bird, and *the
painter became a ghost.*

W. Dreadful. Now I'm becom-
ing a school teacher.

R.V. Help! I'm afraid.

W. Student, name the parts of
the body. (W names 16
parts.)

W. Very fine. Please tell *the
kinds of clothes.*

R.V. Jim has a blue shirt.
Thunder has a yellow
dress. William has a white
hat. Ipolani has red shoes.
A black malo? Boy, no. A
green sarong? *A feather
cloak?* No! (They) are
finished.

W. *What kinds of jobs are
there?*

R.V. As follows, waiter, merchant, farmer, king, priest,
minister, *engineer, cowboy,*
doctor.

W. What day is it?

R.V. Wednesday. There is Hawaiian class three times a
week. That is, Monday,
Wednesday, and Friday.

W. What is good and delicious
food?

R.V. Fish, poi, banana, sweet
potato, *taro,* dog, pig, fruit,
horse, chicken, bread.

K. He aha nā lāhui like
'ole?

W. What are various nation-
alities?

L. *Pukikī, *Pilipino, Pelekane,
Palani, *Paniolo,* a pēlā aku.

R.V. Portuguese, Filipino, English, French, *Spanish,* and
so forth.

K. *Mahalo ā nui loa nō kou
lokomaika'i.*

W. *Thank you very much for
your kindness.*

C. Hawai'i Pono'ī.

Hawai'i's Own.

(Nā Ka-lā-kaua, ka mō'ī, nā
hua'ōlelo. Nā Henry Berger
ka *leo. Ho'opa'ana'au i
keia mele o ke aupuni.)

(Words by King Ka-lā-kaua.
Tune by Henry Berger.
Memorize this song of
the nation.)

Hawai'i pono'ī,
Nānā i kou mō'ī,
Ka lani ali'i,
Ke ali'i.

Hawai'i's own,
Attend your king,
Royal chief,
The ali'i.

Makua lani e,
Kamehameha e,
Nā kāua e pale
Me ka ihe.

Regal father,
Kamehameha,
We shall ward off
With spears.

Hawai'i pono'ī,
Nānā i nā ali'i,
Nā pua muli kou,
Nā poki'i.

Hawai'i's own,
Attend the chiefs,
Children your followers,
Younger brothers.

Hawai'i pono'ī,
E ka *lāhui e,
O kāu hana nui
E ui e.

Hawai'i's own,
O nation,
Your great task
To turn for advice
(to the chiefs).

KANAKOLU-KŪMĀ-WALU

A. Ka lawehala *ʻōpiopio.

'Aihue A. *I ka pō nei,
ʻehia āu *kālā i loaʻa ai?*
(*Loaʻa* is often *loʻa* in
fast colloquial speech.)
ʻAihue B. **ʻEwalu hanele
wale nō kālā. Pohō wale!
Loaʻa ʻelima kaukani
kālā i kuʻu pōkiʻi.* He
ʻaihue mākaukau loa.

A. ʻAʻole ʻoia i loaʻa i ka
mākaʻi?

B. ʻAʻole ʻoia i loaʻa i ka
mākaʻi. Holo ʻāwīwī.

A. Loaʻa iāia he kaʻa?

B. Loaʻa. *ʻAihue ʻia* mamua
o ka hale-mākaʻi.

A. Ua loaʻa anei nā lei momi
iāia?

B. Loaʻa nō. ʻAihue ʻia mai
ka hale o ka mākaʻi.

A. Loaʻa no iāia he mau
mea Hawaiʻi? ʻOia hoʻi,
he ʻahuʻula, he lei palaoa,
he mau *kāhili, he pōhaku
kuʻi ʻai, a pēlā wale aku.

B. Loaʻa. ʻAihue ʻia mai ka
hale-hōʻikeʻike.

A. He wahine nō kāna?

B. ʻAihue ʻoia i kaʻu wahine!

A. He keiki lapuwale maoli ʻoia!
He lawehala ʻōpiopio nohoʻi!

A. The juvenile delinquent.

Thief A. *Last night,* how much
money did you get?

Thief B. Just eight hundred
dollars. Out-of-luck! *My
younger brother* got *five
thousand dollars!* An ac-
complished thief.

A. The police didn't get him
(not he gotten to the
police)?

B. The police didn't get him.
Ran too fast.

A. Did he get a car?

B. Got. *Stolen* in front of the
police station.

A. Has he gotten any pearl
necklaces?

B. Sure has. Stolen from the
house of the policeman.

A. Has he "found" any Ha-
waiian things? Such as
feather cloak, whaletooth
pendant, kāhilis, poi
pounder, *and so forth.*

B. Yes (got). Stolen from the
museum.

A. Has he a wife?

B. He stole my wife!

A. He's really a no-good
youngster. Actually a
juvenile delinquent.

132

Loa'a-type words may be considered inherently passive since they have passive meanings and are never used with the passive voice. Other *loa'a*-type words studied are *maopopo, hiki, lilo.*

B. Another *lilo.*

Lilo ka 'aihue i ka mākaʻi.	The policeman got the thief.
Lilo ka 'aihue i mākaʻi.	The thief became a policeman.
Lilo nā iwi i nā ʻīlio.	The bones went to the dogs.
Lilo ka 'ahuʻula i ka 'aihue.	The feather cloak was lost to the thief.
Lilo nā maiʻa.	The bananas were lost.

In the above sentences, *lilo* is translated "got, became, lost." A single cover meaning is "accrue." Regardless of meaning, the word order is: Verb ± Subject ± *i*-phrase (agentive).

In the following, make substitutions in the appropriate places:

Maopopo ka puke i ka mākaʻi.

(lilo)	Lilo ka puke i ka mākaʻi.
(ka mōʻī)	Lilo ka mōʻī i ka mākaʻi.
(iaʻu)	Lilo ka mōʻī iaʻu.
(ka wahine)	Lilo ka wahine iaʻu.
(loa)	Lilo loa ka wahine iaʻu.
('oia)	Lilo 'oia iaʻu.
(ka moʻolelo)	Lilo ka moʻolelo iaʻu.
(maopopo)	Maopopo ka moʻolelo iaʻu.

KANAKOLU-KŪMĀ-IWA

A.	*Ka uʻi hoʻokano.*	

A.   *The proud beauty.*

Pupuka.   *Ei nei, ke hele nei ʻoe i hea?*

Ugly.   *Darling, where are you going now?*

Uʻi.   Ke hele nei au i loko. Makemake au e lilo i hōkū kiʻi ʻoniʻoni. Pali ke kua, mahina ke alo.

Beauty.   I'm now going to the mainland. I want to become a moving picture star. Back a cliff, front a moon.

P.   Ei nei, ʻaʻole maikaʻi ʻo Hawaiʻi nei?

U.   Darling, isn't our Hawaiʻi any good?

U.   Ke hana nei au i ka hale-holoi-lole. ʻAʻole ia he hana maikaʻi.

B.   I now work in a laundry (house wash clothes). That's not good work!

P.   Ei nei, *e hoʻomanawa nui ʻoe. Inā maʻemaʻe nā lole,* maʻemaʻe ke kino a maʻemaʻe *hoʻi* ka **ʻuhane.*

U.   Darling, *be patient. If clothes are clean,* the body is clean and the soul *too* is clean.

U.   Kulikuli!

B.   Shut up!

P.   Eia au e kali nei. *Ke kali nei au.*

U.   Here I am waiting. *I'm waiting.*

U.   Ke hoʻopaumanawa mai nei ʻoe. Hoʻopaumanawa.

B.   You're wasting your time. Waste time.

P.   Ke kali nei au a hoʻomanawa nui.

U.   I'm waiting and am very patient.

U.   Ke hele nei au i loko. Aloha!

B.   I'm now going to the mainland. Good-by!

Ke (verb) nei indicates action going on at present. *E (verb) nei,* with about the same meaning, is in subordinate clauses after nouns or pronouns. *Ke (verb) nei* is not in constant use. *Nei* after a noun and *eia/ei* frequently have connotations of affection.

B. Nā ʻoihana like ʻole.

Luahine. Ke hele nei
ʻolua i ke kula-nui. Pau
ke kula, lilo ʻolua i aha?

ʻŌpiopio (1). *Kānalua.*

ʻŌpiopio (2). Pēlā au.

L. Lilo paha ʻolua i kumu?
Lilo paha ʻolua i mahiʻai?
I mākaʻi? *I ʻelele?* I hōkū
kiʻi ʻoniʻoni? I koa? I
kālepa? I kahakiʻi? I
wilikī?

B. Various professions/jobs.

Old lady. You two are going
to the University. When
school is finished, what will
you become?

Young man (1). *(I'm) in
doubt.*

Young man (2). So am I.

O. Will you become teachers?
Will you become farmers?
Policemen? *Delegates?*
Movie stars? Soldiers?
Merchants? Painters?
Engineers?

(After every question the young men answer *kānalua, ʻaʻole maopopo,
pēlā paha,* or something else.)

ʻO. (1). E lilo ana paha au i
kahu.

ʻO. (2). ʻO *kuʻu pōkiʻi, e
lilo ana paha ʻoia i
ʻaihue.

L. Auwē nohoʻi e! Maikaʻi
ʻole kēlā ʻoihana!
Hoʻopaumanawa. E
hoʻoponopono ʻoe iāia!

ʻO. (2). Hoʻaʻo nō, akā, *ʻaʻole
hoʻolohe mai.*

ʻO. (1). Pēlā nō. He keiki kāne
kolohe, lapuwale, hūpō,
hoʻokano, naʻaupō, loko
ʻino, ʻaihue, *hoʻopunipuni,*
*pupule, molowā.

L. Auwē nohoʻi e! Nui ka ʻeha
o kuʻu *puʻuwai nona.

Y. (1). Maybe I'll become a
minister.

Y. (2). My younger brother
may become a thief.

O. Goodness! That profession
is no good. A waste of
time. Correct him!

Y. (2). I've sure tried, but (he)
won't listen/obey.

Y. (1). That's right. (He's) a
mischievous boy, no-
good, stupid, proud,
ignorant, evil-hearted,
thieving, *lying,* crazy,
lazy.

O. Goodness! How my heart
aches for him.

KANAHĀ

A. Direction words again.

AʻE. We have thus far learned three direction words (mai, aku, iho). A fourth is *aʻe. Aʻe* is sometimes the reverse of *iho* and means "up." It is also used for movement in an unspecified direction and for bodily processes, and, like other direction words, is usually not translated.

IHO. *Iho* is commonly used reflexively to indicate various sorts of bodily processes, as after the words *manaʻo, ʻai, inu.*

LA. *La* occurs frequently in songs with a vague meaning "there" but more often for rhythmic effect. (Hanohano Hawaiʻi la, lei ka lehua la.) This same *la* also occurs in narration after the four direction words, and seems to replace *ua* and therefore to indicate a single act. This *la* is pronounced as though a part of the preceding direction word and is therefore not separated by a space (aʻela, akula, ihola, maila; *akula* sometimes sounds like *kula*). Still another *la* indicates doubt, as in *pehea la, he aha la.*

Unuhi: *ʻAi ihola* nō ʻoia. Inu iho ke kahuna i ka lama. **Lele aʻela* ka manu i luna o ka lāʻau. Kuahiwi nani la, ʻo Hale-a-ka-lā.

Hele akula ʻo Kiʻi-hele a kū mamua o ka hale o Mākōlea. Aloha akula keia: "Aloha ʻoe." *Aloha maila* ʻo Mākōlea. He aha la ka pane?

Nānā aʻela ke Akua i ka mālamalama (light), ua maikaʻi; a hoʻokaʻawale (separate) aʻela ke Akua mawaena o ka mālamalama ame ka pō uli (Genesis 1:4).

B. Ua mau ke ea.   B. Life/sovereignty is perpetuated.

Nā huaʻōlelo hou o ka moʻolelo me nā manaʻo:

Iulai	July	hoʻihoʻi	to restore
lānui	*holiday*	ʻākoakoa	to assemble
mahina	*month, moon*	haʻiʻōlelo	*speech, make*
Pepeluali	February		*a speech*
hoʻouna	*to send*	*palapala*	*document,*
hoʻohalahala	to protest		*knowledge*
ʻakimalala	admiral	ʻōlelo noʻeau	motto, wise saying

Ka lā *hope loa o Iulai o ka makahiki 'umi-kūmā-walu, kanahā-kūmā-kolu, he lānui ia. Ma ka mahina o Pepeluali o kēlā makahiki, ua *lilo 'o Hawai'i apau iā Pelekane. *Nā Lord Paulet i *hā'awi iā Hawai'i nei. Huhū maila ka mō'ī, 'oia ho'i, 'o Kau-i-ke-ao-uli (Kamehameha 'Ekolu). Ho'ōuna 'oia i nā 'elele iā Pelekane e ho'ohalahala. Mahope iho, ho'ōuna 'o Pelekane iā 'Akimalala Thomas e ho'iho'i i ke ea o Hawai'i nei. Ma Thomas Square keia hana ho'ohanohano. Nui ka hau'oli o nā maka'āinana. 'Ākoakoa lākou ma ka hale-pule o Ka-wai-a-Ha'o. Ha'i'ōlelo akula ka mō'ī, penei: "He aupuni palapala ko'u. Aia i ka lani ke Akua. 'O ke kanaka pono, 'oia ko'u kanaka. Ua mau ke ea o ka 'āina i ka pono."

Ua lilo keia 'ōlelo i ōlelo no'eau nō Hawai'i.

C. Students have difficulty distinguishing the many short particles and words that sound alike or almost alike. A few that cause confusion follow.

a	of (a-class)		ka	the (singular)
a	to, as far as		kā	the-belonging-to (a-class)
a	and			
ā	intensifier		ke	the (singular)
			ke	connective after *hiki*
ai	linking			
'ai	eat		mai	hither
			mai	don't (negative imperative)
e	imperative		ma'i	sick
e	vocative			
e	marker of subordinate verbs, non-past		nā	belonging to, for, by (a-class)
			nā	the (plural)
i	at, in, on; to			
i	object marker		nō	belonging to, for, (o-class)
i	past		nō	intensifier
ia	he, she, it			
ia	this, that		o	of (o-class)
iā	to		'o	subject marker
iā	object marker		'ō	there
'ia	passive, imperative			

D. He Lei nō ka Po'e Aloha 'Āina. Haku 'ia e Ellen Wright Prendergast, January 1893. Kekahi mau inoa o keia mele kaulana: Aloha 'Āina, Kaulana nā Pua, Mele 'Ai Pōhaku. Nā ka po'e kū'ē (oppose) i ka ho'ohui 'āina (annexation). Aia i loko o keia hīmeni nā inoa ali'i kahiko, 'oia ho'i, Keawe o Hawai'i, Pi'ilani o nā Hono- (nā 'āina inoa "Hono-" ma Maui, Moloka'i, a me Lāna'i), Mano o Kaua'i, a me Kākuhihewa o O'ahu.

Kaulana nā pua a'o Hawai'i	Famous are the children of Hawai'i
*Kū pa'a mahope o ka 'āina.	Standing firmly behind the land.
Hiki mai ka 'elele o ka loko 'ino.	*The evil-hearted messenger/ delegate comes.*
Palapala 'ānunu me ka pākaha.	Document of extortion and greed.
Pane mai Hawai'i moku o Keawe.	Hawai'i island of Keawe answers.
Kōkua nā hono a'o Pi'ilani.	The bays named Hono of Pi'ilani help.
Kāko'o mai Kaua'i o Mano, Pa'a pū me ke one o Kākuhihewa.	Kaua'i of Mano lends support, Firmly united with the sands of Kākuhihewa.
'A'ole a'e kau i ka pūlima Maluna o ka pepa o ka 'enemi Ho'ohui 'āina kū'ai hewa	No one will fix a signature On the paper of the enemy With its sin of annexation and sale
I ka pono sivila a'o ke kanaka.	Of the civil rights of the people.
'A'ole mākou a'e minamina I ka pu'u kālā a *ke aupuni.*	We do not value The sums of dollars *of the government.*
Ua lawa mākou i ka pōhaku, I ka 'ai kamaha'o o ka 'āina.	We have enough with stones, The mystic food of the land.
Mahope mākou o Lili'u-lani A kau hou 'ia i ke kalaunu. Ha'ina 'ia mai ana ka puana 'O ka po'e i aloha i ka 'āina.	We are in back of Lili'u-lani That the crown be worn anew. Tell the story Of the people who have loved the land.

KANAHĀ-KŪMĀ-KAHI

A. Ke ana kanahā-kūmā-kahi: *ʻOno ka puaʻa mamua o ka *ʻīlio (pig is more delicious than dog).

Pokipala.	*ʻOi aku ka maikaʻi o ka ʻai Pelekane aiʻole ka ʻai Palani?*	Potipher.	*Is English food better or French food?*
ʻApalahama.	ʻOi ka ʻai Palani mamua o ka ʻai Pelekane.	Abraham.	French food is better than English food.
P.	ʻOi aku ka ʻelele aiʻole ka ʻaihue?	P.	Is the delegate better than the thief?
ʻA.	ʻOi aku ka ʻelele mamua o ka ʻaihue. He lapuwale ia.	A.	The delegate is better than the thief. Heʻs a no-good.
P.	*ʻOi ka mana o ke Akua* aiʻole ka mana o nā lapu?	P.	*Is God more powerful* or the power of ghosts?
ʻA.	ʻOi aku ka mana o ke Akua.	A.	God is more powerful.
P.	ʻOi aku ke onaona o ka lei *aloalo* aiʻole ke onaona o ka lei *ʻawapuhi?*	P.	Is the fragrance of *hibiscus* leis greater or the fragrance of *ginger* leis?
ʻA.	ʻAʻala loa ka ʻawapuhi.	A.	Ginger is very fragrant.
P.	Nui ou mau makahiki mamua o oʻu?	P.	Are you older than I (big your plural year before of my)?
ʻA.	*ʻElemakule nō au.	A.	Iʻm an old man.

B. He kiʻi. E ka haumana, e hoʻomaʻamaʻa ʻoe i ke kamaʻilio ʻana e pili ana i ke kiʻi ma ka haʻawina kanakolu-kūmā-ono. Hoʻomaʻamaʻa a, ʻike loa a mākaukau loa.

A asks B to look at the picture. B asks which picture (ke kiʻi hea).
A says the picture on such and such a page and lesson. B repeats.
A asks how many animals in the picture. B says three live dogs and a dead pig.
A asks how many people. B says an old man and two young men.

A asks what they are doing. B says the old man is pounding poi and the young men are carrying a pig.

A asks what the old man has in his right hand. B answers.

A asks what kind of water is in the picture. B says a waterfall.

A asks what kind of tree there is, and B answers.

A thanks B and says he is smart. B says "you're welcome" but that he is incompetent and lazy.

A asks if the picture is by him (nāu). B says it is by Jean Charlot, that he doesn't know how to draw (kaha), that he likes to look at pictures but (koe keia) he cannot draw.

C.　Drill on *ʻoi aku ka* _____ *mamua o ka* _____ .

Hoʻomaʻamaʻa i keia ana ma keia mau huaʻōlelo:

strength	weakness
goodness	evil
smartness	stupidity
bigness	smallness
newness	oldness (mea kahiko)
kindness	cruelty (loko ʻino)
eating	hunger
that	this
today	yesterday
Thursday	Friday
power of God	power of ghosts
fragrance	bad odors (pilau)
Mary	James
Hawaiian language	English language
taro	sweet potato
life	death (use *ke, ka*)

D.　Substitution drill.

He kanaka *ikaika* ʻo Olomana.

mana	kaulana
akamai	aloha nui ʻia
lākou	hoʻopunipuni
māluhiluhi nō	kahuna
paʻa hana nō	ʻai nui

haumana
kuene
kuene wahine
molowā

ʻelele
ʻawapuhi onaona kā lākou
ʻaʻala
puaʻa

E. Nā ʻano meaʻai Hawaiʻi.

E. Kinds of Hawaiian food.

Kamika. ʻElua ʻano meaʻai
ma Hawaiʻi *nei. ʻOia ka ʻai,
me ka ʻiʻo. ʻO ka ʻai, ʻoia ke
kalo, ka ʻuala, ka *maiʻa, ka
poi, *ka ʻulu.*

Smith. There are two kinds of
food here in Hawaii. These
are vegetable food and flesh.
Vegetable food is taro, sweet
potato, banana, poi, *breadfruit.*

Lopikana. Ua ʻono nō keia
mau meaʻai?

Robinson. Are these foods
delicious?

K. ʻAe, ʻono loa!

S. Yes, very delicious!

L. ʻAʻole ʻono ka poi. *Like
pū me ka library paste.

R. Poi is not delicious. Just
like/same as library paste.

K. Hoʻaʻo ʻoe i ka library
paste?

S. Have you tried library
paste?

L. ʻAʻole loa!

R. Certainly not!

K. A laila, pehea ʻoe i ʻike
ai, ua like me ka library
paste?

S. Then, how do you know,
(it's) the same as library
paste?

L. He aha nā ʻano ʻiʻo?

R. What are the kinds of
flesh food?

K. ʻO nā ʻano ʻiʻo apau,
like me ka *iʻa, *ka heʻe,*
ka ʻīlio, ka lio, ka pipi,
ka puaʻa, ka moa. *Nā
mea like ʻole* e ʻai pū
me ka ʻai.

S. All kinds of meats, like
fish, *squid,* dog, horse,
beef, pig, chicken. *Everything* eaten together with
vegetable food.

F. He kula.

F. School.

Kumu. *E ʻoluʻoluʻoe, e
ka haumana. E hooluhi
iāʻoe. ʻIke anei ʻoe i nā
huahelu paʻakikī?

Teacher. Please, student. Just
to bother you. Do you know
the difficult numbers?

Haumana.	'Ike hemahema *noho'i.	Student.	(I) don't know very well.
K.	He aha: 'eiwa, 'eono, 'umi-kūmā-ono, 'umi-kūmā-kolu, *kana-kolu, 'umi-kūmā-iwa, kanaono-kūmā-lua?	T.	What are: 9, 6, 16, 13, 30, 1962?
H.	*Ho'opa'ana'au 'ia lākou apau.	S.	They are all memorized.
K.	'Ike 'oe i nā 'oihana like 'ole?	T.	Do you know the different jobs?
H.	Pēlā paha.	S.	Maybe so.
K.	He aha: kālepa, hoe wa'a, mea he'e nalu, mea pā'ani *kinipōpō, kahaki'i, kauka, mahi'ai, māka'i, kuene, paniolo, *holo lio, kia'āina, a pēlā aku?	T.	What are: storekeeper, canoe paddler, surfer, ball player, painter, doctor, farmer, policeman, waiter, cowboy, horseman, governor, and so forth?
H.	Pa'a lākou.	S.	They are mastered/known perfectly.
K.	Nā pua, 'oia ho'i, ke aloalo, ka ponimō'ī, ka 'awapuhi 'ula, ka 'awapuhi *melemele?	T.	Flowers such as hibiscus, carnation, red ginger, yellow ginger?
H.	Pa'a.	S.	Mastered.
K.	Nā 'ano hale, 'oia ho'i, ka hale-leka, ka *hale-ma'i, ka *hale-'aina, ka hale-kū'ai, a pēlā aku?	T.	Kinds of houses, namely, post office, hospital, restaurant, store, etc.?
H.	Pa'a lākou apau loa.	S.	They are all known well.
K.	Nā 'ōlelo 'a'ole hana mau, like me: kāhili, malu?	T.	Words not used commonly, such as kāhili, peace?
H.	Māluhiluhi au. Kala mai ia'u. Pono au e moe. Waiho kāua i ka hana. A hui hou aku.	S.	I'm tired. Excuse me. I must lie down/sleep. Let's leave off work. Good-by.

G. Nānā hou i ka ha'awina kanakolu-kūmā-ha, G. Unuhi hou i nā māmala'ōlelo Pelekane, a ho'okomo (insert) "by the father," like me keia: The doctor was loved by the father: Aloha 'ia ke kauka e ka makuakāne. Mahope, ho'okomo "by me" a me "by him." Penei: The doctor was loved by me: Aloha 'ia ke kauka e a'u. The doctor was loved by him: Aloha 'ia ke kauka e ia.

KANAHĀ-KŪMĀ-LUA

A. *Āhea ʻoe e hele aku ai?*

Moke. Āhea ʻoe e hele aku
*ai i *loko?
Lahela. *Ke pau kuʻu hōʻike,*
hele nō au.
M. Āhea e pau ai ka hōʻike?

L. ʻEa?
M. *I ka manawa hea* e pau
ai ka hōʻike?
L. I ka manawa hea la!
M. Āhea e hoʻomaka ai ka
pule o nā hoʻike hope
loa?
L. Ke mākaukau nā kumu.

M. Āhea kāua e holoholo
kaʻa?
L. He kaʻa nō kou?
M. ʻAʻole i keia manawa.
Ke *loaʻa koʻu kaʻa, a
laila, holoholo nō.

A. *When will you go?*

Moses. When will you go to
the mainland?
Rachel. *When my examination
is finished,* I'll go.
M. When will the examination
be finished?
R. Eh? (ʻEa)
M. *At what time* will the
examination be finished?
R. Who knows!
M. When will the week of
final examinations begin?

R. When the teachers are
ready.
M. When will we go riding in
a car?
R. Have you a car?
M. Not now. When I get a
car, then (we'll) go riding.

E ka haumana, nānā pono mai ʻoe! "When" as a question in the
future is translated *āhea . . . e . . . ai* or *i ka manawa hea . . . e . . . ai.* The
linking *ai* is optional. "When" as a statement in the future is translated
ke.

B. Words for "where?": aihea, mahea, i hea, ʻauhea, aia i hea, mai hea mai.

Aia i hea kō kākou makuahine?   Where is our mother?
Mai hea mai kēlā hapa haole?   From where is that hapa haole?
Mai Palani mai.   From France.

Aihea *ka pipi kāne?* Ma 'ō aku.   Where is *the bull?* Over there.
'Auhea wale 'oe? Ma keia wahi.   Where then are you? At this
                                                place.
'Aia i hea ka hale-'aina? Mauka   Where is the restaurant? Far
loa.   inland.

C. Review of passive voice.

Change the following sentences written with the passive voice into the
active voice. All are from the Gospel of Mark. This is practice in distinguishing subject and object.

Passive voice ('ia . . . e)   Active voice ('o . . . i/iā)

1. Ka 'euanelio *i kākau 'ia   Ua kākau 'o Mareko i ka
    ai *e Mareko.   'euanelio.
    The gospel written by Mark.   Mark wrote the gospel.

2. Ho'okahi kanahā lā i ho'owa-
    lewale 'ia mai ('Oia) e
    Satana.
    Forty days (He) was tempted   Forty days Satan tempted Him.
    by Satan.

3. Ua hana 'ia ka lā Sabati (e ke
    Akua) nō ke kanaka, 'a'ole
    ke kanaka nō ka Sabati.
    The Sabbath day was made   The Lord made the Sabbath day
    (by the Lord) for man, not   for man, not man for the
    man for the Sabbath.   Sabbath.

4. A mahope iho, 'ike 'ia mai
    nō Ia e ka po'e 'umi-
    kumamākahi.
    Afterwards He was indeed   Afterwards the eleven people
    seen by the eleven people.   saw Him.

KANAHĀ-KŪMĀ-KOLU

A. Ināhea ʻoe i hele aku ai?

Pua. *Ināhea ʻoe i hele aku ai i Kahiki?*
Kalani. I kēlā makahiki *aku nei.*
P. *Ināhea ʻoe i launa *pū ai me koʻu hoaloha?*

K. I ka manawa o ke kaua. *He aliʻikoa māua maluna o kekahi moku kaua.*
P. Ināhea i piholo ai kō ʻolua moku?
K. I ka makahiki 1943. A laila pakele māua. ʻAʻole i make.
P. I ka manawa hea i launa hou ai ʻolua?
K. I ka makahiki 1950.
P. Āhea ʻolua e launa hou aku ai? **ʻApōpō?*
K. ʻAʻole. *I keia *pule aʻe.* A laila, launa hou ʻoia *me aʻu.*
P. Keia pule aʻe? Maikaʻi kēlā.

A. When did you go?

Pua. *When did you go to Tahiti?*
Kalani. Last year.

P. *When did you meet my friend? (Hoaloha takes o, not the a one might expect.)*

K. At the time of the war. *We were officers on a war ship.*
P. When did your ship sink?

K. In the year 1943. Then we escaped. Did not die.
P. When did you meet again?

K. In the year 1950.
P. When will you meet again? Tomorrow?
K. No. *Next week.* Then he will meet again *with me.*
P. Next week? That's fine.

E ka haumana, nānā pono mai ʻoe! "When" as a question in the past is translated *ināhea . . . i . . . ai* or *i ka manawa hea . . . i . . . ai.* The linking *ai* is optional.

B. Nō ke aha? Nō ka mea.

Kumu. Hiki iāʻoe ke kamaʻilio?
Haumana. ʻAʻole mākaukau loa.

B. Why? Because.

Teacher. Can you converse?

Student. Not very well.

K. *Nō ke aha?*

T. *Why* (not)?

H. *Nō ka mea, 'a'ole hiki ia'u ke lele mai kekahi kumuhana a i kekahi kumuhana.*

S. *Because* (I) can't leap from one subject to another subject.

K. Nō ke aha?

T. Why (not)?

H. Nō ka mea he maka'u. Nō ka mea, ua hilahila au.

S. Because of fear. Because I'm shy.

K. *Nō kou maka'u? Mamuli o ka hilahila?

T. Because of your fear? *Because of shyness?*

H. Nō ka mea, *'a'ole i ma'a!* Nō ka mea, *'a'ohe hoa wala'au.*

S. Because (I'm) *not accustomed.* Because (I have) *no one to talk with* (speaking companion).

K. A laila, kama'ilio pū me nā hoa kula. A laila, pau ka hemahema! Pau ka hilahila. E mahalo 'ia ana 'oe!

T. Then, chat with your schoolmates. Then, no more clumsiness. No more shyness. You will be admired.

E ka haumana: *nō ka mea* is the most common word for "because" but *nō* and *mamuli o* are also used.

C. A'u.

C. Me.

'Ike 'ia ka mahina e a'u.
*Ho'onani 'ia ke *kūlanakauhale e a'u.
'Aihue 'ia *ka moa wahine* e a'u.
'Ike 'ia 'oia e a'u.
Inu 'ia ka lama 'awa'awa e a'u.

Noho 'oia me a'u.
Hele mai lākou me a'u.
Nānā mai ia'u.

The moon was seen by me.
The town was beautified by me.

The hen was stolen by me.
She was seen by me.
The bitter liquor was drunk by me.

He stayed with me.
They came with me.
Look at me.

A'u, me, follows *e* (agent marker), *me* (with), and *i/iā* (object marker). *Au* follows *'o* (subject marker). The other pronouns have invariable forms after these four case markers.

D. Nā pule mamua o ka 'aina.

Kakolika: E ku'u Akua e *ho'omaika'i (bless)* mai 'oe ia'u, a me ka'u *wahi (some/a little)* *mea'ai.

Kalawina: E ke Akua *hemolele (perfect)*, ka mea i *hana i ka lani a me ka honua, ho'omaika'i mai 'oe i keia mea'ai i mua o mākou i loa'a mai iā mākou *ke olakino (health)*.

Nō keia mau mea'ai a kou aloha i ho'olako (supply) mai ai, ke ho'omaika'i nei mākou iā'oe, e ke Akua mana loa.

E.   He *oli (chant: not for dancing)* ho'ohanohano ali'i mai ka wā kahiko.

Nō ka lani ka *moku, ka honua, (lani: chief; *honua: land*).
Ka uka, ka moana, nō ka lani,
Nona ka po, nona ke ao,
A, nona ke kau, ka ho'oilo, ka makali'i (seasons, winter, summer),
Ka malama, ka huihui *hōkū* lani e kau nei (the moon and clustering *stars* of the heavens placed here).

[Fornander, vol. 4, pp. 374-375]

KANAHĀ-KŪMĀ-HĀ

A. Ke ana kanahā-kūmā-hā: *ua kau nei;* ua kau la (*this aforementioned semester/summer/season;* that aforementioned season). This construction is common in writing but rare in conversation. The translation "aforementioned" is awkward; in English one says often "this" or "that."

Kiʻekiʻe ua kuahiwi la.	*That mountain under discussion is tall.*
I ua wā la, nui ka poʻe Lukia.	At that aforementioned time, there were many Russians.
ʻAʻahu ua *kahuna la i ka ʻahuʻula.	That priest we've been talking of was wearing the feather cloak.
Nou, ua kāhili la.	That aforementioned kāhili is for you.
Kaulana ua lama nei i ka ikaika.	This aforementioned rum is famous for its strength.
Lōʻihi ua papa heʻe nalu nei.	This aforementioned surfboard is long.

B. ʻOia ala (pronounced ʻoiyala): he, she. (He huaʻōlelo hana mau ʻia; perhaps it is more specific than *ʻoia.*) Do not confuse this *ala* (after ʻoia), *ala,* road, *ala,* wake up, and *ʻala,* fragrant.

Nānā ʻoia ala i ka pū hala.	*He looked at the pandanus tree.*
Kūʻai ʻoia ala i wahi iʻa.	He bought some/a little fish.
Nīele ʻoia ala nō kona maopopo ʻole.	She was inquisitive because of her not understanding.
Kāhea aku ʻoia ala: "E aho ia!"	*He called out: "That's better!"*
ʻAi ʻoia ala i nā laulau ʻono.	She ate the delicious laulaus.
Hele ʻoia ala i ke ala loa.	She went on the long road.
Ua ala ʻoia ala i ke kakahiaka.	hᵤ woke up in the morning.
Ua ʻala ʻAʻala Paka?	Is ʻAʻala Park fragrant?

C. *Pule kamali'i (children's prayer).*

Pule au, pule au,
Pule i nā lā apau.
*Inā *moe, pule nō.
Inā ala, pule hou.

Noi au, noi au,
I ku'u Haku, ku'u Iesū,
Ho'oma'ema'e (clean) i ku'u
na'au.
Hana hou i pono mau.

D. Make sentences translating the English words and fitting them into the two patterns, first the future, and then the past.

Ahea +	Pronoun + *e*	Verb *ai*	±	(Object Phrase (Locative Phrase
	you	go		
	you	fly		
	he	practice		the lesson.
	they (3)	learn		the hula.
	they (2)	surf		
		ride horseback		
		memorize		the lesson.
		fly		in a plane.
		stay permanently		in Honolulu.
Inahea +	Pronoun + *i*	Verb *ai*	±	(Object Phrase (Locative Phrase

E. Unuhi.

He sat	with me.	with us.
He lived	with me.	with us.
He ate	with me.	with us.
He came	with me.	with us.
He read	with me.	with us.
He washed	with me.	with us.

F. Ho'oma'ama'a.

this)
that) aforementioned { liquor, waterfall, prayer, hen, friend, breadfruit, governor, examination, thief, pandanus tree, season. }

G. Ho'oma'ama'a.

(Ua) came   'oia ala me + pronoun object.
(Ua) played ball   'oia ala me + pronoun object.
(Ua) stayed   'oia ala me + pronoun object.

(Ua)	chatted	ʻoia ala me + pronoun object.
(Ua)	studied-lesson	ʻoia ala me + pronoun object.
(Ua)	rode-horseback	ʻoia ala me + pronoun object.
(Ua)	drank-liquor	ʻoia ala me + pronoun object.

H. Nā ʻōlelo *nane (riddles)*.

  1. Kuʻu hale, hoʻokahi oʻa (beam), *ʻelua puka (doors)*.
  2. *Kakahiaka ʻehā *wāwae, awakea (noon) ʻelua wāwae,
      *ahiahi ʻekolu wāwae.
  3. Kuʻu wahi manu, kiaʻi (guard) hale.
  4. Kuʻu manu mahiʻai.
  5. Kuʻu manu aia a makani, lele.
  6. He mau kūpuna kou, he ʻai kō uka, a he iʻa kō kai. He aha ka
      inoa o ka pua?
  7. *ʻEkolu pā (walls)*, loaʻa ka wai.
  8. Kuʻu pūnāwai (spring) kau i ka lewa (air).
  9. Uliuli *mehe (like/as)* mau *ʻuala, *keʻokeʻo mehe hau (snow)
      la, *ʻula *mehe ahi (fire)* la.
 10. He lāʻau hele i ke kaua.

Nā haʻina: ihu, kanaka, nā maka, ʻōʻō (ʻelua manaʻo o ʻōʻō, ʻoia hoʻi,
he *honey eater bird*, a he *digging stick*), lupe (kite), ʻawapuhi (ka ʻawa a
me ka puhi, *eel*), *niu (coconut)*, niu, ipu haole (watermelon), koa.

I. Table of demonstratives (for reference).

	Distance unspecified (this, that)	Near speaker (this)	Near addressee (that)	Far (that)
Without *ke:*	ia	nei	na/ana	la/ala
With *ke:*		keia (neia: rare)	kēnā	kēlā
With *pe:*	peia (rare)	penei		pēlā
With *ua:*	ua . . . ia	ua . . . nei	ua . . . na (rare)	ua . . . la/ala

KANAHĀ-KŪMĀ-LIMA

A. Ka haole.

A. E B, noho ʻoe i laila. E C, noho ʻoe malaila. A laila, kamaʻilio pū kākou.

B, C. Hiki.

A. He aha ka manaʻo o kēlā huaʻōlelo, ʻoia hoʻi: ka haole?

B. He aha la. ʻAʻole mākaukau. *Nō laila, ʻaʻole au i ʻike.*

A. Nō laila, ʻaʻole ʻike. Pehea ʻoe, e C?

C. Penei paha ka wehewehe ʻana. Aia ʻelua huaʻōlelo, ʻoia hoʻi, "ha" ame "ole." No laila mai ka inoa.

A. "ʻOle," ua like nō me "ʻaʻole." He aha ka manaʻo o "ha"?

C. ʻO "breath."

A. No laila, "no breath" he haole? Pupule kēlā!

B. Eia kekahi wehewehe ʻana. Komo ka poʻe kānaka i loko o ka heiau, ua kolo a ʻōlelo "ha!" ʻO ka poʻe haole, ʻaʻole lākou i ʻōlelo "ha!"

A. Nō laila ka inoa? ʻAʻole pololei kēlā.

B, C. Nō ke aha?

A. Haole.

A. O B, you sit there. O C, you sit there. Then we'll talk together

B, C. Okay.

A. What's the meaning of that word, I mean: haole?

B. How should I know. (I'm) not clever. *Therefore, I don't know.*

A. Therefore (you) don't know. What of you, o C?

C. This is maybe an explanation. There are two words, namely, "ha" and "ole." That's where the name is from.

A. "Ole" is like "ʻaʻole." What's the meaning of "ha"?

C. "Breath."

A. So the haole is "no breath"? That's crazy!

B. Here's another explanation. The Hawaiians went into a heiau and crawled and said "ha!" The haole people did not say "ha!"

A. Thence the name? That's not right.

B, C. Why (not)?

A. Nō ka mea, ʻaʻohe ʻokina ma ka huaʻōlelo "haole."

A. Because *there's no glottal stop* in the word "haole."

B. ʻOia?

B. Is that so?

C. Kekahi mea, he ʻōlelo *kahiko. Heluhelu au i ka moʻolelo o Kamapuaʻa.

C. Another thing, (it's) an old word. I read the story of Kamapuaʻa.

B. ʻO wai ʻo Kamapuaʻa?

B. Who is Kamapuaʻa?

C. He hapa puaʻa, he hapa kanaka. Aia he mele e pili ana iāia. Penei: "He haole nui, maka ʻālohilohi."

C. Half pig, half man. There's a song about him. Like this: "A big haole, bright eyes."

A. Nō laila, ʻaʻole he ʻōlelo hou, he ʻōlelo kahiko. Mamua o ka hele ʻana mai o ka poʻe haole. ʻAʻole anei?

A. So, not a new word, an old word. Before the coming of the haole people? Isn't that so?

C. Pololei nō ʻoe. He inoa kahiko ia. Nō laila, ʻaʻole au i hilinaʻi i nā wehewehe ʻana hakuwale ʻia.

C. You're right. It's an old name. Therefore I don't believe in made-up explanations.

ma laila	there	a laila	then
i laila	there	nō laila	therefore, for
mai laila	from there		for that reason

(Study of tapes shows that *laila* is commonly pronounced *leila* and sometimes *lila*.)

B. *Ka hola.*

B. *The hour/time/o'clock.*

Luka. Hola ʻehia ke *kiʻiʻoniʻoni?

Ruth. What time is the movie?

Mele. Hola ʻewalu.

Mary. Eight o'clock.

L. I ke kakahiaka?

R. In the morning?

M. Tsa! I ke ahiahi. *Kala mai iaʻu. ʻAʻole i ka hola ʻewalu. Ua hewa au.

M. Gracious! In the evening. Excuse me. Not at eight o'clock. I was wrong.

L. Āhea?

R. When?

M. *Hapalua hola 'ewalu.*

L. E aho ia. Pau i ka hola 'ehia?

M. Hapalua hola 'umi.

L. E hele kāua i ka pō'aono!

M. Pa'a hana nō au!

L. Maika'i ka lāpule?

M. Hiki. Koe keia, ho'omaka i ka hapalua hola 'eiwa.

L. Hapalua hola 'eiwa. E aho ia. Pau āhea?

M. Hapalua hola 'umikūmā-lua.

L. Auwē! Maka'u nō au i nā lapu 'ino o ka pō uli!

M. Mai maka'u! Na'u e *mālama* pono iā 'oe!

L. Koa loa 'oe. Nō laila, 'a'ole au e maka'u. Mālama mai 'oe ia'u.

M. *8:30.*

R. That's better. When will it be finished (finished at what hour)?

M. 10:30.

R. Let's go on Saturday!

M. I'm busy!

R. Is Sunday okay?

M. Okay. But (it) begins at 9:30.

R. 9:30. That's better. When finished?

M. 12:30.

R. O dear! I'm afraid of the sinful ghosts of the black night!

M. Don't be afraid! I'll *protect* you well!

R. You are so brave. Therefore I'm not afraid. You protect me.

KANAHĀ-KŪMĀ-ONO

A. Ke ana kanahā-kūmā-ono: inā e ua (if it rains).
This pattern is used only in the future.

Inā e ʻauʻau ʻoe, ʻaʻole maʻi.	*If you bathe,* no sickness.
Inā e *ʻaihue ʻoe, pepehi!*	If you steal, a *beating!*
Inā e hiki iā mākou, e oli ana.	If we can, (we) will chant.
Inā e holoholo ʻoe *a pō ka lā,*	If you ride *until day becomes*
huhū maila ka *mākaʻi.	*night,* the policeman will be angry.
Inā e hoʻopunipuni *mau ʻoe,	If you lie all the time, the devil
e lilo i ke kiapolō.	will get you.

B. Mataio (Matthew) 22:36–40.

36. E ke kumu, heaha ke *kauoha (order/commandment)* nui iloko o ke *kanawai (law)*?
37. I aku la o Iesu ia ia, E aloha aku oe ia Iehova i kou Akua me kou *naau a pau, a me kou uhane a pau, a me kou manao a pau.
38. O ka mua keia a me ke kauoha nui.
39. Ua like hoi ka lua me ia. E aloha aku oe i kou hoa-launa (neighbor) me (as) oe ia oe iho.
40. Maluna o keia mau kauoha elua, ke *kau nei ke kanawai a pau a me na kaula (prophets).

C. Pule a ka Haku.

E kō mākou Makua i loko o ka lani,
E hoʻano ʻia (hallowed) kou inoa.
E hiki mai kōu aupuni.
E mālama ʻia (be done) kou
makemake ma ka honua nei,

E like me ia i mālama ʻia ma ka lani la.
E hāʻawi mai iā mākou i keia lā
i ʻai na mākou no neia (keia) lā.

E kala mai hoʻi iā makou i kā
   mākou lawehala ʻana (sins),
Me (as) mākou e kala nei i ka
   poʻe i lawehale i kā mākou.
Mai hoʻokuʻu (permit) ʻoe iā
   mākou i ka hoʻowalewale ʻia
   mai (temptation).

E hoʻopakele nonaʻe (but
   deliver) iā mākou i ka ʻino.
No ka mea, nou ke aupuni, a me
   ka mana, a me ka hoʻonani ʻia.
A mau loa aku. ʻĀmene.

KANAHĀ-KŪMĀ-HIKU

A. Aia nō ia iāʻoe.

Keiki. E māmā, hiki iaʻu
ke hele i ke kiʻiʻoniʻoni?
Māmā. *Aia nō ia iāʻoe.*

K. Hiki iā Pua ke hele
pū me aʻu?
M. Aia nō ia iāia.
K. (Iā Pua.) Hiki nō?
Pua. Aia nō i koʻu pāpā.
*ʻI mai ʻoia, aia a pau ka
hana,* a laila hiki.
M. He *wahi kenikeni* nō
kā ʻolua?
K. *He hapahā kaʻu.*
P. *He ʻumi keneka kaʻu.*
M. ʻAʻole lawa! Eia ʻumi-
kūmā-lua keneka. E hele.
P. (Iāia iho.) Pī loa ka māmā
o kuʻu hoaloha! (Iā Māmā.)
Mahalo nō kou lokomaikaʻi.

A. Suit yourself/it's up to you.

Child. Mamma, can I go to the
movie?
Mamma. *Suit yourself/it's up
to you.*

C. Can Pua go with me?

M. It's up to him.
C. (To Pua.) Can (you)?
Pua. It depends on my papa.
*He says, only if the work is
done,* then okay.
M. Have you (2) *any change?*

C. *I have a quarter.*
P. *I have ten cents.*
M. Not enough. Here's twelve
cents. Go on.
P. (To himself.) My friend's
mamma is certainly stingy!
(To M.) Thank you for
your kindness.

B. Ke ana kanahā-kūmā-hiku: inā i ua (if it had rained).
This pattern is used only in the past.

Inā i ʻauʻau kai ʻoe, ʻaʻohe maʻi.

If you had bathed in the sea, no
sickness.

Inā i hānai ʻia ʻoe e ka Palani,
ʻike i ka walaʻau Palani.

If you had been reared/fed by the
Frenchman, (you) would have
known the French language.

Inā i piʻi aku ʻoe i ka mauna,
a laila, ikaika nō ʻoe.

If you had climbed/gone inland
on the mountain, then you
would have been strong.

157

Inā ʻaʻole ʻoe i moe i ka lepo, ʻaʻohe lepo.	If you had not slept/lain on the dirt, (you) would not have been dirty.
Inā ʻaʻole i kapu, leʻaleʻa nō i ka lāpule.	*If it hadn't been forbidden/kapu,* (there would have been) *fun* on Sunday.
Inā i hoʻomau a hoʻomanawanui, paʻa ke oli.	*If (you) had persevered/contin-ued* patiently, the chant would have been mastered.

C.   Hoʻomaʻamaʻa: nā ana like ʻole. E kākau ʻoe i nā huahelu ana.

(1)   Ke ana _____ . (*N*-words) Nō wai ka hale? Who did this sentence (by whom)? Let me have that white shirt. The name song is for him: for you: for me.

(2)   Ke ana _____ . (*K*-less possessives) ʻEhia āna kālā? How many pigs has he? (He has) sixteen horses. They have no sarongs. The doctor has two kegs of rum.

(3)   Ke ana _____ . (*Loaʻa*-type words) Loaʻa ka ʻaihue i ka mākaʻi. They found a gift. He acquired a sweetheart. Pua found twenty-one dollars. The dog got an owl bone. I got ten dollars.

(4)   Ke ana _____ . Aia nō ia iāʻoe. It's up to the delegate. Suit yourself. It depends on that distant land.

KANAHĀ-KŪMĀ-WALU

†Laukia-manu-i-Kahiki. (Nānā i ka mea kōkua i ka haʻawina kanahā-kūmā-iwa.)

ʻO Makiʻiʻoeʻoe ka makuakāne. Mai Kuai-he-lani ʻoia. Ua hele ʻoia ala a hiki i Kauaʻi. Ua noho pū lāua me ka wahine. ʻO Hina kāna wahine. A laila, ua makemake ʻo Makiʻi e hoʻi i kona ʻāina ponoʻī. ʻŌlelo akula ʻoia i ka wahine iā Hina:

"E hoʻi ana au i koʻu ʻāina ponoʻī. ʻOia hoʻi, ʻo Kuai-he-lani. E noho paʻa oe i Kauaʻi. Inā e hānau he *keiki kāne, kapa (call) ʻoe i kuʻu inoa. Inā e hānau he kaikamahine, kapa ʻoe i ka inoa o Laukia-manu-i-Kahiki (snare that lures the far-flung birds). E hāʻawi aku ʻoe i ke keiki i keia mau hōʻailona (recognition tokens, emblems): he lei palaoa, he kūpeʻe (bracelets), he ʻahuʻula, he waʻa nui, he waʻa iki, he kanaka nui, he kanaka iki, he waʻa ʻula, he ʻaha (sennit) ʻula, he kanaka ʻula. E *pono i ke keiki ke lawe mai iaʻu i keia mau mea."

Hoʻi akula ʻO Makiʻiʻoeʻoe i kona ʻāina ponoʻī.

Hānau ka wahine. He kaikamahine. Kapa ʻia ʻoia ʻo Laukia-manu-i-Kahiki. Hānai ihola ʻo Hina me kāna kāne hou i ke keiki ʻuʻuku †a nui. Pali ke kua, *mahina ke alo. Lawe mai ʻo Laukia i kona mau hoaloha i ka home (home). Hāʻawi akula iā lākou i ka meaʻai apau. Huhū maila ka makuakāne kōlea (foster). Pepehi ʻoia ala i ke kaikamahine ʻuʻuku.

Manaʻo ihola ʻo Laukia: "ʻAʻole kēlā, ʻo koʻu makuakāne ponoʻī. He makuakāne kōlea ia. Aihea koʻu makuakāne ponoʻī?"

Hele akula ʻo Laukia i ka ʻohe (bamboo).

Nīnau akula: "ʻO ʻoe paha koʻu makuakāne ponoʻī?"

Pane maila ka ʻohe: "ʻAʻole loa! ʻO Makiʻiʻoeʻoe kou makuakāne. Ua hoʻi i Kuai-he-lani."

*Hiki ʻo Laukia i mua o Hina. ʻĪ akula: "Mai hoʻopunipuni ʻoe iaʻu! ʻO Makiʻiʻoeʻoe koʻu makuakāne la, ua hoʻi i Kuai-he-lani."

Pane maila ka makuahine, "ʻAe, ʻo kō makuakāne ia."

Hele akula ʻo Laukia. Nānā akula ʻoia i nā luāhine ʻelua e pūlehu (roasting) maiʻa ana i ke alanui. ʻO keia mau luāhine ʻelua, he mau kūpuna wāhine nō Laukia.

ʻĪ mai nā luāhine: "He alanui, eia la ʻo ka ʻohe. E piʻi ʻoe *i luna."

†See page 161.

Pi'i a'ela 'o Laukia a luna. Kupu (grow) a'ela ka'ohe. Moe akula ka wēlau (tip) a hiki i Kuai-he-lani. Hele ka wahine i laila.

Hele akula ke kaikamahine a hiki i kekahi māla (garden) *pua nani loa. Ua kapu nā pua apau loa, †i lei o Laukia: ka 'ilima, ka maile, ka melekule (marigold), ame nā pua like 'ole. 'Aihue akula 'o Laukia i keia mau pua kapu. Nānā ihola 'oia ala i kekahi wai kapu. 'Au'au ihola 'oia *maloko o keia wai kapu.

'O kēlā ka 'āina o Maki'i'oe'oe, ka makuakāne o Laukia. 'A'ole maopopo iāia, 'o wai keia wahine e 'a'e (break) kapu ana. Huhū maila 'oia mamuli o kēlā 'au'au 'ana maloko o ka wai kapu. Ha'i akula 'oia i nā kānaka ona, 'apōpō e hō'ā (light) i ka imu e make ai ke kaikamahine.

'A'ahu i ka 'ahu'ula

Lele ihola kekahi manu, he pueo (owl). 'O keia pueo, he kupuna nō Hina. Mai Kaua'i †ka lele 'ana aku a hiki i Kuai-he-lani, nō ka 'ike e make ana ka mo'opuna. †Aia iāia nā *makana (gift/present)* a Maki'i'oe'oe i hā'awi ai iā Hina, i †hō'ike nō Laukia-manu e hele ai i Kuai-he-lani.

Kāhea maila ua pueo nei iā Laukia:
"E Laukia-manu-i-Kahiki e,
Kaikamahine a Hina,
Make 'oe, make 'oe."
Aloha akula 'o Laukia i ka pueo.

Pau ke kāhea 'ana a ka pueo ame ke kaikamahine, maopopo ihola iā Maki'i'oe'oe, 'o ke kaikamahine nō, 'o Laukia-manu-i-Kahiki. Lālau (take) maila i ke kaikamahine, a uwē ihola.

Lele ihola ua pueo nei, a pa'i (strike) ihola i nā 'ēheu (wings) ona i luna o ke kaikamahine, †a lei ihola i ka lei palaoa, 'a'ahu i ka 'ahu'ula. (E nānā 'oe i ke ki'i.)

Kapu a'ela 'o Laukia. 'A'ole e hele i waho. 'A'ohe kānaka komo i loko o kona hale noho, 'a'ohe mea *kama'ilio iāia. He wahine maika'i loa ia ke nānā aku. Ua puka (come out) †kona 'ula mawaho o ka hale, like me ke ahi.

A laila, ua holo maila ho'okahi keiki kāne a Maki'i'oe'oe, mai ka mokupuni o Kahiki-kū. 'O Kahiki-'ula kona inoa. Hele mai 'oia me ka wa'a 'ula, ka pe'a (sail) 'ula, ke kaula (line) 'ula, ka hoe 'ula, ke kanaka 'ula, ka wa'a nui, ka wa'a iki, ke kanaka nui, ke kanaka iki. 'O Laukia kona kaikuahine. †Ho'okahi nō kō lāua makuakāne, a 'elua makuahine.

Nānā akula 'o Kahiki-'ula i keia mea 'ula mawaho o ka hale, a 'ī akula: "E! Pau kō hale i ke ahi!"

Pane maila ka makuakāne: " 'A'ohe ahi, he kanaka, aia i loko, 'o kō kaikuahine."

Nānā maila ke kaikamahine, a aloha akula: "Aloha 'oe."

Nani nō a nani, u'i nō a u'i, 'a'ala nō a 'a'ala, onaona nō a onaona. Ua like a like. Ua noho pū lāua, he kāne a he wahine.

Nā Wehewehe 'Ana (items marked by†)

†From Fornander, vol. 4, pp. 596-609. For translation helps, see notes below and ha'awina kanahā-kūmā-iwa, B. It is suggested that students write out the translation, and use consistently either past or historical present tenses.

a nui: until grown.
i lei o: as leis for.
Mai Kaua'i ka lele 'ana (she flew from Kaua'i): translate by a verb.
Aia iāia: she had.
i hō'ike: as tokens.
a lei ihola: and put on.
kona 'ula: this is the subject of the verb phrase *ua puka*.
ho'okahi: same.

KANAHĀ-KŪMĀ-IWA

A. Ke ana kanahā-kūmā-iwa: inā he pilikia, haʻi mai (if there is trouble, tell me).

Inā he lānui, maikaʻi ia.	If there's a holiday, that's good.
Inā he lā *ua, noho paʻa i ka home.	If it's a rainy day, stay all-the-time (*paʻa*) at home.
Inā he kālā, leʻaleʻa nō.	If there's money, lots of fun.
Inā he kānāwai, pono e lohe.	If there's a law, it must be obeyed.
Inā he hokele, kauoha i meaʻai.	If there's a hotel, order food.
Inā he *hua ʻai, haʻi mai.	If there is fruit, tell me.

B. E ka haumana, unuhi i nā ʻōlelo o lalo nei. Hiki no ke nānā i ka haʻawina kanahā-kūmā-walu. A laila, hoʻopaʻanaʻau ʻoe i kāu unuhi ʻana. Hiki ke nānā i ka ʻōlelo Pelekane wale nō.

1. Makiʻiʻoeʻoe is the father, Hina the mother. Makiʻi is from Kuai-he-lani. He and Hina (lāua ʻo Hina) live at Kauaʻi.

2. The father says to his wife: "If a boy is born, call him by my name; if a girl is born, call her Laukia-manu-i-Kahiki."

3. He gives her gifts for the child: a whaletooth pendant, bracelet, feather cloak, big canoe, small canoe, big servant, small servant, red canoe, red sennit, red servant.

4. Maikiʻiʻoeʻoe goes back to his own land.

5. A girl is born. She is called Laukia-manu-i-Kahiki.

6. She gives food to her playmates.

7. The foster father is enraged and beats her.

8. She thinks he is not her real father.

9. She asks the bamboo if he is her real father and he says no and tells her who her father is, and where. (Change to direct discourse.)

10. Laukia sees two old ladies roasting bananas on the road. They are grandmothers.

11. They tell her to climb the bamboo. Then she will go to Kuai-he-lani.

12. She climbs and goes to Kuai-he-lani.
13. She sees flowers (maile, 'ilima, melekule) and steals the flowers. They are taboo flowers.
14. She bathes in fresh water. It is taboo water.
15. Maki'i'oe'oe sees her. He doesn't know she is his own daughter. He is angry because she does not observe (nānā) the taboos.
16. He tells the people to light (hō'ā) the oven so the girl will die.
17. An owl flies down: a grandmother of Laukia-manu.
18. She has (aia iāia he mau) gifts.
19. The owl chants the name of the girl, daughter of Maki'i'oe'oe, daughter of Hina, you die, you die.
20. Maki'i'oe'oe understands the girl is his daughter. He greets her. They weep.
21. The owl strikes the girl and gives her the whaletooth pendant and feather cloak.
22. Laukia-manu-i-Kahiki was tabooed. She might not go outside.
23. She was a very good-looking woman (good to look at).
24. Kahiki-'ula sailed in from Kahiki-kū with a red canoe, red paddle, red servant, large canoe, small canoe, large servant, small servant.
25. Laukia was his sister.
26. He saw the redness (red thing) outside the house and said: "Goodness! Your house will be consumed in fire!"
27. The father said: "(It's) not a fire! (It's) a person; there inside, is your sister."
28. The girl greeted him.
29. (One was) as beautiful as (the other) was beautiful, as youthful as youthful, strongly fragrant as strongly fragrant, sweet as sweet, like as like.
30. They lived together, man and wife.

KANALIMA

A. Ke ana kanalima: Ke mākaukau, haʻi mai (when prepared, tell me). *Ke* means "when" only for a statement (not a question) in the future.

Ke anu, komo mai i loko.	*When cold,* come inside.
Ke wela, hele aku i waho.	*When hot/warm,* go outside.
Ke ala, ʻauʻau wai nō.	When getting up, bathe.
Ke pōloli, ʻai.	*When hungry,* eat.
Ke pau, *hōʻike mai.	When finished, let me know/ inform me.

B. *Nā manaʻo kūʻē.*

B. *Opposite meanings.*

*kokoke, mamao	near, far
mākaukau, hemahema	prepared, unprepared
naʻauao, naʻaupō	wise, ignorant
wela, anu	hot, cold
ua, lā	rain, sun
lā, pō	day, night
hema, ʻākau	left, right
hāʻawi aiʻole noi	give or ask
momona, ʻawaʻawa	sweet, bitter
koʻu *wā liʻiliʻi, koʻu wā ʻelemakule aiʻole luahine	my youth, my old age (male or female)
aloha kakahiaka, aloha ahiahi	good morning, good evening
he makahiki hou, he makahiki kahiko	a new year, an old year
he poʻe *waiwai, he poʻe ʻilihune	rich people, poor people
he kākau-ʻōlelo kolohe aiʻole *hoʻomanawanui	a secretary/clerk naughty or patient
he manawa malu aiʻole kaua	a time of peace or war
he kauka paʻa hana aiʻole molowā	a doctor busy or lazy
he ʻelele *māluhiluhi aiʻole ʻeleu*	a messenger *tired or active*

C. āhea, ināhea.

Āhea ʻoe e pupule ai?	When will you be crazy?
Ināhea ʻoe i hoʻomanawanui ai?	When were you patient?
Ināhea lāua i kāhea mai ai?	When did they call?
Āhea e wehewehe ai ke kumu i ke kaua?	When will the teacher explain the war?
Ināhea ʻoia i kūʻai ai i wahi kalo?	When did she buy some taro?

D. Ke kiʻi.

D. The picture.

A.	E Pī, hiki nō ke hoʻoluhi iāʻoe?	A.	Say, B, may (I) bother you?
B.	Hiki.	B.	Certainly.
A.	E nānā aku ʻoe i ke kiʻi.	A.	Look at the picture.
B.	Ke kiʻi hea?	B.	Which picture?
A.	(Haʻi aku i ka haʻawina kanahā-kūmā-walu; haʻi aku hoʻi i ka ʻaoʻao.)	A.	Says lesson 48; also tells the page.)
B.	Loaʻa.	B.	Found.
A.	ʻO wai ka wahine i waena o ke kiʻi?	A.	Who is the woman in the middle of the picture?
B.	ʻO Laukia-manu-i-Kahiki.	B.	Laukia-manu-i-Kahiki.
A.	He aha kēlā mea ma kona lima ʻākau?	A.	What is that thing in her right hand?
B.	He pua ia. He pua kapu.	B.	That's a flower. A kapu flower.
A.	He aha ka mea ma kona lima hema?	A.	What is the thing in her left hand?
B.	ʻAʻohe mea. Aia ma kona ʻaoʻao.	B.	Nothing. There (it) is at her side.
A.	He aha kēlā mea i luna ma ka ʻaoʻao hema?	A.	What is that thing above on the left side?
B.	Ma ka *lani? He mahina ia.	B.	In the sky? That's a moon.
A.	He aha kēlā manu?	A.	What's that bird?
B.	He pueo.	B.	An owl.
A.	He mana kona?	A.	Has it magic power?
B.	ʻAe, nui ka mana. He kupuna nō Laukia.	B.	Yes, much power. (She's) a grandmother of Laukia.
A.	Lawe mai ʻoia ala i ke *aha?	A.	What is she bringing?

B. He mau makana. He
*'ahuula, a pēlā aku.

A. He kāma'a nō kō Laukia?

B. Aloha 'ino! 'A'ohe ona
kāma'a!

A. 'Eha kona wāwae?

B. 'A'ole.

A. Nō ke aha?

B. Nō ka mea, pa'akikī loa
kona wāwae. No laila, 'a'ole
'eha iki. Ua ma'a 'oia.

A. 'O wai kēlā po'e *'u'uku ma
nā 'ao'ao o ke ki'i?

B. He po'e maka'u i ke *ali'i
wahine.

A. Nā wai i kaha ke ki'i? Nāu?

B. 'A'ole loa. Tsa! Nā Jean
Charlot, he kahaki'i
*kaulana loa.

B. Presents. A feather cloak,
and so forth.

A. Has Laukia shoes?

B. How pathetic/pitiable! She
has no shoes!

A. Do her feet hurt?

B. No.

A. Why?

B. Because her feet are very
tough. Therefore, not even
a little pain. She's used
to it.

A. Who are those little people
on the sides of the picture?

B. People afraid of the
chiefess.

A. By whom is the picture?
By you?

B. Certainly not. Heavens!
By Jean Charlot, a famous
painter.

HA'AWINA

KANALIMA-KŪMĀ-KAHI

A. Ke ana kanalima-kūmā-kahi: i ka manawa/wā 'oe i hele mai ai (at the time when/when you came).

I ka manawa i hele mai ai ke *kua'āina*, *pa'a hana au.
I ko'u wā li'ili'i, nui kō mākou le'ale'a.
I ka manawa i kū'ē ai ka po'e, pōmaika'i *'ole.
I ka wā i 'imi na'auao ai, lokomaika'i ka po'e apau.

When/at the time that the *rustic* came. I was busy.
When I was small, we had a lot of fun.
When the people opposed, there was no good fortune.
When I was seeking education, everyone was kind.

B. He mo'olelo nō Pele.

B. A story about Pele.

1. Nui nā mo'olelo e pili ana iā Pele, ka wahine 'ai honua.
2. Penei ka 'ōlelo a kekahi.
3. Hele mai he *luahine malihini. *Noi 'oia i wai, ai'ole i 'ai. I laulau paha. Inā he aloha kō ke kama'āina, 'a'ole he pilikia. Akā inā 'a'ohe aloha, *nalowale ka wahine!* Mahope, *he 'ā Pele.* Pau nā hale i ka 'ā 'ia. Pau *ho'i* ka po'e na'au aloha 'ole!
4. Pēlā kekahi 'ōlelo 'ana.
5. Penei ka 'ōlelo o ka wā kahiko.

1. There are many stories about Pele, the earth-devouring woman.
2. The story of some goes this way.
3. A strange old lady comes. She asks for water or food. Laulaus? If the natives have aloha, no trouble. But if there is no aloha, the *woman disappears!* Later *there is Pele's fire/lava/burning.* The houses are consumed by being burned. Finished *too/also* the people with hearts without aloha.
4. Such is one story.
5. This is the story of olden times.

6. Noho 'o Pele i kona 'āina
pono'ī, 'oia ho'i, 'o
Kīlauea, *mokupuni
o Hawai'i.

6. Pele lived in her own land,
namely, Kīlauea, island
of Hawaii.

7. Lilo 'o Pele *i ka hiamoe loa.*
He moe'uhane kāna.

7. Pele was engrossed (lilo)
*in a deep sleep. She had
a dream.*

8. Hele akula iā Kaua'i a launa
me Lohi'au, he u'i.

8. (She) went to Kaua'i and
met Lohi'au, a hand-
some youth.

9. Mahope mai ala a'ela 'o
Pele. Nui kona makemake
iā Lohi'au.

9. Afterward Pele woke up.
Great was her desire for
Lohi'au.

10. Nō laila, ho'oūna a'ela i kona
pōki'i aloha, 'oia ho'i, 'o
Hi'iaka-i-ka-poli-o-Pele,
e ki'i iā Lohi'au.

10. Therefore, (she) sent her
beloved younger sister,
namely, Hi'iaka-in-the-
bosom-of-Pele, *to fetch*
Lohi'au.

11. Hele akula 'o Hi'iaka mai Hawai'i a hiki i Kaua'i.

11. Hi'iaka went on from Hawai'i as far as Kaua'i.

12. Kaua 'oia ala *me nā mo'o
nui loa.* Lanakila mau 'o
Hi'iaka.

12. She fought *with many
water supernaturals.*
Hi'iaka always won.

13. Hiki *ā Kaua'i. Auwē noho'i
e! Ua *make loa 'o Lohi'au
nō kona makemake nui iā
Pele!

13. (She) came to Kaua'i.
Goodness! Lohi'au had
died for his great desire
for Pele!

14. Ola 'oia iā Hi'iaka.

14. Hi'iaka brought him back
to life.

15. Ho'i lāua i Hawai'i. 'A'ole
kolohe ike.

15. The two returned to Hawai'i. (They) didn't
misbehave in the least
(bit).

16. Akā, lili 'o Pele. Huhū
wela loa.

16. But Pele was jealous. Very
hot anger.

17. Ua 'ā ka Pele a luku wale
i nā lehua *punahele* a
Hi'iaka.

17. Pele's lava flowed and destroyed the *favorite*
lehuas of Hi'iaka.

18. Luku wale noho'i iā
Lohi'au-ipo. Pau loa i ke
ahi a Pele.

18. Destroyed indeed Lohi'au-
ipo. Finished/completed
in Pele's fire.

19. Hulihia ka *mauna, wela i ke ahi.	19. The mountain was overturned (hulihia), hot with fire.
20. Aloha wale iā Lohiʻau! He meʻe meʻe ʻole!	20. Alas for Lohiʻau! An unheroic hero!
21. Aloha wale iā Hiʻiaka! Luku ʻia nā lehua punahele!	21. Alas for Hiʻiaka! Favorite lehuas destroyed!
22. Pau wale i ka wahine ʻai honua!	22. Consumed wantonly by the earth-devouring woman!

Note: *Moʻo* in verse 12 has been translated "Water supernaturals." The word also means "lizard." *Meʻe meʻe ʻole* (verse 20) is a nonhero. Lohiʻau is not the only unheroic hero in Hawaiian stories. See Elbert, 1960, in the bibliography.

Huhū wela loa ʻo Pele

C. *Loaʻa*-type words again (review page 133).
    Ola in verse 14 is a *loaʻa*-type word:

Verb	±	Subject	±	*i*-phrase (agentive)
ola		ʻoia		iā Hiʻiaka
saved		he		by Hiʻiaka

In the following, make substitutions in the appropriate places. *Make* and *ʻeha* are also *loaʻa*-type words.

Ola ka mōʻī i ke akua.	God save the king.
(ʻo Pele)	Ola ʻo Pele i ke Akua.
(i ka moeʻuhane)	Ola ʻo Pele i ka moeʻuhane.
(lilo)	Lilo ʻo Pele i ka moeʻuhane.
(make)	Make ʻo Pele i ka moeʻuhane.
(ʻeha)	ʻEha ʻo Pele i ka moeʻuhane.
(i ka luku ʻia)	ʻEha ʻo Pele i ka luku ʻia.

KANALIMA-KŪMĀ-LUA

A. *Ke kauwā.*	**A.** *The slave.*

Ali'i. Ki'i mai i *wahi kalo a i wahi i'a *na'u.	Chief. Fetch some taro and some fish for me.
Maka'āinana. Nāu wale nō?	Commoner. Just for you?
A. Ki'i aku i wahi mai'a nā ku'u wahine.	Ch. Fetch some bananas for my wife.
M. 'A'ole *kapu nā mai'a?	Co. Aren't bananas taboo?
A. 'Ae, poina. Ki'i aku he he'e nāna.	Ch. Yes, (I) forgot. Fetch her a squid.
M. E ke kauwā, lawe mai i i'a, *kalo, a he he'e. Inā 'a'ole 'oe hana *āwīwī mai, lilo 'oe i mōhai ola. He limu pae wale 'oe.	Co. Slave, bring fish, taro, and a squid. If you don't do this fast, you'll be a live sacrifice. You are just drifted seaweed.
Kauwā. ('Ae mai me ke ku'ehu'e maka.) Iāia iho: *Pau Pele, pau manō!* Aloha 'ino!	Slave. (Assents with eyebrows.) To himself: *Death by Pele, death by sharks!* Woe!

B. He *leka.

Ke'ena Kia'āina (Governor's office) o Hilo
'Aperila 10, 1855

Aloha 'oe,
  Ke hō'ike aku nei au iā'oe, ua pau kā Geo. L. Kapeau noho 'ana ma
ka 'oihana kia'āina o Hawai'i, a ua ho'olilo 'ia ka mea Hanohano R.
Ke'elikōlani i kia'āina nō Hawai'i nei. A 'o Hilo nei nō kona wahi i *koho
(choose/vote)* ai e noho, e hana aku i nā hana apau e pili ana i kāna
'oihana kia'āina.
  Nō laila, ke kauoha aku nei au iā'oe, e ho'oūna *koke (quickly)* mai i
kou palapala hō'ike (report) hapahā (quarterly), lāua pū me nā dālā apau

i loa'a iā'oe ma kāu 'oihana *luna kānāwai (judge)*. Mai kali 'oe o hihia
auane'i (or there will be law suits).
'O wau nō me ka mahalo iā'oe.

L. L. Austin
Hope (deputy) Kia'āina o Hawai'i

C.   Luka Ke'elikōlani.

Kamuela. 'O wai 'o Luka Ke'elikōlani?	Sam. Who is Ruth Ke'eli-kōlani?
'Elikapeka. He ali'i wahine ia. Nānā aku 'oe i kona ki'i. (Ha'i aku 'o E. i ka 'ao'ao.)	Elizabeth. She was a chiefess. Look at her picture. (E tells the page.)
K. 'Ae, he maika'i. Nāu keia ki'i?	S. Yes, fine. Is this picture by you?
E. 'Ae, na'u. He *kahaki'i au.	E. Yes, by me. I'm an artist.
K. He aha ka 'oihana o Luka?	S. What was Ruth's position?
E. He kia'āina o Hawai'i.	E. Governor of Hawai'i.
K. He wahine u'i?	S. A beautiful woman?
E. Pēlā paha. Aia nō i kou mana'o. He wahine momona loa. He maka ikaika. 'A'ole pupuka.	E. Maybe so. Depends on your likes. (She was) a very fat woman. A strong face. Not ugly.
K. Pehea kona 'ano?	S. What was her character?
E. He lokomaika'i. Nui ke kōkua i ka po'e *'ilihune*.	E. Good-hearted. Much help to *poor* people.
K. He wahine hele pule?	S. A church-going woman?
E. Pēlā paha. I kekahi manawa, 'auwana nō.	E. Maybe so. Sometimes she went wandering.
K. He aha ka makahiki o kona make 'ana?	S. What was the year of her death?
E. *'Umi-kūmā-walu, kanawalu-kūmā-kolu.	E. 1883.

D.   He aha nā mana'o kū'ē o: ho'omaka, 'awa'awa, hema, 'ele'ele, anu,
mā'ona, 'ōpiopio, mākaukau, 'eleu, pī, pupule, 'ākau, nehinei, iki, moa
wahine, kuli, *pi'i, ho'opau, like pū, li'ili'i, pipi kāne, ho'omau, 'apōpō,
*pōloli, 'elemakule, nalowale, kauwā, kaumaha, ma'ema'e, molowā,
pōkole.

Luka Keʻelikōlani, he mea aliʻi

E. Ke ki'i e pili ana iā Pele.

Palani. E ka *Pelekane, e nānā aku 'oe i ke ki'i e pili ana iā Pele. Loa'a ka 'ao'ao?

Pelekane. Loa'a.

Pa. 'O wai 'o Pele? Mahea kona home? He aha kona 'a'ahu? He *pā'ū? He kapa? He mu'umu'u? He kāma'a? He pāpale nō kona? He aha kēlā mea maka'u loa kokoke i kona lima hema? He aha ka holoholona? 'Ehia po'e 'u'uku? (A pēlā aku nā nīnau. Pane mau 'o Pelekane.)

E. The picture concerning Pele.

Frenchman. Say, Englishman, look at the picture concerning Pele. Found the page?

Englishman. Found.

F. Who is Pele? Where is her home? What are her clothes? Sarong? Tapa? Mu'umu'u? Shoes? Has she a hat? What is that fearful thing close to her left hand? What is the animal? How many little people are there? (Questions like these. E keeps answering.)

KANALIMA-KŪMĀ-KOLU

A. Nā huaʻōlelo *paʻakikī.

   hoʻi: to come back (hoʻi lākou, ua hoʻi lāua, e hoʻi ana au)
          indeed, very, too (lākou hoʻi, maikaʻi hoʻi, nui hoʻi)
   mai: from (mai Maui, mai Honolulu aku)
          donʻt (mai hele, mai *noho paʻa)
          direction toward (hoʻi mai)
   mau: plural marker (keia mau iʻa, koʻu mau lole)
          always (hana mau, *ʻoia mau nō)
          continue (ua mau ke ea, hoʻomau ʻia)
   ʻai: food, eat (kāna ʻai, ua ʻai ʻoia) versus *ai* (linking: ka manawa i ʻai
          ai, pehea e hana ai)
   lā (day) versus *la* (there, doubt)
   ʻala (fragrance) versus *ala* (road) and *ala* (there: *ʻoia ala)
   wahi (place, some)
   pule (week, prayer)
   hou (new, fresh, again)

Lono. *Ei nei,* HOʻI koke MAI, i ka pōʻalima o keia pule.

Ku. ʻOia ka LĀ? No ke aha LA?

L. *No ka mea, he lānui a he *ʻano nui.*

K. Kānalua HOʻI. Paʻahana paha inā he LĀ. MAI kali. Mahea e launa pū ai kākou?

L. Ma koʻu keʻena i keia kūlanakauhale. Ma ke ALA Maui. Aia malaila ka Luna Kānāwai, ka mea Hanohano Kanaloa. Hele

Lono. *My friend,* come back quickly on Friday of this week.

Ku. Thatʻs the day? But why?

L. Because itʻs a holiday and *important.*

K. Really doubtful. Busy maybe if (itʻs) sunny. Donʻt wait. Where are we to meet together?

L. At my office in this town. On Maui street. The judge will be there, his Excellency Kanaloa. Heʻs coming. We must

MAILA 'oia ALA. Pono e
ho'omaika'i kākou iāia.

K. 'Ae nō wau.

L. E hele mai ana HO'I
kekahi MAU po'e 'ē
a'e paha.

K. Aia kekahi pilikia. He
WAHI *mamao MAI ko'u
home mai.

L. A laila, holo lio MAI. Koe
keia. 'Ilihune maoli au.
Lawe mai i WAHI i'a!

K. 'Ae HO'I au.

L. Mahalo nō kou
lokomaika'i.

K. He mea *iki. 'A'ole
pilikia. Ka hola *hea e
launa pū ai kākou?

L. Hapalua hola 'ehiku.

K. Kakahiaka nui! 'A'ole
paha e ALA.

L. Pono e ALA. MAI hiamoe
loa. Loa'a ke ola i ka
ho'omanawanui MAU.

congratulate him.

K. I certainly agree.

L. Maybe some *other/differ-
ent* people will be coming
too.

K. One other trouble. It's a
place far from my home.

L. Then ride horseback. This
remains/one other thing.
I'm really poor. Bring a
few fish!

K. I'll surely agree.

L. Thank you for your kind-
ness/good heart.

K. You are welcome/just a
trifle. No trouble. What
time are we to meet?

L. Seven thirty o'clock.

K. Early morning! Maybe
(I'll) not wake up.

L. Must get up. Don't sleep
late. Life comes from constant patience (gets the life
in the patience constant).

B. Ho'oma'ama'a i ka hua'ōlelo *lilo*. Nānā hou i nā ana kanakolu-kūmā-
hiku ame kanakolu-kūmā-walu. Unuhi. He turned into stone, into a pig.
She won five dollars. They got much taro. Lilo nā niu apau loa. Lilo loa
nā niho o ka 'elemakule. Nalowale! Aloha 'ino. He minamina noho'i.

C. Ho'oma'ama'a i nā hua'ōlelo e pili ana i ka *honua, 'oia ho'i: wailele,
moana (open sea), lā, hōkū, mahina, mauna, kuahiwi, pōhaku, 'ili'ili
(pebble), one, *pali, 'ā Pele, mo'o, moa wahine, pipi wahine, pipi kāne,
moa kāne, lepo, *pō, ao, mokupuni, pū hala, niu, pua'a, pueo, ahi, 'ulu,
a pēlā aku.

KANALIMA-KŪMĀ-HĀ

Ke kiʻi o ka poʻe hula.

Palani. E Kini, komo mai. He
papa Hawaiʻi keia. Pehea ʻoe?

Kini. ʻOia mau nō.
P. E nānā aku ʻoe i ke kiʻi.
K. Ke kiʻi hea? Ma ka ʻaoʻao
hea?
(Haʻi aku ʻo P. i ka ʻaoʻao.)
P. He aha nā mea Hawaiʻi ma
ke kiʻi?
K. *ʻO ka ipu,* nā ʻiliʻili, *nā pūʻili,
ka pahu,* *a pēlā aku.
P. He aha nā ʻano lei?

K. ʻO ka maile paha, *ka hulu
manu* paha, ka ponimōʻī paha.
ʻAʻohe aloalo. Aʻohe hoʻi he
ʻawapuhi keʻokeʻo *aiʻole
melemele.
P. He aha kou lei punahele? He
aha ka lei *aʻala* loa?

K. ʻO koʻu makemake nui, ʻoia
hoʻi, ka lei pīkake. ʻOi aku
kona ʻaʻala mamua o nā lei
ʻē aʻe.
P. ʻĀ ʻoia. He aha nā ʻano lāʻau
ma ke kiʻi?

K. ʻElua. Ka niu me ka maiʻa.
P. He mau pāʻū nō kō ka poʻe?
K. Pēlā paha.

Picture of the hula dancers.

Frank. O Jean, come in. This
is a Hawaiian class. How are
you?
Jean. Same as ever.
F. Look at the picture.
J. Which picture? Which
page?
(F tells the page.)
F. What are the Hawaiian
things in the picture?
J. *Gourd,* pebbles, *bamboo
rattles, drum,* and so forth.
F. What kinds of leis are
there?
J. Maybe maile, maybe *bird
feathers,* maybe carnation.
No hibiscus. Neither is
there white or yellow
ginger.
F. What's your favorite lei?
What lei is the most
fragrant?
J. What I like very much, it's
this, the pīkake lei. It's
more fragrant than other
leis.
F. That's right. What kinds of
plants are there in the
picture?
J. Two. Coconut and banana.
F. Have the people sarongs?
J. Maybe so.

P.   ʻIke ʻia nā māhele kino, ʻoia
     hoʻi, nā kuli, nā pepeiao, nā
     *niho, ka lauoho, nā kua?
     Nā waha? Nā *ihu? Nā ʻōpū?
     Nā maka?
(Pane ʻo K. ʻIke ʻia nā kuli, ʻike ʻia
     nā pepeiao hema o nā kāne ma
     ka ʻaoʻao ʻākau, a pēlā wale aku.)

P.   Nā wai ke kiʻi? Nāu?

K.   ʻAʻole naʻu. Nā kekahi kahakiʻi
     kaulana loa. ʻAʻole hiki iaʻu
     ke kahakiʻi.

F.   Are the body parts visible,
     namely, knees, ears, teeth,
     hair, back? Mouths? Noses?
     Stomachs? Eyes?

(J answers. The knees are seen,
     the left ears of the men on the
     right side are seen, and so
     forth.)

F.   Who is the picture by?
     You?

J.   Not by me. By a famous
     painter. I can't draw.

Ka poʻe hula

P. Hiki iā'oe ke pā ipu? 'Ike nō
'oe i ka hula pū'ili? Ka hula
'ili'ili? He lei hulu manu kou?

F. Can you beat the gourd
drum? Do you know the
bamboo-rattle hula? The
pebble hula? Have you a
feather lei?

KANALIMA-KŪMĀ-LIMA

A. *Ke ana ʻāina.*

He ʻano nui ke ana ʻāina. No ke aha la? No ka mea, hōʻike ʻia ka *nui* o nā ʻāina like ʻole ma ka ʻōlelo Hawaiʻi. Pono i ka poʻe wilikī ke heluhelu Hawaiʻi a hiki i keia lā. Pono hoʻi i ka poʻe loia ke heluhelu Hawaiʻi. Nui nā hihia ʻāina i nā ʻaha hoʻokolokolo. Penei nā huaʻōlelo hou:

ʻākau (ak), north
hema (he), south
hikina (hik), east
komohana (kom), west

A. *Land surveying/measuring.*

Land surveying is important. But why? Because the *size* of various lands is reported in the Hawaiian language. It is necessary for engineers to read Hawaiian until this day. It is also necessary for lawyers to read Hawaiian. There are many land cases in the courts. Here are the new words:

ʻāpana, parcel of land
kaula, chain in surveying, usually 66 feet
pā, lot, yard, fence
puʻu, pile, hill

Pahale.

E hoomaka ma ke kihi Akau o keia ma ke Alanui Beritania, pili ana me Capt. Carter, a e holo Hema 48 kekele Hik 2 kaul 50 pauku ma ke Alanui Beritania, a laila Hema 78 kekele Kom 2 kaul 45 pauku ma ke Alanui Huiʻna, a laila Ak 22 kekele Kom 20-1/2 pauku ma ko Bishop, a laila Ak 53 kekele Kom 1 kaul ma ko Bishop, a laila Akau 43-3/4 kekele Hik 1 kaul 98 pauku ma ko Capt. Carter a hiki i kahi hoomakaʻi.

ʻMa ia Apana 429 Anana.. Anaia e R. W. Meyer. 5 Okatoba, 1850.

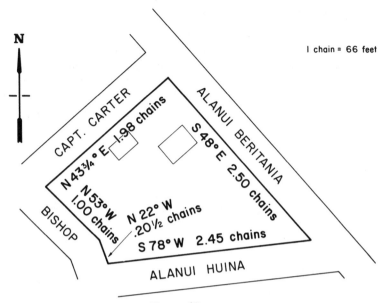

He ana ʻāina

B.   *-na.*

This is a nonproductive suffix that transforms words ordinarily used as verbs to nouns. Only a few are introduced in this elementary text.

Verb	*Noun*
hāʻawi, to give	haʻawina, lesson
helu, to count	heluna, number
hiki, to come	hikina, east (The reference is to the rising sun; *komohana* refers to the setting sun and means "west"; see C.)
holoholo, to go about	holoholona, animal
kahu, to care for	kahuna, expert, sorcerer
ʻoki, to cut	ʻokina, glottal stop

The functions of *-na* and *ʻana* are similar, but *ʻana* may follow an indefinite number of verbs, whereas *-na* is associated with a fixed number of verbs (that is, it is nonproductive). Particles and words may be inserted between the base and *ʻana (ka noho wale ʻana mai)*, but not between bases and *-na*.

C.   *-hana, -lana.*

These are nonproductive suffixes that, like *-na,* act as nominalizers. Those noted are listed below; bases taking *-hana* also take a passive/imperative suffix *-hia;* similarly *-lana* and *-lia* are attached to the same bases. Only a few of the bases with *-hia* and *-lia* derivatives, however, have *-hana* and *-lana* derivatives. Unless indicated, the meanings of the *-hia* and *-lia* derivatives are the same as the meanings of the bases plus passive or (rarely) imperative meanings.

Base	*Nominalizer*	*Passive/imperative*
kilo, look	kilohana, lookout	kilohia
kau, place	kaulana, resting place	kaulia
komo, enter	komohana, west	komohia
kū, stand	kūlana, position	kūlia, strive
mana'o, think	mana'olana, thought	mana'olia

D.   He mau leka.

Ke'ena Kia'āina
Hilo, Aug. 8, 1878

A. G. Judd,

Aloha 'oe. Ua kauoha 'ia mai au e ka mea *Hanohano S. Kipi, Kia'āina o Hawai'i, e hō'ike aku iā'oe, a iā 'oukou 'o nā luna kānāwai ki'eki'e, 'oia keia: ua ho'okohu (appoint) 'ia 'o D. D. Nae'ole i luna kānāwai nō Hilo-'ākau, me ka lā 8 o 'Aukake, A. D. 1878. Me ka pono.

W. Ke-ao-makani

Ke'ena Kia'āina
Kailua, Hawai'i
26 October 1853

Aloha 'oe,

Ua loa'a mai nei ia'u kāu palapala o ka lā 5 o keia malama (mahina) nō ka ho'onoho 'ana (appointment) mai o J. H. Conny ka Māka'i Nui, i Hope (deputy) 'oe nona ma Ka'ū.

Ke 'ae aku nei au e pono nō 'oe ke mālama (nānā) i kēlā 'oihana, ame nā lawehala (prisoners) pū ho'i o nā 'āpana la ma Ka'ū, a e hō'ike mai ho'i ia'u i ka pono o kou mālama 'ana i nā pa'ahao (prisoners).

Geo. L. Kapeau

E. Lele iho ka pueo.

Lopaka. Nānā i ke ki'i ma ka ha'awina kanahā-kūmā-walu.

Lei-aloha. Loa'a.

L. He aha ke 'ano manu? 'O wai ka manu? 'O wai ka wahine? He mu'umu'u anei kō ka wahine? He lei palaoa kona? He kāma'a? He aha ka pua i ka lima 'ākau o ka wahine? He ponimō'ī? He aloalo? He 'awapuhi? He aha ka *a'ahu o ke kāne? He aha nā 'a'ahu o nā wāhine? He aha kēlā mea ma ke kihi hema o ke ki'i i luna loa? He aha kēlā mea u'i i ke kua o ka wahine? He aha kona waiho'olu'u? 'Ehia *pepeiao o ka pueo?

Lei-aloha. (Pane mai 'oia ala.)

E. The owl flies down.

Robert. Look at the picture in lesson 48.

Lei-aloha. Found.

R. What kind of bird is there? Who is the bird? Who is the woman? Does the woman have a mu'umu'u? Has she a whaletooth pendant? Shoes? What is the flower in the right hand of the woman? Carnation? Hibiscus? Ginger? What is the man wearing? What are the women wearing? What is that thing at the left corner of the picture on top? What is that beautiful thing at the back of the woman? What is its color? How many ears has the owl?

L. (She answers.)

KANALIMA-KŪMĀ-ONO

A. Ma ke alanui.

Kuaʻāina. Kara mai iaʻu. ʻAʻole au tamaʻāina i teia wahi. Mai Niʻihau
nō au. E ʻoluʻolu ʻoe, e haʻi mai, mahea ketahi hale-ʻaina maitaʻi?
Akamai. Kekahi hale-ʻaina *pipiʻi (expensive)?* Aia ma ke alanui Ka-
lā-kaua. Mauka aku. (Pronounce: maukaku.) Kokoke i ka hale
kiʻiʻoniʻoni.
K. Mahalo a nui loa nō tou lotomaikaʻi.
A. He mea iki. He mea ʻole.

B. Ma ka hale-ʻaina.

Haku hale. Komo mai. Aloha.
K. Aloha ahiahi.
Haku. Makemake ʻoe i keia *pākaukau* kokoke i ka puka?
K. ʻAʻole. Maitaʻi tērā pākaukau kokoke i tēlā wahine uʻi.
Haku. Eia nō.
(Hele mai ke kuene wahine ʻōpiopio.)
Kuene. Aloha ʻoe. Makemake ʻoe e *inu lama?
K. Sya! Kūʻē nō au i nā mea inu *ikaika. Ua pōrori au. Matemate au
e ʻai a māʻona.
Kuene. Makemake ʻoe i ka meaʻai Pākē?
K. ʻAʻole loa! He aha tetahi ʻano ʻē aʻe?
Kuene. Aia nā ʻano like ʻole. He Kōlea, haole, Kepanī, Hawaiʻi.
K. Matemate i ka mea Hawaiʻi nō ka mea, ua nui roa tona ʻono.
Kuene. A laila, e *kauoha ʻoe i ka poi, heʻe, pipi kaula (jerked beef),
moa, *laulau, iʻa, ʻulu, haupia (coconut pudding), a pēlā wale aku.
K. ʻĀ ʻoia.
(Ua ʻai ʻo Kuaʻāina a māʻona.)
Kuene. Ua lawa ka meaʻai? Māʻona ʻoe?
K. ʻAe. Māʻona piha. Piha ka ʻōpū. Ua piha ka rua o ka inaina (pit of
wrath, i.e., hunger pains are pau). Ua holo ʻo Hanalē, tomo mai ʻo
Keoni Pulu. Eia he makana *nāu. He mea iki wale nō. (Hāʻawi aku
i ʻumi keneka. Huhū ke kuene. A laila, hāʻawi aku i hapahā. Huhū
nā maka o ke kuene. A laila, hāʻawi aku i hapalua.)

Kuene. Mahalo a nui loa nō kou *lokomaikaʻi.

K. Aloha pumehana (warm). (Iāia iho.) Pipiʻi teia ʻāina o Waitītī! Hoʻi nō au i ka ʻāina aloha o Niʻihau e ʻai i talo moʻa (cooked taro, figuratively, a life of ease). ʻAʻohe tulituli, ʻaʻohe pilikia, uʻi ka ʻāina, aloha te tamaʻāina.

C. E ka haumana, hoʻomaʻamaʻa ʻoe i keia kamaʻilio ʻana. E lilo ʻoe i Kuaʻāina. Ke paʻa, lilo ʻoe i Akamai, i haku hale, i kuene wahine, a pēlā aku. Eia kekahi huaʻōlelo hou: *pākaukau, table.*

1. K asks A where a good restaurant is. K says he is not familiar with Wai-kīkī because he is from Niʻihau.
2. A says there is an expensive restaurant up on Ka-lā-kaua Avenue near the movie.
3. K thanks A for his kindness and A says he is welcome.
4. In the restaurant, the manager greets K, and asks if he wants the table near the door.
5. K prefers a table near a beautiful woman.
6. The waitress asks if he wants a drink.
7. K strongly disapproves of liquor.
8. W asks if he wants Chinese food.
9. K refuses and asks what other kinds of foods there are.
10. W answers, and K wants Hawaiian food.
11. W suggests an order. After he has eaten she asks if he's full.
12. K replies with two favorite Hawaiian expressions, that the pit of wrath is full, and that Henry (hungry) has run off and John Bull (full) has come.
13. K is returning to Niʻihau to eat cooked taro. There is no noise and no trouble. The land is beautiful. The people know the meaning of aloha.

D. Improvise other dialogues on this theme.

E. The *k*-less possessives follow locatives. See haʻawina ʻumi-kūmā-kolu.

Unuhi: i mua oʻu (in my presence, before me); mahope o lākou; i mua ona; i hope o ka niu; maluna ou; i mua oʻu. Mahope o ka *ʻaina (meal).* *Mawaho o ka pā pōhaku.

F. Nā ʻōlelo like ʻole e pili ana i ka hoʻokani pila (music playing). E hoʻ-omaʻamaʻa ʻoe: leo, oli, ʻiliʻili, pūʻili, ipu, pahu, kīkā (guitar), ʻukulele.

KANALIMA-KŪMĀ-HIKU

Liholiho lāua ʻo Kamāmalu

Hele mai ka poʻe mikanele i Hawaiʻi nei i ka makahiki 1820. Nā lākou i *haku (compose)* i nā hua palapala pīʻāpā (letters of the alphabet). ʻAʻole i ʻike mua ka poʻe Hawaiʻi i ka palapala. ʻAʻole i hiki ke heluhelu. ʻAʻole hoʻi hiki ke kākau. Aʻo nā mikanele i ke kamaʻilio Hawaiʻi. Hoʻoholo (decide) lākou e kākau i ka ʻōlelo Hawaiʻi. Wae (select) kekahi komike (committee) i nā hua palapala pīʻāpā mai ka ʻōlelo haole. ʻAʻole paʻakikī nā hua palapala leokahi (vowel), ʻoia hoʻi, ʻa, ʻe, ʻi, ʻo, ʻu. Paʻakikī nā hua palapala leokanipū (consonant), ʻoia hoʻi, l aiʻole r, t aiʻole k, v aiʻole w. (ʻAno like *ka hoʻopuka ʻana, pronunciation.*) He aha ka mea pololei?

Ma ka lā ʻehiku o Ianuali 1822, ua paʻi (print) mua ʻia kekahi pepa ma ka ʻōlelo Hawaiʻi e ʻElika Lomika (Elisha Loomis). Hoʻopaʻi ʻia ka inoa o ka mōʻī Liholiho, ʻoia hoʻi, ʻo Kamehameha II, ʻelua manawa: LIHOLIHO, RIHORIHO. Hōʻike ʻia i ka mōʻī. ʻŌlelo aku ka mōʻī penei: " ʻOi aku ka maikaʻi o Rihoriho."

A laila aʻo nā aliʻi e heluhelu a e kākau leka. Aʻo koke a aʻo maikaʻi. Aia malalo nei kekahi leka i kākau ʻia e Liholiho:

Novema (Nowemapa) 17, 1823 a ke makaiki (makahiki).
OAHU, Honolulu. Malaila makou i holo mai nei. *Uwe mai ou *kahu i ka holo i Kahiki. Ka makaainana kekahi aloha ia kakou. Akolu po makou i ka moana. Maikaʻi wale no makou e holo nei ma ka moana, aohe maʻi. O makou he *lealea wale no makou Liliha ka maʻimaʻi i ka luaʻi (vomit), o laua me Kekuanaoa. Aha (ʻehā) po *makani (wind)* maikaʻi loa, hookahi po inoino (stormy) loa. ʻElima o makou po o ka moana. He olelo inoino (slander) wale no kana i ka poe mikanele o Luahine. He i mai o Luahine e ai ke keiki ka mikanele.

Nānā pono! He lā, he kē, he wē.
ʻElua pilikia nui. ʻAʻole i kākau ʻia ka ʻokina. ʻAʻole hoʻi i kākau ʻia nā macrons.

I ka lā 27 o Nowemapa 1823, holo aku nā aliʻi mai Hawaiʻi aku a holo loa i Pelekane. Lawe ka mōʻī i kāna wahine punahele, ʻoia hoʻi, ʻo Kamāmalu.

Liholiho (courtesy of the Honolulu Academy of Arts)

Kamāmalu (courtesy of the Honolulu Academy of Arts)

Penei ka ʻōlelo a Hailama Binamu (Hiram Bingham), he mikanele
Kalawina, e pili ana iā Kamāmalu:

"Kamāmalu distinguished herself as she was wont to do. This Amazonian
lady, about 26 years of age, tall and portly, of queen-like air, yet affectionate,
filial, courteous, patriotic, and friendly to the missionary cause, . . . Standing
on the stone quay near the boats, looking around with open countenance,
in a tender and plaintive strain—an elevated and poetic impromptu, poured
forth eloquently her parting salutation—her last farewell."

> Penei ke oli:
> E ka lani, e ka honua, e ka mauna, e ka moana,
> E ka hū (citizens), e ka makaʻāinana, aloha ʻoukou!
> E ka lepo, aloha ʻoe.
> E ka mea a kuʻu makuakāne i ʻeha ai, auwē ʻoe!

> ʻO Kamehameha ʻEkahi kona makuakāne. Aloha ʻino!

Penei kekahi ʻōlelo hou e pili ana iā Kamāmalu. Nā mea kamaʻilio: Kini
ka-pahu-kula-o-Kamāmalu Wilikona a me Kawena Johnson. Hoʻopaʻa ʻia i ka
tape recorder, 1956.

Kawena. Aunt Kini, e kamaʻilio paha kāua e pili ana i kou inoa.	Kawena. Aunt Jennie, let's talk perhaps concerning your name.
Aunt Kini. ʻAe.	Aunt Jennie. Yes.
K. Pehea i loaʻa ai?	K. How was it gotten?
A. He lōʻihi ka wehewehe ʻana.	A. The explanation is long.
K. ʻAʻole pilikia. ʻO wai kou inoa Hawaiʻi?	K. No matter. What is your Hawaiian name?
A. Ka-pahu-kula-o-Kamāmalu.	A. The-golden-casket-of-Kamāmalu.
K. Pehea i loaʻa ai?	K. How was it gotten?
A. Loaʻa koʻu inoa i ka make ʻana o Kamāmalu.	A. My name was gotten on the death of Kamāmalu.
K. ʻO wai Kamāmalu?	K. Who was Kamāmalu?
A. Ka wahine a Kamehameha ʻElua, ʻoia hoʻi, Liholiho.	A. The wife of Kamehameha II, that is, Liholiho.
K. ʻAe. A laila . . .	K. Yes. Then . . .
A. Hele aku lāua, ʻo Liholiho me kāna wahine. Hele aku lāua i Pelekane, a make lāua i laila.	A. The two went away, Liholiho and his wife. The two went to England, and the two died there.

K. Aloha ʻino!

A. Hoʻihoʻi ʻia nā kino kupapaʻu o lāua i Hawaiʻi nei. Kō lāua pahu, he pahu keleawe. Kō lāua kino i loko o ka ʻalekohola. He ʻāpana kula ua kau ʻia maluna o ka pahu. Keia ʻāpana kula ua kau ʻia me ka inoa, Kamāmalu, ka mōʻī wahine. Mai loko mai o laila i loaʻa ai ka inoa o koʻu makuahine, Kapahu-kula-o-Kamāmalu.

K. ʻĀ ʻoia! ʻO kou māmā ponoʻī kēlā?

A. ʻAʻole. ʻO koʻu kahu hānai kēlā. Koʻu makuahine ia.

K. A tragedy!

A. The corpses of the two were returned here to Hawaiʻi. Their casket, a brass casket. Their two bodies were in alcohol. A golden crest was placed on top of the casket. This golden crest was engraved with the name Kamāmalu, the queen. From within there was gotten the name of my mother, The-golden-casket-of-Kamāmalu.

K. That's it! Your own mamma that?

A. No. That was my foster mother. She was my mother.

Note: Infants were often named for an event occurring at their birth. Aunt Jennie says that her foster mother was born at the time that Queen Māmalu's casket was brought from London (1824). Aunt Jennie considers her foster mother her "mother."

KANALIMA-KŪMĀ-WALU

A. Nā hua'ōlelo: brother, sister.

Written form	Usual spoken form	
kaikua'ana	keiku'ana	*older brother* of a male, *older sister* of a female (i.e., older sibling of the same sex)
kaikaina	keikeina	*younger brother* of a male, *younger sister* of a female (i.e., younger sibling of the same sex)
kaikuahine	keikuahine	*sister* of a male
kaikunāne	keikunāne	*brother* of a female

Hawaiian sibling terms are not at all like English. The terms depend on the relative sexes of the persons involved, and of the relative ages (of persons of the same sex). Cousins may be called by the same terms, although another word for cousin is *hoahānau*. Sibling terms take the *o*-possessive.

Rule: After numbers, *'ehia*, locatives, and *'a'ole*, the *k*-less possessive is used.

In the blanks fill in "he" or "she." A laila, ho'opa'ana'au nō.

1. 'Ehiku *ona kaikuahine.
2. 'Elima ona kaikunāne.
3. 'A'ohe ona kaikaina.

4. *Hanele ona kaikunāne.*

5. 'A'ohe ona kaikua'ana.

6. 'Eiwa ona kaikua'ana.

1. _____ has seven sisters.
2. _____ has five brothers.
3. _____ has no younger sisters.
4. _____ *has a hundred brothers.*
5. _____ has no older sisters.
6. _____ has nine older brothers.

7. ʻEhia ona kaikunāne?

8. *ʻEono ona hoahānau.

7. How many brothers
   has _____?

8. _____ has six cousins.

B. He kamaʻilio ʻana e pili ana
   i *ka ʻohana.*

B. A conversation relating to *the
   family.*

Paniolo kāne.   Ei nei, ʻehia
*ou kaikaina?

Paniolo wahine.   ʻAʻohe
*oʻu kaikaina. ʻEhia ou
kaikaina?

K.   ʻElua oʻu kaikaina, akā,
     ʻaʻohe oʻu kaikuaʻana.
     ʻO koʻu kaikaina hope
     loa, *he moho.* Mamake
     ʻoia i ka ʻoihana luna
     kānāwai kiʻekiʻe. E koho
     ʻoe iāia.

W.   Hiki nō. He paniolo pono
     kou pōkiʻi. ʻO ʻoe ka mua
     loa o kou ʻohana. ʻAʻole
     anei?

K.   ʻAʻole. Hoʻokahi oʻu
     kaikuahine. ʻOia ka mua.

W.   ʻEhā ʻoukou. ʻAʻole anei?

K.   Pēlā nō. ʻEhia ʻoukou?

W.   ʻO au ka pōkiʻi. ʻElua oʻu
     kaikuaʻana.

K.   Pehea? ʻAʻohe kaikunāne?

W.   ʻAʻole. ʻEkolu o mākou
     keiki. Noho mākou ma ka
     hale o ke kaikuahine o
     koʻu makuakāne. *Mālama*
     ʻoia iā mākou, no ka mea,
     ua make kō mākou
     makuahine *ponoʻī.*

Cowboy.   Sweetheart, how
many younger sisters have
you?

Cowgirl.   I haven't any
younger sisters. How many
younger brothers have you?

B.   I have two younger
     brothers, but no older
     brothers. My youngest
     brother is *a candidate.*
     He aspires to the office
     of supreme judge. Vote
     for him.

G.   I agree. Your kid brother
     is an honest cowboy.
     You're the oldest in your
     family, aren't you?

B.   No. I have one sister. She's
     the oldest.

G.   You are four, aren't you?

B.   That's so. How many are
     you?

G.   I'm the youngest. I have
     two older sisters.

B.   What about it? No
     brothers?

G.   No. We are three kids. We
     live in my father's sister's
     house. She *looks after* us,
     because our own mother
     is dead.

K. Aloha ʻino. He minamina
nohoʻi.

B. How pathetic! Sure too
bad.

C. Ke ana _____.

'Oi aku anei ka ʻoi o ka niho
pueo mamua o ka niho ʻīlio?

Are owl teeth sharper than dog
teeth?

'Oi aku anei ke kulikuli o
Nuʻuanu aiʻole Mānoa?

Is Nuʻuanu noisier than Manoa?

'Oi anei ka ʻaʻala o ka ponimōʻī
mamua o ke aloalo?

Is carnation more fragrant than
hibiscus?

'Oi anei ka ʻono o ka puaʻa
mamua o ka ʻono o nā
holoholona ʻē aʻe?

Is pork more delicious than the
taste of other animals?

'Oi aku anei ka ʻeleu o ka
wilikī mamua o ka ʻeleu o
ke kākauʻōlelo?

Is the engineer more active than
the *clerk?*

'Oi aku anei ou makahiki mamua
o oʻu?

Are you older than I?

'Oi aku paha ka nani o Mele
mamua o ka nani o kono
kaikaina?

Is Mary more beautiful than her
younger sister?

KANALIMA-KŪMĀ-IWA

A. He haʻiʻōlelo.

Ka haʻiʻōlelo poni (inaugural) a ke Kiaʻāina Kamuela W. King, i kēia lā 28 o ka mahina o Pepeluali, makahiki 1953.

E nā kini (multitude) o kuʻu ʻāina aloha, nā mamo (descendants) Hawaiʻi ponoʻī, o nā mokupuni apau o kēia paeʻāina (island group), mai Hawaiʻi a Kauaʻi, ke hāʻawi aku nei au i koʻu aloha pumehana (warm) nui loa, iā ʻoukou apau, ke aloha nō.

Ke kū nei au ma keia kahua (platform), ke kahua i hoʻohanohano ʻia (exalted), e kō kākou aliʻi i hala (departed).

Ke kahua i hoʻano ʻia (hallowed) no ka paio (struggle) ʻana, i kō kākou pono.

I keia lā, ke kū aku nei au, me ka haʻahaʻa (humility), ka moho i hoʻohiwahiwa (honor) ʻia ai, e kō kākou *makua nui, ka palekikena o ke aupuni makua nui, ʻo Amelika, Dwight D. Eisenhower, he kiaʻāina nō keia teritori.

Ke pule aku nei au, me ka haʻahaʻa o koʻu ʻuhane, i ke Akua ma ka lani, me ka mahalo, nō kāna hana hiwahiwa (esteemed act), i koho ai iaʻu, he ʻōiwi (native) Hawaiʻi, i kiaʻāina nō kō kākou *home aloha.

*Nō laila, e nā Hawaiʻi apau, ke nonoi (*noi) aku nei au, me ka haʻahaʻa nō kā ʻoukou pule, e hoʻoikaika ʻia koʻu ʻuhane, a me koʻu kino, a me ke alakaʻi (lead) mau ʻana i kaʻu hana, i nā wā apau, nō kō kākou pono.

ʻAneʻane (almost) e piha nā makahiki, he kanalima-kumamā-lima, ʻo ka hui ʻana o kō kākou ʻāina, me ka ʻāina makua.

Keia ka maka (time) mua loa, i *lohe ʻia ai kā kākou pule, e hoʻohanohano ʻia kekahi o nā pua Hawaiʻi.

No laila, ke noi aku nei au, iā ʻoukou apau, e hui, a e huki (pull) like kākou apau, e mau ai keia hanohano, maluna o kākou apau.

A ke hōʻike aku nei au, i nā manaʻo pōmaikaʻi (blessed) loa, i haku ʻia ai e kō kākou Aliʻi, Kau-i-ke-ao-uli, Kamehameha ʻekolu:

"Ua hana mai ke Akua i nā lāhui kānaka apau i ke koko hoʻokahi, e noho like lākou ma ka honua nei, me ke kuʻikahi (united), a me ka pōmaikaʻi. Ua hāʻawi mai nohoʻi ke Akua i kekahi mau waiwai (endowment) like, nō nā kānaka apau, me nā aliʻi apau, o nā ʻāina apau loa."

A i loko o keia ʻuhane, kaʻu pule e noho mau ai kākou. Me ka mahalo nui loa, nō kō ʻoukou ʻae ʻana, e ʻākoakoa (assemble) i keia lā, nō ka hoʻohanohano ʻana iaʻu, i koʻu hāpai (exalted) ʻia ʻana i kiaʻāina nō kō kākou ʻāina aloha.

Ke aloha nō.

B. Nā nīnau like ʻole.

1. He aha ke kumu o ka haʻiʻōlelo?
2. He aha ka mahina o ka haʻiʻōlelo? Ka makahiki?
3. He aha ke ʻano o ke aloha i hāʻawi ʻia aku ai?
4. Kū ke aliʻi *i hea?
5. Nā wai i koho iā Kini?
6. He aha nā mea i noi ʻia ai i ke Akua i ka lani?
7. ʻO wai ka makua nui o ka poʻe Hawaiʻi?
8. Pule ke kiaʻāina hou iā wai?
9. ʻEhia makahiki o ka hui ʻana o Hawaiʻi me ka ʻāina makua?
10. ʻO wai ka *pua (child, descendant)* Hawaiʻi mua loa i hoʻohanohano ʻia e ka ʻāina makua ma ka ʻoihana kiaʻāina?
11. ʻO wai ka inoa Hawaiʻi o Kamehameha ʻekolu?
12. Like ʻole ke koko o nā lāhui like ʻole?
13. Pehea ka ʻōlelo pololei, kāna pule aiʻole kona pule?

C. *He pāʻina.*

Palani. Ei nei, keia koʻu hoaloha, ʻo Keoni Pulu.

Hina. Hauʻoli koʻu *hui* ʻana, me ʻoe.

Keoni. Hauʻoli pū nō au, i koʻu hui ʻana, me ʻoe.

H. *Holo mai ʻolua i ka moana? Pehea ke *kai?

P. Maikaʻi, akā, nui ka makani. (Pāʻina pū lākou.)

K. Mahalo ā nui, nō nā meaʻai ʻono, a me nā mea maikaʻi o keia pāʻina.

C. *A feast/luncheon/dinner.*

Frank. Darling, this is my friend, John Bull.

Hina. I'm happy to *meet* you.

John. I'm happy too to meet you.

H. You sailed on the open sea? How was the sea?

F. Good, but a big wind. (They eat together.)

J. Thank you very much for the delicious food and all the good things of this dinner.

H.   Hau'oli au i kō 'olua   H.   I'm glad you (2) came.
     hele 'ana mai. E hele   Come again.
     hou mai 'olua.

D.   He leka.

                                          Pi'ihonua, Hilo
                                          28 Iulai 1849
     Aloha 'oe,
        E ha'i aku 'oe i ka'u mau 'ōlelo *i mua o nā luna (bosses) a nā
     konohiki (overseers) e waiho nei i keia manawa, e lawe mai lākou i ka
     pua'a, moa, manu, hua moa (eggs), poi, 'aka'akai (onions), 'opihi, limu
     (seaweed), me ia mea aku, ia mea aku, i mua o'u i ka lā 30 o Iulai.
        A inā e lawe 'ole mai kekahi, na'u nō e ha'i i ka ho'opa'i (punish-
     ment). 'O nā 'āina na'e (indeed) e lilo i ke *Aupuni.

                                          George L. Kapeau

     'O wau nō,
     Iā Rev. T. Coan, Punahoa, Hilo.

HAʻAWINA

KANAONO

A. Hoʻolaha i ka poʻe koho pālota, ʻāpana luna-makaʻāinana ʻehā:
   announcement to voters (people select ballot), fourth representative
   district.

   Nā māhele i hui ʻia—6, 7, 12, 13, 14, ame 16. E koho ka poʻe koho
   pālota maloko o keia māhele i ka *heluna (number)* nō nā moho i hōʻike
   ʻia malalo nei, ʻaʻole hoʻi e *ʻoi aku mamua o ia heluna, ʻeono *ʻelele
   laulā (at large), ʻekahi ʻelele mai nā māhele i hui ʻia.

B. He haʻiʻōlelo a ka moho.

   Aloha kākou. E Hilo i ka Ua-kani-lehua, ka mea nāna i hoʻokau aku i ka
   lei o ka hanohano maluna o nā *poʻohiwi o ke kanaka nāna e hoʻokele
   (guide) nei i ke aupuni kalana (county) o Hawaiʻi, e nānā i ke kanaka e
   ʻike mau ʻia ana i mua ou i kēlā a me keia lā e nānā ana hoʻi i nā pono o
   ke kalana. E ʻike i kou ēwe (lineage) e Hawaiʻi nui kua uli.

   E Puna paia (bowers) ʻala i ka hala, ʻo ka mea nāna i hoʻoʻaʻala aku i
   kona inoa i mua ou mau makaʻāinana, e ʻike iho a e hoʻomau iho i ke
   ʻala onaona o ka hala a me ka hīnano (pandanus), ma o ka hāʻawi ʻana
   iho i ko ʻoukou pāloka ma ka lā 5 aʻe nei o ʻOkakoba.

   Ua nui loa koʻu mau makahiki i lawelawe ai nō ka lehulehu (serve the
   public). ʻAʻole ʻaihue. ʻAʻole hoʻopunipuni. ʻAʻole kolohe.

   Eia ka pua (child) i mua o ʻoukou e noi aku ana i kā ʻoukou kākoʻo
   (support) ʻana mai i ka lā koho e hiki mai ana. Me ka mahāāālo.

C. E ka haumana, e kākau ʻoe i kekahi haʻiʻōlelo *kālaiʻāina (political).* Lilo
   i *kiaʻāina, kenekoa (senator), luna-makaʻāinana (representative), luna-
   kānāwai, mākaʻi nui (sheriff), puʻukū (treasurer), meia (mayor), ʻohi
   (catch) ʻīlio, hope kiaʻāina, a pēlā aku.

   Hoʻokomo i nā inoa haʻaheo o ka ʻāina.

   Nā ua kaulana: Oʻahu: ua Tuahine (Mānoa), Waʻahila (Mānoa,
   Nuʻuanu), Kūkala-hale (Honolulu), Pōʻai-hale (Kahaluʻu). Maui: ua
   Lani-haʻahaʻa, ua kea (Hāna), Kaua-ʻula (Lahaina). Hawaiʻi: ua
   Kanilehua ("rain that lehua flowers drink," Hilo), ua Kīpuʻupuʻu
   (Waimea).

Nā makani kaulana: A'e (tradewind), 'Āpa'apa'a (Kohala), 'Eka (Kona, Hawai'i), Kēhau (Kona, Hawai'i), Kuehu-'ale ("billow-scattering," Kawaihae), Kuehu-lepo (Na'alehu, Hawai'i), Ma'a'a (Maui), Moa'e (tradewind), Mumuku (Kona, Hawai'i), Ulumano (Hawai'i).

Nā kuahiwi: (Hualālai, Mauna Kea (Hawai'i), Hale-a-ka-lā (Maui), Ka'ala (O'ahu), Wai'ale'ale (Kaua'i).

Nā ali'i: Keawe (Hawai'i), Pi'ilani (nā Hono- o Maui, Lāna'i, a me Moloka'i), Kākuhihewa (O'ahu), Mano-ka-lani-pō (Kaua'i). (Nānā i ka 'ao'ao 138.)

Nā akua wahine: Hina (ka makuahine o Moloka'i), Ka-'ahu-pāhau (o nā manō, sharks, ma Pearl Harbor), Li'a (o ka nahele, forest), Pele, Uli (ka hana 'anā'anā, sorcery).

Eia malalo iho he mele, *Hilo Hanakahi*, me nā inoa ha'aheo o nā moku (district) o ka mokupuni o Hawai'i. Hanakahi, he inoa ia o kekahi 'āina ma ka 'ao'ao Hāmākua o Hilo; he inoa ho'i o kekahi ali'i o ka wā kahiko —he hō'ailona o ka la'i (symbol of peace).

Hilo, Hanakahi, i ka ua Kani-lehua.
Puna, paia 'ala, i ka paia 'ala i ka hala.
Ka'ū, i ka makani, i ka makani kuehu (scattering) *lepo.
Kona, i ke kai, i ke kai mā'oki'oki (streaked).
Ka-wai-hae, i ke kai, i ke kai hāwanawana (whispering).
Wai-mea, i ka ua, i ka ua Kīpu'upu'u.
Kohala, i ka makani, i ka makani 'Āpa'apa'a.
Hāmākua, i ka pali lele koa'e (tropic bird).
Ha'ina ka *puana, i ka ua Kani-lehua.

KANAONO-KŪMĀ-KAHI

A. He *palapala mai Fatu Hiva. (Ka ʻElele Hawaiʻi, Novemaba 15, 1854.)
(He mokupuni keia i ka Marquesas Islands, kapa ʻia ʻo Nuʻuhiwa ma ka
ʻōlelo Hawaiʻi.)

ʻOʻomoa, Fatu Iva, Aug. 5, 1854

Aloha ʻoe, e Mr. Kalaka (Clark), ame nā makamaka (hoaloha) o
mākou mai Hilo, *a hiki i Niʻihau. Eia mākou nā kumu mai Hawaiʻi
mai, ke noho nei ma Fatu Iva ka ʻāina o Matunui i noho ai.

Eia ʻo Fatu Iva ma ka ʻaoʻao hema o ka Pōʻaiwaena (equator) 18 27
degrē a ma ke komohana 138 49 degrē.

He ʻāina *wela ʻo Fatu Hiva. He nui ka wela ma ka malama (mahina)
o Sep. Nov. Dec. Ja. Feb. ʻO ka wā e wela ana ʻo Hawaiʻi, ʻoia kō ʻoneʻi
(here) hoʻoilo (winter); a ʻo ka wā e hoʻoilo *malaila, ʻoia ke kau (wela)
maʻaneʻi (here). He ʻāina ua nui e like me kuʻu ʻāina hānau. Kelekele
(muddy) wale nā alanui a ʻinoʻino (bad) nohoʻi.

He ʻano poepoe (somewhat round) ʻo Fatu Iva e like nō me Lānaʻi;
he ʻāina pali ʻo Fatu Iva, he pali ma nā ʻaoʻao ʻāpuni (apau); hoʻokahi
naʻe (only) alanui mawaena o ka ʻāina; a maluna o ka waʻa e hele ai
mākou.

He ʻāina kahawai (streams), he wai ʻono . . . o puni (go around) nō ʻo
Fatu Iva i ka lā hoʻokahi ke holo ma ka waʻa.

Nā kānaka ma Fatu Iva. Hoʻokahi nō ʻano o keia lāhui me kō Tahiti
ame kō Hawaiʻi, ʻano like loa nā ʻili; nā ʻōlelo ʻana, ame kekahi mau
tabu a i koʻu manaʻo wale ʻana, hoʻokahi kupuna o keia moana.

He ʻano puʻipuʻi (stocky) nā kino o nā kāne ame nā wāhine; he ʻano
nunui nā kāne; a ʻo nā wāhine ka (mea) i ʻuʻuku. He poʻe makemake i
ke kākau uhi (tattooing), ʻoia kō lākou mea makemake loa.

He malo kō nā kāne, a he pāʻū kō nā wāhine. He ʻano like me
Hawaiʻi mamua, ʻaʻole lākou i nele (without) i nā mea ʻaʻahu.

He ʻulu kā lākou ʻai nui, ʻo ka hua o nā ʻulu; a i (inā) pau ia aia hoʻi
ka ʻulu i waiho ʻia (deposited) ma ka lepo; ʻoia ka ʻai e ʻai ai i ka wā
ʻaʻole i hua ka ʻulu; ua kapa ʻia he "mā." He wai *ʻawaʻawa.

Nā hana *leʻaleʻa. ʻO ka hula ka mea nui, hula ka pō, hula ke ao; ʻoia
kā lākou la leʻaleʻa nui . . .

B. Ho'opa'a manawa.

Ka-'eu-o-Kalihi.   'O wai
kekahi huapala maika'i?
Na'auao.   Kama'āina 'olua
me Lei-momi?

K.   'Ae! Pali ke kua, mahina
ke alo. 'A'ohe pu'u,
'a'ohe ke'e. Kīnā 'ole.
N.   Pono!
K.   He aha kāna huahelu?
N.   'Ole lima, ono 'ole kolu.
(Wili 'o K.)
K.   Aloha kāua.
Lei-momi.   Aloha. 'O wai
keia?
K.   'O Ka-'eu-o-Kalihi. E
Lei, ka'awale 'oe i ka
lā 18?
L.   Keia mahina?
K.   'A'ole. Keia mahina a'e.
Ka hulahula o ka po'e
pepehi 'ia.
L.   Kala mai ia'u. Pa'a hana
nō au. *Minamina loa.
Kāhea hou mai i kekahi
manawa. He keiki 'olu'olu
'oe. (Iāia iho.) He keiki
lapuwale! (Kau i ke
kelepona.)
K.   Tsa! He wahine *kolohe!
E Na'auao, 'o wai kekahi
kūmū maika'i?
N.   Pehea la 'o 'Alanohea?

K.   Auwē noho'i e! Pali ke
kua, mahina ke alo. 'A'ohe
pu'u, 'a'ohe ke'e. Kīnā 'ole.
E kelepona aku ana au iāia.

B. Making a date.

Rascal-of-Kalihi.   Who's a good
date (lit., ripe fruit)?
Wise.   Are you acquainted
with Shell Lei (acquainted
you [2] with)?

R.   Yes! Back a cliff, front a
moon. No pimples, no
crooks. Without a blemish.
W.   Right!
R.   What's her number?
W.   05-603. (R dials.)

R.   Hello.
Shell Lei.   Hello. Who is this?

R.   Rascal-of-Kalihi. Say Lei,
are you free on the 18th
day?
S.   This month?
R.   No. Next month. The
dance of the beatniks.

S.   Pardon me. I'm busy. So
sorry. Call again some
other time. You are such
a nice boy. (To herself.)
No-good boy! (Hangs up.)

R.   Say! Rascal woman. Say,
Wise, who is another fine
date?
W.   What about Pretty
Fragrance?

R.   Man! Back a cliff, front a
moon. No pimples, no
crooks. Without a blemish.
I'm going to phone her.

(Wili.) E 'Alanohea. Aloha!

'Alanohea.   Aloha nō. 'O wai
  keia?
K.   Kāu ipo, Ka-'eu-o-Kalihi.

A.   Pehea 'oe?
K.   'Oia mau nō. Ei nei,
    ka'awale 'oe i ka lā 18?
    Keia mahina a'e?
A.   Ka'awale loa!
K.   Maika'i. Hele kāua i ka
    hulahula o ka po'e
    pepehi 'ia!
A.   Hiki nō. E ku'u milimili,
    e ki'i mai 'oe ia'u. 'A'ole
    anei?
K.   Hiki nō, e ku'u pua mae
    'ole. Hiki nō, e ke kole
    maka onaona. Hiki nō, e
    ku'u nūnū maka onaona.

(Dials.) O Pretty Fragrance.
  Hello!
Pretty Fragrance.   Hello. Who
  is this?
R.   Your sweetheart, Rascal-
    of-Kalihi.
P.   How are you?
R.   Same as usual. Darling, are
    you free on the 18th day?
    Next month?
P.   Very free!
R.   Fine. Let's go to the dance
    of the beatniks!

P.   Okay. My toy, you'll come
    and get me. Won't you?

R.   Sure, my flower that never
    wilts. Sure, sweet-eyed
    surgeon fish. Sure, my
    sweet-eyed dove.

C.   An important but not common idiom is *ka i,* short for *ka mea i,* the one
who did/was/is: 'o ke aloha ka i 'oi aku, aloha is the best. For future
and imperative, the form is *ke,* short for *ka mea e:* 'o wau ke hele a'e,
I'm the one who should go (for reference).

KANAONO-KŪMĀ-LUA

A. He kama'ilio 'ana nō ke koho 'ana.

Kamuela. *Ei nei, e hele kāua e koho. Keia ka pō'alua.

Samuel. Honey, let's go and vote. This is Tuesday.

Luka. 'A'ole hiki ia'u ke koho.

Ruth. I can't vote.

K. *Nō ke aha?

S. Why?

L. 'Ōpiopio loa au.

R. I'm too young.

K. 'Ehia ou mau makahiki?

S. How old are you?

L. 'Umi-kūmā-walu o'u mau makahiki.

R. I'm eighteen years old.

K. A laila, hele ho'okahi au.

S. Then I'll go alone.

L. 'O wai kou moho punahele e lilo ai i *wilikī kūlanakauhale?

R. Who is your favorite candidate to become city engineer?

K. Maika'i *ka hapa nui* o nā moho. 'O ko'u kaikua'ana ku'u punahele.

S. *Most/the majority* of the candidates are good. My favorite is my older brother/cousin.

L. He aha ke kumu o kou makemake 'ana iāia?

R. What's the reason for your liking him?

K. He 'eleu, na'auao, hana ' pono, ho'omanawanui. He keiki hānau o ka 'āina. 'O kona one hānau, aia ma Hilo. 'A'ole 'oia e puhi paka. 'A'ole 'aihue. 'A'ole *ho'opunipuni. 'A'ole kolohe.

S. He's active, wise, honest, patient. A son born of the land. His birth place (sands) is at Hilo. He does not smoke tobacco. Nor steal. Nor lie. Nor misbehave.

L. Aia no iā'oe ke koho 'ana. Akā, ko'u kaikunāne, he moho maika'i.

R. The choice is up to you. But my brother is a good candidate.

B.   Ka *'imi lumi 'ana.

Koa.	Aloha 'oe.	K.	'Ae. Hele mau.
Haku hale wahine. Aloha.		H.	*E hele lawai'a 'oe? (Do*
K.	He lumi anei kāu?		*you go fishing?)*
H.	Aia paha.	K.	'Ae. Akamai i ka lawai'a.
K.	Hiki ia'u ke nānā aku?		E hā'awi aku ana au i nā
H.	Pēlā paha. He aha kāu		i'a iā'oe.
	'oihana?	H.	Komo mai! Ho'okahi a'u
K.	He koa au.		lumi.
H.	He inu 'oe i ka lama?	K.	Ehia kālā no ka lumi?
K.	'A'ole loa.	H.	'Umi kālā no ka pule
H.	He puhi paka 'oe?		ho'okahi.
K.	'A'ole loa.	K.	Pipi'i.
H.	He hele pule?	H.	Tsa! He kanaka pī loa 'oe!

Act out this drama. 1. Soldier asks for a room. 2. Landlady says maybe and he asks to see it. 3. She asks his profession, and then if he drinks, smokes, goes to church, and fishes. 4. He doesn't drink or smoke, and he goes constantly to church, and he fishes. He offers to give her fish, including squid. 5. He asks the price of the room. 6. She says ten dollars and when he says it's expensive she chides him for being stingy.

Practice variations of the dialogue. The soldier drinks, smokes, and does not go to church. The landlady drives him away. Or the soldier says he hasn't any money. The landlady has pity (aloha) and says he may pay later, or stay for free (manuahi).

C.   He leka.

Keena Kiaaina
Hilo, July 3, 1879

Hon. P. Mamakala
*Luna Kanawai
Kohala Akau

Aloha oe,

Ua loaa mai nei kau hoike (report) no ka hapaha (quarter) o June 30th me na bila (bills) dala no na dala eono haneri kanakolu kumamalua.

O wau no me ka aloha,

L. Lyman

D.   He leo.

E hea (kāhea) i ke kanaka e komo maloko,
E hānai ai a hewa waha (mā'ona piha).
Eia nō ka uku (payment) la, 'o ka leo.
A he leo wale nō, e!
          [Emerson 1909:41]

I 'elua maila; pono au.
'Ōlelo i ke aka (shadow)
Ka hele ho'okahi e,
Mamina (minamina) ka leo,
He leo wale nō, e.
          [Emerson 1915:19]

KANAONO-KŪMĀ-ĶOLU

A. *K*-less possessives.

Nānā hou i ka haʻawaina iwakālua-kūmā-ono. The rules for the *k*-less possessive are summarized below:

(1) After numbers and words of quantity (nui).

(2) After negatives (ʻaʻole, ʻaʻohe).

(3) After locatives (mua, hope, luna, lalo, a pēlā aku).

(4) If a *k*-word (ka, ke; keia, kēnā, kēlā; nā, ua ... nei) precedes the noun. This is rather common if more than one object is possessed, as *nā keiki *āna,* his children.

Prefix *k*- if it is needed to the possessives underlined below. If the k-less possessive is appropriate, leave the sentence as it is. Unuhi.

Ua ʻaʻala _____ oʻu lei *ponimōʻī keʻokeʻo. Hānai ka paniolo i _____ āna pipi wahine. ʻElua _____ ona kaʻa *Palani. ʻEhā keiki _____ a ke *kauka Kakolika. I luna _____ o ka imu. ʻEhia _____ ou mau makahiki? Iwakālua oʻu mau makahiki. ʻAʻohe _____ oʻu ʻahuʻula. Nui _____ ona lei *aloalo. Ka mana _____ o ke Akua. I mua _____ ona he wailele. E pili ana ua moeʻuhane la i _____ āna pōhaku kuʻi ʻai i *nalowale ʻia. Nā mea _____ aʻu i lohe ai nō Lono. ʻAno maʻi au mamuli o ka pōloli loa. E lohe māua i nā kauoha _____ āu. Nui loa _____ aʻu mau *pōpoki (cats).* ʻEhia _____ ou pepeiao? ʻElua _____ āna ipo. ʻElua ipo _____ a ke kolohe. ʻEhia _____ a ʻoukou *pahu? ʻAʻohe mea _____ o loko. ʻAʻohe mea _____ o *laila. Aia _____ oʻu hoahānau malaila.

B. Nā nīnau e pili ana i ka palapala mai Fatu Hiva.

1. He aha ka makahiki o ka leka?

2. Iā wai i kākau ʻia ai ka leka?

3. Nā wai i kākau ka leka?

4. Mahea ʻo Fatu Hiva?

5. ʻElua kau ma Fatu Hiva. He aha ka inoa o ke kau anu?

6. I ka wā ua, pehea ke ʻano o nā alanui?

7. Mahea nā pali ma Fatu Hiva?

8. Pehea ke ʻano o ka *ʻili o ka poʻe Fatu Hiva?

9. Pehea ka lole o nā wāhine?
10. Pehea ka 'ai *punahele?

C. Ka Wai a Kāne.

Mai unuhi kāpulu (carelessly)! Ha'eha'e, he 'āina ma Puna, Hawai'i.
Nihoa, he mokupuni mawaena o Kaua'i me Midway. Lehua, he moku
li'ili'i i ka 'ao'ao komohana o Ni'ihau.

He ui (query), he nīnau,
E ui aku ana au iā'oe.
Aia i hea ka wai a Kāne?
Aia i ka hikina a ka lā.
Puka i Ha'eha'e.
Aia i laila ka wai a Kāne.

E ui aku ana au iā'oe,
Aia i hea ka wai a Kāne?
Aia i ke kuahiwi, i ke kualono
   (mountain ridges),
I ke awāwa (vales), i ke kahawai
   (streams).
Aia i laila ka wai a Kāne.

E ui aku ana au iā'oe,
Aia i hea ka wai a Kāne?
Aia i luna ka wai a Kāne,
I ke ao (cloud) uli, i ke ao
   *'ele'ele,
I ke ao panopano (jet black),
I ke ao pōpolo hua mea a Kāne
   la, e!
Aia i laila ka wai a Kāne.

E ui aku ana au iā'oe,
Aia i hea ka wai a Kāne?
Aia i kaulana (setting) ka lā,
I ka pae 'ōpua (cloud bank) i
   ke kai
Ea (rising) mai ana ma Nihoa
Ma ka mole (root) mai o Lehua.
Aia i laila ka wai a Kāne.

E ui aku ana au iā'oe,
Aia i hea ka wai a Kāne?
Aia i kai, i ka *moana,
I ke kua-lau (rains), i ke ānuenue
   (rainbow),
I ka pūnohu (pink cloud) i ka
   uakoko (rainbow patch),
I ka 'ālewalewa (floating mist).
Aia i laila ka wai a Kāne.

E ui aku ana au iā'oe,
Aia i hea ka wai a Kāne?
Aia i lalo, i ka honua, i ka wai
   hū (gushing),
I ka wai kau a Kāne me Kanaloa.
He wai puna (spring), he wai e
   inu,
He wai e mana, he wai e ola,
E *ola no, eā.
[Emerson 1909:257–258]

KANAONO-KŪMĀ-HĀ

A. Particles that sound alike and nearly alike were listed in haʻawina kanahā, C. Nānā hou iā lākou. Below are listed some content words that cause confusion.

ai	linking	*hoʻi	indeed, also
ʻai	to eat; food; poi	hoʻi	go back
		lā	day; sun
ʻaina	meal	la	there
ʻāina	land	la	doubt
ʻaʻole	no; not	mau	plural marker
aiʻole	or	mau	continue, always
ana	pattern, survey, measure	nui	many, much, number, quantity, size, big
āna	his, her	ʻoi	*sharp*
ʻana	noun-making	ʻoi	best
e (verb)	progressive	pono	righteous
ana	action	ponoʻī	own
ʻano	kind; fairly	wahi	place
hiki	can, able	wahi	a little, some
hiki	go, come, arrive		

B. He hoʻomaʻamaʻa ʻana: he aha nā haʻina?

1. ʻOi ka molowā aiʻole ka *ʻeleu?

2. ʻOi aku ka nani o nā *wailele o Kauaʻi aiʻole nā wailele o ʻAmelika-hui-pū-ʻia (United States)?

3. ʻOi aku ka waiwai o ka pū hala aiʻole ka *niu?

4. ʻOi aku ka maikaʻi o ka leʻaleʻa aiʻole ka hiamoe?

5. ʻOi ka lānui aiʻole ka lā hana, ka lāpule aiʻole ka pōʻaono?

6. ʻOi ka hōkū aiʻole ka mahina?

7. ʻOi aku ka nani o ka pālule polū aiʻole ʻōmaʻomaʻo?

8. ʻOi ka pūʻili aiʻole ka ipu aiʻole ka ʻiliʻili?

9. ʻOi ka lei hulu aiʻole ka
   *lei palaoa?
10. ʻOi aku ka *ʻaʻala o ka lei
    *ʻawapuhi aiʻole ka lei
    ponimōʻī? (Kānalua.)
11. ʻOi ka ʻoihana lawaiʻa aiʻole
    ka ʻoihana *paniolo?

12. ʻOi ka paʻakikī o nā mele
    kuaʻāina aiʻole nā mele
    Pelekane?
13. ʻOi aku ka pono o ka
    waiwai aiʻole ka
    ʻilihune?

C. Unuhi: He aha ka nui o nā pōpoki ʻeleʻele? Ke hele mai ka *moho punahele, haʻi mai iaʻu. Inā e *hoʻomau ʻoe i kāu hana ʻino, pau ʻoe i ke *ahi o Pele. He aha ka lā i ʻai ʻia ai ka heʻe? Ka pōʻakahi aiʻole ka pōʻahā? Hāʻawi mai he wahi niu naʻu. He ʻano pipiʻi ke kumu kūʻai (price) o kēlā wehi (adornment) kahiko. ʻEhia āna ʻano papa? Inahea ka ʻaina awakea? Ahea ka ʻaina ahiahi? Hiki iāʻoe ke ana ʻāina? E puhi paka mau ana koʻu kaikaina, nō laila mai ka ʻilihune. Ua hiamoe loa kona kaikunāne i ka hale i luna o ke kuahiwi *kiʻekiʻe loa. Aia ma ka ʻaoʻao komohana o ka pā kokoke i ka puʻu pōhaku. Kiʻi mai i wahi kalo no ke kaikuaʻana o koʻu makuakāne. ʻEhia ona *hoaloha? Hoʻoūna mai i nā mea like ʻole i koe (remaining). ʻOi aku ka pipiʻi o kēlā kāhili mamua o keia. ʻAʻole anei?

D. E hoʻokomo mai ʻoe i nā ʻokina a me nā macrons in the following. This means that you will have to analyze every o (ʻo subject marker or o of), ia (iā, ia, ʻia, iʻa), ana (e X ana, k-word X ʻana, āna, k-less possessive).

Hoʻolaha (advertisement)

O kou no ka oi. Aohe wa makepono (bargain) *e ae e like me keia, oia hoi: e *kuai makepono (cheaply) loa aku ana au i na PAPALE BIVA (beaver) wahine he ehiku haneri, no ke kumu kuai emi (cheap) loa i ike ole ia mamua ma na hale-kuai e ae o keia kulanakauhale.
Elua Dala *hapalua wale no!
A e loaa pu no me na hulu pikake (peacock) nani.
E hoomaka ana keia kuai ana ma ka poaono, Aperila 11, 1884, ma kou mau Hale-Kuai Lole nani, ma ke kihi o Alanui Pāpū (Fort) me Hokele, a ma ke kihi o Alanui Kalepa me Nuuanu. (Na La o Hawaii.)

Aohe ana keiki. Aohe ana makana maikai, he mau makana kapulu wale no ana. He keiki ikaika loa ma ka ai ana, hookahi umu (imu) hookahi ai ana.

KANAONO-KŪMĀ-LIMA

A. *Loaʻa*-type words. A list of common *loaʻa*-type words follows. (Refresh your memory: nānā i ka haʻawina kanakolu-kūmā-walu.) *ʻEha, hiki, lilo, loaʻa, make, maopopo, nalowale, ola.* These words can be thought of as inherently passive: they are never followed by *ʻia.* In many instances, translation by an English active is better than by a passive: maopopo iaʻu, understood to me; I understand. Ola ka mōʻī i ke Akua, the king should be saved by God; God save the king. Words with *hoʻo-* may be followed by *ʻia* and are never used as *loaʻa*-type words.

(1) Ua ola au.
Ola ka mōʻī i ke Akua.
Ola ʻoia iaʻu.
Make lākou.
Make ʻo Kama i ka moho.

(1) I am saved. (ola)
God save the king. (ola)
I saved him. (ola)
They are dead. (make)
Kama was killed by the candidate. (make)

(2) Ua ʻeha ka *Paniolo.*

Ua hōʻeha au i ke kākau ʻōlelo.
Ua ʻeha ka loko i ke aloha.
Ola ka honua i ka ua.

Lilo ka pākaukau i ka mea holo lio.

(2) The *Spaniard* is in pain. (ʻeha)
I hurt the clerk. (hōʻeha)

The heart hurts with love. (ʻeha)
The land gets life from rain. (ola)
The horseback rider got the table. (lilo)

(3) Lilo ka *ʻiliʻili i ka moʻo.

Loaʻa iāia he niho ʻoi.
Lilo ka hulu manu i ka makani.
Loaʻa he ahi iā Pele.
Maopopo ka haʻina i ka lawaiʻa.

(3) The lizard took the pebbles. (lilo)
He got a sharp tooth. (loaʻa)
The wind took off the bird feather. (lilo)
Pele got a fire. (loaʻa)
The fisherman understood the answer. (maopopo)

B.   'Ē.

A'o kākou i ka hua'ōlelo "'ē": *strange, astonishing, amazing, other, foreign.* Eia kekahi mana'o o 'e: *beforehand, already, had.*

(4) Mai ka 'āina 'ē.
He hana 'ē loa.

He mea 'ē ka le'ale'a o ka
pā'ina.
*Hānai 'ē 'oia i ka pōpoki.
*Ki'i 'ē 'ia ka pōhaku ku'i
'ai.

(5) Ana 'ē 'ia ka *pā e ka hapa
haole.
'Imi 'ē i ka na'auao.
Loa'a 'ē i ka *lapu he
*makana.
He mea 'ē ka maka'u i ka
*lā'au.
He pōloli 'ē 'o ka moa
wahine.
Kekahi lā 'ē a'e.

(4) From the foreign land.
Astonishing/strange pro-
cedure.
The fun at the feast was
terrific.
He had already fed the cat.
The poi pounder had already
been fetched.

(5) The hapa haole had already
surveyed the lot.
Seek wisdom/education first.
The ghost had already
obtained a gift.
The fear of the plant was
amazing.
The hen was astonishingly
hungry.
Another day.

C. Mele hōʻole (refuse) rama.

'Aʻole au e inu rama.
'Aʻole inu waina hoʻi.
Pau ke gini, pau ka ʻawa.
'Aʻole loa lālau (take) hou.
Pēlā hoʻi ka *puhi paka*
  (smoke tobacco).
'Aʻole au e puhi hou.
*'Ino maoli kēlā hana,
Pono ʻole maoli nō.

E nānā i nā kānaka,
Nā kāhiko me nā hou,

Nā pūʻali (army) puhi paka
Mai ka wā naʻau-a-pō.
Puhi, puhi, puhi, puhi,
'Oia nō ka hana mau.

Lilo (nalowale) nō ka hale
  maoli,
Kapa, lole, iʻa, ʻai
No ke kumu kūʻai paka
A pau ʻino ka waiwai.
Puhi, puhi, puhi, puhi.
'Ilihune mau nonaʻe (indeed).
[Mele pūʻali inu wai, 1849]

KANAONO-KŪMĀ-ONO

A.

† Lā‘ie-i-ka-wai
(Nā Hale-‘ole i haku. Ua ho‘opōkole ‘ia keia māhele.)

‘O ‘Aiwohi-kupua, he ali‘i ia o Kaua‘i. I kekahi lā, hiamoe ihola ke ali‘i, loa‘a ihola kekahi wahine u‘i loa iāia ma ka moe‘uhane. ‘O Lā‘ie-i-ka-wai keia wahine. I loko o ia ala ‘ana a‘e, aia ho‘i (behold!) he mea minamina loa i ke ali‘i i kona ‘ike ‘ana iā Lā‘ie-i-ka-wai ma ka moe‘uhane, nō ka mea, ua *ala ‘ē mai ka hiamoe. A laila, ‘ī aku ke ali‘i i ‘ōlelo pa‘a (determination, oath) i mua o kona mau mea apau, penei, e hele aku ‘oia e ‘imi i keia wahine ma Pali-uli, ma ka mokupuni o Hawai‘i.

Holo akula ke ali‘i me kona po‘e a hiki i Hawai‘i. Pi‘i *a‘ela i uka loa. A laila, ‘ike akula i ka hale o Lā‘ie-i-ka-wai. Ua uhi (cover) ‘ia ka hale me nā hulu melemele o ka ‘ō‘ō, he manu kaulana a waiwai. Iā (while) ‘Aiwohi e nānā ana i kēlā hale, he mea ‘ē ke kāhāhā (astonishment) a me ka hilahila. He ‘ahu‘ula kona, he makana no ke ali‘i wahine. He aha keia mea! He hale ‘oko‘a (entire) o ka wahine i uhi ‘ia me nā hulu melemele.

Nō laila, ho‘i koke ‘o ‘Aiwohi i Kaua‘i a noi i kona mau kaikuahine e ho‘i pū lākou i Hawai‘i he mea kōkua iāia. ‘Ae mai kona mau kaikuahine. ‘Elima † kō lākou nui, ‘o Maile-ha‘i-wale, ‘o Maile-kaluhea, ‘o Maile-lau-li‘i, ‘o Maile-pākaha, a ‘o Ka-hala-o-māpuana, kō lākou *pōki‘i. Holo akula he iwakālua-kūmā-kolu kō lākou nui. Ha‘alele (leave) lākou iā Kaua‘i, hiki ma Pu‘uloa (Pearl Harbor), a malaila aku a kau (arrive) ma Hanauma. I kekahi lā a‘e, kau i Moloka‘i, ma Kaunakakai. Malaila aku a pae (land) i Mala, ma Lahaina. Malaila hiki aku i Ke-one-‘ō‘io, a malaila i noho lō‘ihi ai ‘ekolu anahulu (ten-day period) nō ka mea, ua nui ka ‘ino (storm) ma ka moana. Mai laila aku, holo a Kea‘au, Hawai‘i, a pi‘i aku i uka o † Pali-uli.

Kū (stopped) *maila ‘o ‘Aiwohi-kupua, lāua pū me ke kaikuahine, ‘oia ho‘i, ‘o Maile-ha‘i-wale. Ku‘u (release) aku keia wahine i ke ‘ala (*‘a‘ala), a ua ho‘āla (awaken) keia onaona iā Lā‘ie-i-ka-wai. Nīnau akula ke ali‘i wahine i kona kahu: "He ‘ala, eia la, he ‘ala ‘ē wale nō keia, he ‘ala anuanu, he ‘ala hu‘ihu‘i (chilly), eia la i ka pu‘uwai."

†See page 216.

Pane maila ke kahu: "ʻAʻole nō he ʻala ʻē, ʻo nā kaikuahine ʻaʻala o ʻAiwohi-kupua i kiʻi maila iāʻoe i wahine ʻoe, a i kāne ia."

ʻĪ aku ʻo Lāʻie-i-ka-wai: "Tsa! ʻAʻole au e male (marry) iāia!"

A laila, he mea ʻē ka hilahila o ʻAiwohi-kupua. Hoʻi koke i kai a kau i luna o ka waʻa. Iho maila nā kaikuahine ona, a mele akula iāia. A ka pōkiʻi o lākou, ʻoia ʻo Ka-hala-o-māpuana, ua hele loa aku a paʻa mahope o ka waʻa, a *kāhea aku me ka mele penei:

† "Kō mākou kaikunāne *haku, kaikunāne kapu . . .
Nāu ka huakaʻi (journey), ukali (follow) aku mākou i nā pali . . .
He aloha ʻole e,
He aloha ʻole paha kou iā mākou,
Nā hoa ukali o ka moana.
ʻO ka ʻale (billow) nui, ʻale iki,
ʻO ka ʻale loa, ʻale poko (pōkole),
ʻO ka ʻale kua loloa (long) o ka moana.
Hoa ukali o kēlā uka,
ʻO kēlā nahele liʻuliʻu (distant).
ʻO ka pō ʻiu anoano (awesome distant).
E huli mai (turn), e huli mai . . .
I hea la hoʻi kāu haʻalele (abandon), haʻalele iho iā mākou i kahi
    (wahi) hāiki (narrow).
Nāu i waele (open) ke alanui mamua,
Mahope aku mākou ou.
ʻIkea (behold) ai he mau pōkiʻi.
*I laila la haʻalele aku ka huhū,
Ka inaina (wrath), ka *ʻōpū aloha ʻole.
Hō (give) mai ka ihu i ou mau pōkiʻi, aloha wale . . . e!"

ʻAʻole lohe ʻo ʻAiwohi-kupua. Kauoha akula i nā †hoe waʻa e hoe ikaika. A laila, hoʻi aʻe nā kaikuahine a Pali-uli, noho ihola lākou maloko o nā pūhā (hollow) lāʻau. Hiki iā lākou ke nānā mau i ka hale o Lāʻie-i-ka-wai. I kekahi lā aʻe, wehe (open) aʻela ke kahu o ke aliʻi wahine i ka puka o ka hale aliʻi. Hoʻopūʻiwa ʻia (startled) nā wāhine. ʻIke akula lākou iā Lāʻie-i-ka-wai e kau mai ana i luna o ka ʻēheu (wings) o nā manu e like me kona ʻano mau, ʻelua hoʻi mau manu ʻiʻiwi e kau ana ma nā poʻohiwi o ke aliʻi, e lū (pour) ana i nā wai ʻala ma ke *poʻo o ke aliʻi.

ʻĪ aku ke kahu i ka pōkiʻi o nā wāhine: "Mai makaʻu ʻoe, e kū ʻoe a e komo aku e *launa pū me kuʻu aliʻi."

E kau mai ana i luna o ka ʻēheu

ʻĪ mai ke kaikamahine: "He makaʻu." Akā, hele aku lākou a e lilo he mau kiaʻi (guards) nō ke aliʻi wahine.

Hoʻi ʻo ʻAiwohi-kupua i Kauaʻi a hoʻohalahala (complain) nō ka paʻakikī o Lāʻie-i-ka-wai. A laila, hui ʻoia me Haua-ʻiliki, he keiki leo maikaʻi o Mānā, he keiki kaukau-aliʻi (lesser chief) nohoʻi. ʻOia ka ʻoi i ka maikaʻi. A laila, *hoʻoūna ʻo ʻAiwohi iā Haua-ʻiliki i Hawaiʻi e kiʻi iā Lāʻie. A laila, holo aku ʻo Haua-ʻiliki a pae (land) ma Keaʻau, Hawaiʻi.

Ma ka puka (appear) ʻana a ka lā, uhi ʻia ka ʻāina me ka noe (mist), a i ka mao (clearing) ʻana, aia hoʻi, ʻehiku mau wāhine e noho ana ma ke one. A laila, holoholo aʻela ʻo Haua-ʻiliki i mua o lākou, e hōʻike ana i kona ʻano kanaka uʻi. A he aha la ʻo Haua-ʻiliki iā Lāʻie-i-ka-wai? "He ʻōpala (trash) paha."

Hōʻike ʻo Haua-ʻiliki i kona akamai ma ka heʻe nalu. ʻO Haua-ʻiliki nō ka ʻoi ma Kauaʻi no ke akamai i ka heʻe nalu. He keiki kaulana hoʻi ʻoia ala nō kona uʻi. A laila, heʻe aku ʻo Haua i kona nalu, a walaʻau nā kamaʻāina, a me nā kaikuahine, akā, ʻaʻole kāhea mai ʻo Lāʻie iāia.

A laila, hoʻi ʻo Haua me ka loko kaumaha. Huhū wela loa ʻo
ʻAiwohi-kupua a hoʻoūna aku i kekahi manu ʻelele e ʻike iā
ʻLāʻie-i-ka-wai. Lele akula ka manu a ʻike i ke aliʻi wahine. Auwē nohoʻi!
Kiaʻi ʻia ʻoia ala e ka moʻo nui! ʻOia hoʻi, ʻo Kiha-nui-lūlū-moku. He
pahu (staff) kapu a he moʻo he mau kiaʻi a ka wahine.

Hōʻike ka manu i ka mea hou weliweli (terrifying) loa iā
ʻAiwohi-kupua. A laila, hoʻoūna aku ʻo ʻAiwohi i kona ʻīlio ʻai kanaka,
ʻo Kalahumoku nō Kahiki mai. Piʻi aʻela ka ʻīlio i uka o Pali-uli. E moe
ana ka moʻo. Akā, nō ka hohono (stench) o ka ʻīlio, ala aʻela ʻo ka moʻo.
Wehe aʻela ka moʻo i kāna waha e nahu (bite). Ia wā, hōʻike ʻo ka ʻīlio i
kona mau niho ʻoi loa. Ia wā lāua i hele ai me ka weliweli loa, e nahu
kekahi i kekahi, a lanakila (win) ka moʻo maluna o ka ʻīlio. Pau nā
pepeiao a mumuku (cut off), moku ka huelo (the tail was cut off). A
laila, hoʻopau loa ʻo ʻAiwohi-kupua i kona manaʻo ʻana nō Lāʻie-i-ka-wai.

Kiaʻi ʻia e ka moʻo nui

Nā Wehewehe 'Ana (items marked by †)

†He puke nui keia, nā Martha Warren Beckwith i ho'oponopono (see bibliography). Keep your translation in a consistent tense, either all historical present or consistently past.

kō lākou nui: their number. These are names of varieties of *maile*, personified plants. The youngest sister is Ka-hala-o-māpuana, the pandanus of wafted fragrance.

Travels in legends often contain a succession of places visited; they attest the teller's knowledge and memory, and add verisimilitude. Pali-uli is an imaginery paradise, probably in the Puna District, Hawai'i.

The following traditional elements are noted in the song: the recounting of shared tribulations, repetition with metathesis *('ale nui, 'ale iki, 'ale loa, 'ale poko)*, a traditional tribute to an older brother (*nāu i waele ke alanui mamua*, you opened up the pathway = you were born first).

nā hoe wa'a: canoe paddlers.

B.   *Iho* is used in at least four ways: (1) as a directional meaning "down," as in lessons 19 and 40; (2) as a reflexive denoting bodily processes, as after such verbs as *'ai, aloha, inu, mana'o,* or *no'ono'o* (in this position it is usually not translated into English); (3) as a modifier of a preceding pronoun with the meaning "self"; (4) as a verb in its own right meaning "go down."

    (1) Hele iho lākou mai ke kuahiwi.   They went down from the hill.

    (2) 'Ai ihola 'oia i ka pua'a.   He ate pork.

         Ua no'ono'o iho lāua i ke aloha.   They thought of love.

    (3) Pa'akikī ma kāna iho.   Stubborn with himself.

         Ke nānā nei au ia'u iho.   I am looking at myself.

         Namu 'oia iāia iho.   She talks to herself.

         E hana ana 'oia nona iho.   He works for himself.

    (4) Ua iho maila 'oia.   He came down.

KANAONO-KŪMĀ-HIKU

A. Nā ʻōlelo noʻeau (traditional sayings).

Ka ua

Luʻuluʻu (burdened) Hanalei i ka ua nui, kaumaha i ka noe (mist) o
Alakaʻi. (*Kaumaha ka puʻuwai.)
ʻO ka ua o Hilo e mao (clear) ana, ʻo ke aloha i ka ipo, mea pau ʻole.
He lā ua nō Hilo a pō ka lā. (He pilikia?)
I Kahiki ka ua, ʻako (thatch) ʻē ka hale. I kahi (wahi) ʻē ka ua, waele
(clear off) ʻē ka pulu (mulch). (Hana ʻē, mahope iho he ua. Make
hay while the sun shines.)

Ka wahine uʻi

Pali ke kua, mahina ke alo.
Kau ka ʻiwa (frigate bird), he lā *makani. Kīkaha (soars) ka ʻiwa i nā pali.
Pua ka wiliwili (a tree), ʻai ka manō. Pua ka wahine uʻi, nanahu (bites)
ke kānāwai. Uliuli ke kai a holo ka manō, a uʻi ka wahine, makaleho
(eager) nā kāne a kiʻi i ka wahine.

Ke aloha

I ka noho pū ʻana, ʻike i ke aloha.
ʻO ke aloha ka mea i ʻoi aku ka maikaʻi mamua o ka ʻumeke (bowl) poi
a me ka ipu kai (fish).
He aliʻi ke aloha, he kilohana (outer tapa; the best) e *paʻa ai.

Ke kanaka

Kuʻu hōʻikeʻike (guide) o nā kai ʻewalu. (He kumu maikaʻi, he haku
maikaʻi.)
ʻO ke kanaka ke kuleana o ka moe (moeʻuhane).
E hele ka ʻelemakule, ka luahine, a me ke keiki a moe i ke ala. (Ke
kānāwai māmala hoe.)
I ʻike ʻia nō ke kanaka i ka noho mai o ke kanaka.
Ua ola a ʻō kō kea (until sugarcane tassels, of age).
Liʻiliʻi ka ʻōhiki (sand crab), loloa ka lua (long hole). (Good in small
packages.)
I (inā) uʻi nō ka hula, inā nā ka maka e kiʻi.

Ka waʻa
Hoe aku ka waʻa. (Hoʻomau i ka hana.)
ʻAʻole make ka waʻa i ka ʻale (waves) o waho; aia nō i ka ʻale o loko o ka
waʻa. (Ka makaʻu o loko.)
Pae maila koʻu waʻa i ka ʻāina. (*Māʻona, *piha ka ʻōpū.)

Ka poʻe naʻaupō
Ka poʻe unaunahi (scale) heʻe o Kula, ʻo Kula hoe hewa.

Ikaika ʻole
Nui pū maiʻa, ʻōhaka (empty) o loko.

B.   Ka lāhui Hawaiʻi, kona ʻano. Nā Kepelino (1830-1878?) (Beckwith,
      1932).

      He lāhui kanaka nui keia i kinohi (ka hoʻomaka ʻana), ua nui a piha
      pono nā mokupuni Hawaiʻi iāia. He lāhui kino maʻemaʻe (clean), he
      puʻipuʻi (stout), ua nunui nā lālā (large-limbed), a me ka ikaika, mehe
      liona (like a lion) la malalo iho o ka ikaika o ka lā, a ua lōʻihi kona ola
      ʻana ma ka honua. He lāhui aloha, he ʻoluʻolu, he lokomaikaʻi, a he poʻe
      aulike (treat kindly) i nā malihini. He lāhui kanaka hōnēnē (attracted)
      i nā mea ʻino a nā haole hoʻokano a hilahila ʻole o ʻAmerika mai, mai
      iā Lono (Captain Cook) a hiki i keia wā, a lākou i hoʻolaha (spread) ai
      i nā maʻi ʻino a hilahila, pau ʻole i ka helu ʻia ke haʻi aʻe. He lāhui
      haʻahaʻa (modest), naʻau pēpē (humble spirit), leo ʻoluʻolu, mehe mau
      keiki la nā ka moa i ka nahele, a mehe ʻuaʻu (petrels) la nō ka lua (pits),
      a me he nūnū (cooing) la hoʻi ma nā pali pōhaku, pēlā aku, ke ʻano o ka
      lāhui Hawaiʻi.

C.   E ka haumana, e *haʻiʻōlelo kālaiʻāina (political) mai ʻoe. E lilo ʻoe i
      moho. He moho aha? Aia nō ia iāʻoe. Hōʻike mai paha i kou *one
      hānau. Pehea i hoʻonaʻauao ʻia ai? Hoʻopunipuni ʻoe, ʻaihue, kolohe,
      kūʻē i ka ʻino, mamake i ka hana pono, kākoʻo (support) i nā kānāwai
      maikaʻi, inu lama, puhi paka, he ʻohana keiki, a pēlā aku, pēlā aku,
      pēlā aku. Nānā pono: keʻena, office (room); ʻoihana, office (political);
      ka ʻoihana kiaʻāina, the office of governor.

D.   Systematically review all dialogues memorized this semester.

KANAONO-KŪMĀ-WALU

A. Hana Kahuna.

I ka make ʻana o ka hoaloha, e mālama ʻia nā iwi me ka lauoho maloko o kekahi pūʻolo (bundle). E mōhai (sacrifice) ana ke kahuna. Eia kāna mōhai: ka *malo kea (keʻokeʻo), ka malo puakai (ʻula), ke kapa, ke ʻapu (*ipu) ʻawa, ka ipu poi. Mamua o nā ʻāina apau, e pule ana ke kahuna i ka ʻuhane o nā iwi:

E Puhi, e hoʻi mai.	Eia kou malo.
Eia kou ʻai.	E hoʻi mai a ʻai a māʻona
Eia kou iʻa.	A hele a pāʻani a lelele.
Eia kou kapa.	ʻĀmama, ua noa (taboo is lifted).
Eia kou ʻawa.	[J. S. Emerson, 1892]

B. Antithesis. Hawaiian narrative art makes rich use of antitheses, or paired opposites: "A hiki keia (Kai-palaoa) i Kohala, ao ihola me ka makuahine, apau na mea apau loa, o ko luna o ko lalo, o ko uka o ko kai, o ko ke ao o ko ka po, o ka make o ke ola, o ka hewa o ka pono, lolo (expert) ihola apau." [Fornander, vol. 4, p. 575]

C. Hoʻomaʻamaʻa i ke ana ʻāina. Nānā hou i ka haʻawina kanalima-kūmā-lima.

ʻĀpana ʻelima. Ana ʻia ka pā e Kalani. Hoʻomaka i ka puʻu pōhaku ma ke kihi ʻākau a e holo ak, *kanahā ma ka hapalua kekelē hikina. A laila hoʻomau hikina kanakolu hema, a laila holo i ke komohana. Ana ʻia e Keawe.

D. Words not used for five lessons. Be sure you know them.

(1) *Words commonly used as nouns.*
Nā kānaka: haku hale, hoa, hoahānau, kaikaina, kaikuaʻana, kaikuahine, kaikunāne, kākau-ʻōlelo, kālepa, kamaliʻi, kuaʻāina, kuene wahine, lani, lawaiʻa, makaʻāinana, mākua, mea heʻe nalu, mea pāʻani kinipōpō, mōʻī wahine, ʻohana, Paniolo.
Nā mea Hawaiʻi: ʻawa, inoa, kapa, oli, pahu, papa heʻe nalu, pōhaku kuʻi ʻai, pūʻili, ʻukulele.

Nā holoholona: heʻe, ʻiole, lio wahine, manō, moa wahine, moʻo, pipi kāne, ʻuku.

Nā māhele kino: ʻiʻo, iwi, koko, kuli, lauoho, papālina, poli.

Nā mea pili i ke aʻo ʻana: hanele, heluna, huapalapala, kaukani, kulanui, kumuhana, māmalaʻōlelo, ʻokina.

Ke ana ʻāina: ʻākau, ʻāpana, hema, hikina, komohana.

Nā lā o ka pule; ka manawa, hola, lānui, lāpule, neihinei, pōʻahā, pōʻakahi, pōʻakolu, pōʻalima, pōʻalua, pōʻaono.

Nature: anuanu, ao, hōkū, uka.

Nā mea ʻē aʻe: ʻaina, ala, ʻala, hale-kūʻai, hale-pule, hapa nui, hīmeni, kānāwai, keʻena, keneka, kenikeni, kihi, kumu, lālani, mana, nane, pāʻina, pālule, pū hala, ʻulu, waihoʻoluʻu, wehewehe ʻana.

(2) *Words commonly used as adjectives.*
ʻākau, ʻano nui, anu, hema, kaʻawale, Kakolika, Kalawina, kāpulu, kilakila, koke, kuaʻāina, kuli, maʻa, maʻemaʻe, makapō, maloʻo, momona, ʻoi, ʻomaʻomaʻo, pī, pipiʻi, pōkole, polū, pōmaikaʻi, uliuli.

(3) *Words commonly used as verbs.*
ʻauʻau, hiamoe, hīmeni, hoe, hoʻokani, hoʻokano, hoʻokomo, hoʻolohe, hoʻomaikaʻi, hoʻopau, hoʻopaumanawa, hoʻopili, hui, ʻī, kaha, kali, kānalua, kapa, kuʻi, make wai, mālama, moe ʻuhane, namu, pepehi, poina, waiho, wehewehe.

(4) *Others, including words of special distributions.*
Possessives: āu, aʻu, nāna, nona, nou, noʻu.
Others: aʻe, āhea? aia, aia i hea? aihea? akula, ala, ʻano, ʻauhea? ʻē, hoʻi, ihola, i ka manawa hea? ināhea? ke, ke . . . nei, la, mai, mamuli o, mehe, ʻo.

Hawaiian – English Vocabulary

Note: Only common glosses are given; many words are used as nouns, verbs, adjectives, and adverbs, but not all such meanings are included. Students at other than elementary levels will need to consult dictionaries.

a. And, then; of.

ā. To, until, as far as.

'ā. To burn; lava.

'a'ahu. Clothing; to wear clothes.

'a'ala. Fragrance, perfume, sweet scent; fragrant.

a'e. Nearby; then (direction unspecified).

'ae. Yes; to agree.

a'ela. There (direction unspecified).

aha? What?

āhea? When (future)?

ahi. Fire.

ahiahi. Evening.

a hiki i. As far as, until.

a hui hou aku. Good-by.

'ahu'ula. Feather cloak.

ai. Linking particle.

'ai. To eat; food; poi.

aia. There is, there are; to depend.

aia i hea? Where?

aia nō ia. It's up to, it depends on.

Aia nō ia iā 'oe. It's up to you, suit yourself.

aihea? Where?

'aihue. To steal; thief.

'aina. Meal.

'āina. Land.

ai'ole. Or.

akā. But, however, nevertheless.

akamai. Smart.

'Akamu. Adam, Adams.

'ākau. Right; north.

aku. Away, thither (particle expressing direction away from speaker).

akua. God, ghost.

akula. There, away.

aku nei. Last.

ala. Road, path; wake up; awake; to rise up; there.

'ala. Fragrant.

a laila. Then.

alanui. Street, road.

ali'i. Chief; royal.

ali'i wahine. Chiefess.

alo. Front, presence.

aloalo. Hibiscus.

aloha. Love, affection, pity, compassion, mercy; hello; good-by; to greet.

aloha ahiahi. Good evening.

aloha 'ino! Oh dear! How dreadful! How pathetic!

aloha kakahiaka. Good morning.

a me. And.

ana. Pattern, model, measure, survey. See *e . . . ana.*

āna. His, hers, its.

'ana. Noun-maker.

anei. Particle indicating a question that can be answered yes or no.

'ano. Kind, likeness, nature; somewhat, rather.

'ano nui. Important.

anu. Cold.

anuanu. Cold.

ao. Cloud; light.

a'o. To learn.

'ao'ao. Side, page.

'a'ohe. None, no, not; to have none.

'Ā 'oia. That's right.

'a'ole. No; not.

'A'ole loa! Certainly not!

'Apalahama. Abraham.

'āpana. District.

apau. All.

a pēlā aku. And so forth.

'apōpō. Tomorrow.

au. I.

a'u. My, mine, me.

āu. Your.

'au'au. To bathe.

'auhea? Where?

aupuni. Government.

Auwē! Alas! Oh!

Auwē noho'i e! Goodness!

'awa. *Piper methysticum,* a drink.

'awa'awa. Brackish, bitter.

'awapuhi. Ginger.

'āwīwī. Fast; quickly.

e. By; vocative particle; particle introducing nonpast subordinate verbs.

'ē. Different, other, strange, foreign; beforehand, already.

'ē a'e. Another, different, strange.

e . . . ana. Marker of incompleted action and future tense.

'eha. To hurt, pain; sore.

'ehā. Four.

'ehia? How many?

'ehiku. Seven.

eia. Here is, here are.

ei nei. You there, the one here, darling.

'eiwa. Nine.

'ekahi. One.

'ekolu. Three.

'ele'ele. Black.

'elele. Delegate, messenger.

'elemakule. Old man; old.

'eleu. Lively, active, alert.

'elima. Five.

'elua. Two.

e 'olu'olu 'oe. Please.

'eono. Six.

'ewalu. Eight.

ha'aheo. To cherish; proud; pride.

hā'awi. To give, grant.

ha'awina. Lesson.

ha'i. To tell, relate, say.

ha'ina. To tell; answer.

ha'i'ōlelo. To make a speech; speech.

haku. Lord, boss, master, employer; to compose.

haku hale. House owner, landlord.

haku mele. Poet, composer of songs.

hala. Pandanus; to sin, err, pass by or on, miss.

hale. House.

hale-'aina. Restaurant.

hale-kūʻai. Store.

hale-leka. Post office.

hale-maʻi. Hospital.

hale-pule. Church.

hana. Work, job, action, activity; to work, do.

hānai. To nourish, raise, foster, adopt, feed; adopted child.

hana nui. Hard work, much work; difficult.

hānau. To give birth; born.

hanele. Hundred.

hanohano. Glorious, honorable; glory.

haole. Caucasian, white person; English (language).

hapahā. Quarter; quarterly.

hapa haole. Part-Caucasian.

hapalua. Half, half-past; 50 cents.

hapa nui. Most, majority.

haumana, haumāna. Student.

hauʻoli. Happy.

Hawaiʻi. Hawaii; Hawaiian.

he. A, an; is a.

hea? Which?

he aha? What?

heʻe. Squid, octopus; to slide, surf.

heʻe nalu. To surf.

hele. To go.

hele aku. To go.

hele mai. To come.

helu. To count, number.

heluhelu. To read.

heluna. Number, total.

hema. Left; south.

hemahema. Awkward, unskilled; not to know well.

he mea iki. You are welcome; just a trifle.

hewa. Mistake; to make a mistake; wrong, incorrect.

hiamoe. To sleep.

hiki. To be able, can; O.K.; to arrive, approach.

hikina. East.

hiki nō. Certainly, O.K., surely.

hilahila. Ashamed, shy, bashful; shame, embarrassment.

hīmeni. Hymn, song not for dancing; to sing hīmeni.

hoa. Friend, associate.

hoahānau. Cousin.

hoaloha. Friend.

hoʻaʻo. To try.

hoe. Paddle; to paddle.

hoe waʻa. To paddle a canoe.

hoʻi. Indeed, very, also, too; to return, come back.

hōʻike. To show, exhibit; test, report.

hōkū. Star.

hola. Hour, time, oʻclock.

holo. To run, go, sail, ride.

holoholo. To walk, ride, sail, go out for pleasure.

holoholona. Animal.

holo lio. To ride horseback.

home. Home.

honua. Earth, land, world.

hoʻokahi. One, same.

hoʻokani. To play (music).

hoʻokano. Proud, conceited.

hoʻokomo. To insert, enter.

hoʻolohe. To listen.

hoʻoluhi. To bother, disturb.

hoʻomaʻamaʻa. To practice.

hoʻomaikaʻi. To congratulate, bless, thank.

ho'omaka. To begin, start.

ho'omanawanui. Patient; to be patient.

ho'omau. To continue, persist.

ho'onani. To beautify, glorify, exalt.

ho'opa'ana'au. To memorize.

ho'opau. To finish.

ho'opaumanawa. To waste time; a waste of time.

ho'opili. To mimic, imitate.

ho'oponopono. To correct.

ho'opunipuni. To lie.

ho'oūna. To send.

hope. Last, after, behind, stern.

hope loa. Last, youngest.

hou. New, fresh; again.

hua. Fruit; to bear fruit.

huahelu. Number, figure.

hua'ōlelo. Word.

hua palapala. Letter.

huhū. Anger, wrath; angry.

hui. Club; to join, meet.
A hui hou aku, good-by.

hula. Dance, hula; to dance the hula; song, chant for dancing.

hūpō. Ignorant, foolish; fool.

i. Object marker; to, at; he, she, it; particle marking completed (definite) or past action; because.

'ī. To say.

ia. He, she, it, this, that.

iā. Object marker; to, at.

i'a. Fish.

'ia. Marker of passive voice.

iāia. Him, her; to him, to her.

iā'oe. You; to you.

ia'u. Me; to me.

'Iesū. Jesus.

i hea? Where?

iho. Down, below; self; to go or come down; marker of reflexive action.

ihola. Downward; then; marker of reflexive action.

ihu. Nose.

ikaika. Strong, powerful; strength.

'ike. To know, see.

iki. Little, small. See *He mea iki.*

i laila. There, at that place.

'ili. Skin.

'ilihune. Poor.

'ili'ili. Pebble.

'īlio. Dog.

i luna. High, above, up, on, over.

'imi. To seek, look for.

imu. Earth oven.

i mua. Forward, before, in front of.

inā. If.

inahea? When (past)?

'ino. Wicked, sinful, harmful; sin.

inoa. Name; name chant.

inu. To drink.

'i'o. Flesh, meat.

'iole. Rat, mouse.

ipo. Sweetheart.

ipu. Gourd, gourd drum.

iwakālua. Twenty.

iwakālua-kūmā-kahi. Twenty-one.

iwi. Bone.

ka. The.

kā. Belonging to, of.

ka'a. Car.

ka'awale. Unoccupied, free, not busy; to separate.

kaha. To draw, paint.

kahaki'i. Artist, painter; to draw a picture.

kāhea. To call.

kahiko. Ancient, old.

kāhili. Feather standard.

kahu. Guardian, attendant, minister.

kahuna. Priest, expert.

kai. Sea, sea water.

kaikaina. Younger brother of a male, younger sister of a female.

kaikamahine. Girl, daughter, niece.

kaikua'ana. Older brother of a male, older sister of a female.

kaikuahine. Sister of a male.

kaikunāne. Brother of a female.

kakahiaka. Morning.

kākau. To write.

kākau-'olelo. Secretary, clerk.

Kakolika. Catholic.

kākou. We (3, inclusive).

kālā. Money, dollar.

kalaiwa ka'a. To drive a car; driver.

Kalaka. Clark.

Kala mai ia'u. Excuse me.

Kalawina. Protestant, Calvinist.

Kale. Charles.

kālepa. Merchant, trader, storekeeper.

kali. To wait.

kalo. Taro.

kāma'a. Shoe, shoes.

kama'āina. Native, native-born person; to know.

kama'ilio. To converse, talk, chat.

kama'ilio 'ana. Conversation.

kamali'i. Children.

Kamika. Smith.

Kamuela. Samuel, Sam.

kāna. His, her.

kanahā. Forty.

kanahā-kūmā-kahi. Forty-one.

kanahiku. Seventy.

kanahiku-kūmā-kahi. Seventy-one.

kanaiwa. Ninety.

kanaiwa-kūmā-kahi. Ninety-one.

kanaka. Human being, man, person.

kānaka. Human beings, men, persons.

kanakolu. Thirty.

kanakolu-kūmā-kahi. Thirty-one.

kanalima. Fifty.

kanalima-kūmā-kahi. Fifty-one.

kānalua. Doubt.

kanaono. Sixty.

kanaono-kūmā-kahi. Sixty-one.

kānāwai. Law.

kanawalu. Eighty.

kanawalu-kūmā-kahi. Eighty-one.

kāne. Male, husband, man.

kapa. Tapa; to call, give a name to.

kapu. Taboo, sacred.

kāpulu. Untidy, messy, slovenly.

kau. To place, put, rest on, get on, perch; season, summer, semester.

ka'u. My, mine.

kāu. Your.

kaua. To make war; war, battle.

kāua. We (2 inclusive).

kauka. Doctor.

kaukani. Thousand.

kaulana. Famous.

kaumaha. Heavy; sad.

kauoha. To order, command; order, command.

kauwā. Slave, outcast, servant.

ke. The; when; marker of subordinate verbs.

ke'ena. Office.

keia. This.

keiki. Child.

keiki kāne. Boy, son.

kekahi. A, some, another, other; too.

kēlā. That (far).

kēnā. That (near).

ke . . . nei. Marker of present tense.

keneka. Cent.

kenikeni. Ten cents; small change.

ke'oke'o. White.

Keoki. George.

Keoni. John.

Kepanī. Japanese.

kia'āina. Governor.

ki'eki'e. Height; lofty, majestic, superior, high.

kihi. Corner.

ki'i. Picture, statue, image; to fetch, procure.

ki'i'oni'oni. Moving picture.

kilakila. Majestic.

Kini. King, Jean, Jeannie, Jennie.

kinipōpō. Ball; to play ball.

kino. Body.

kō. Belonging to, of; your.

koa. Soldier, warrior; brave; bravery.

koe keia. Except for this, however, but.

koho. To elect, vote, choose, select.

koke. Quickly.

koko. Blood.

kokoke. Near, close.

kōkua. To help, assist.

Kōlea. Korean.

kolohe. Mischievous, naughty; rascal, prankster.

komo. To enter, go or come in.

komohana. West.

kona. His, her, its.

kou. Your.

ko'u. My.

kū. To stand; upright, standing.

kua. Back.

kua'āina. Countrified, rustic; country person.

kuahiwi. Mountain.

kū'ai. To buy, sell.

kū'e. To oppose, resist; objection; opposite.

kuene. Waiter.

kuene wahine. Waitress.

ku'i. To punch, pound.

kūkū. Granny.

kula. School.

kūlanakauhale. Village, town, city.

kula-nui. University.

kuli. Knee; deaf.

kulikuli. Noise, din; to make a noise; noisy, deafening; shut up!

kumu. Teacher; reason.

kumuhana. Subject, topic.

kupuna. Grandparent, ancestor.

kupuna kāne. Grandfather.

kupuna wahine. Grandmother.

ku'u. My

la. There; doubt.

lā. Day, sun.

lā'au. Plant, tree, stick, club, wood; forest; medicine.

Lahela. Rachel.

lāhui. Race, nation, people, nationality.

laila. There.

lākou. They (3).

lālani. Line.

lalo. Down, below, under.

lama. Rum, liquor; torch.

lani. Heaven, sky; royal chief.

lānui. Holiday.

lapu. Ghost.

lāpule. Sunday.

lapuwale. Worthless, foolish.

lāua. They (2).

laulau. Steamed leaf package of food.

launa. To associate, meet, fraternize.

lauoho. Hair.

lawa. Enough.

lawai'a. To go fishing; fisherman.

lawe. To carry, bring, take.

le'ale'a. Pleasure, joy, merriment, fun; to have a good time.

lei. Lei, wreath; child; to wear a lei.

lei palaoa. Whale-tooth pendant.

leka. Letter.

lele. To fly, leap, jump.

leo. Voice, tune, sound.

lepo. Dirt, earth, ground; dirty.

li'ili'i. Small, little.

like. Like, similar, same.

like 'ole. Various, varied, different.

like pū. Same, just alike.

lilo. To become, turn into, get, accrue to, lose.

lima. Hand, arm; five.

lio. Horse.

lio wahine. Mare.

loa. Very, too, very much; long.

loa'a. To get, obtain, find.

lohe. To hear.

lohi. Slow, late, tardy.

lō'ihi. Long, tall; length, height.

loko. Inside, within; interior, mainland; heart.

lokomaika'i. kindness, generosity, good will.

lole. Dress, clothes.

Lopaka. Robert, Bob.

Lopikana. Robinson.

luahine. Old woman; old.

Luka. Ruth, Luke.

Lukia. Russia; Russian.

lumi. Room.

luna. Boss, foreman; above, up.

luna kānāwai. Judge.

ma. At, in, on (indefinite).

ma'a. Accustomed, used.

ma'ema'e. Clean.

mahalo. Thanks; to thank; to admire; admiration.

mahea? Where?

māhele. Part, division.

mahi'ai. Farmer; to farm.

mahina. Moon; month.

mahope. After, behind, last, back.

mai. Hither, direction toward the speaker; don't (negative command); from.

ma'i. Sick, ill; sickness.

mai'a. Banana.

maika'i. Good, fine, beautiful, well.

maila. Then, there, direction this way.

maka. Eye, face.

maka'āinana. Public, common people, citizen.

makahiki. Year.

māka'i. Policeman.

makana. Gift, present.

makani. Wind.

makapō. Blind.

maka'u. To fear; frightened, afraid.

mākaukau. Clever, proficient, prepared.

make. To die; killed, dead.

makemake. To want, wish, like, desire.

make wai. Thirsty.

mākou. We (3, exclusive).

makua. Parent.

mākua. Parents.

makuahine. Mother.

makuakāne. Father.

malaila. There.

malalo. Below, under, down.

mālama. To protect, care for, keep.

malihini. Newcomer, stranger, visitor, tourist.

malo. Loincloth.

maloko. Inside.

malo'o. Dry.

māluhiluhi. Tired, weary, tiresome.

maluna. On, on top of, above, over.

māmala'ōlelo. Sentence.

mamao. Far, distant.

mamua. Before.

mamuli o. Because.

mana. Supernatural power.

mana'o. Meaning, idea, opinion, thought; to think.

manawa. Time, season, turn. *I ka manawa hea?* When?

manō. Shark.

manu. Bird.

maoli. Native, real, true, genuine, very.

mā'ona. Satisfied, sated, full; to have eaten.

maopopo. To understand.

mau. Plural marker; to continue, persevere; constant, continual, always, steady.

māua. We (2, exclusive).

mauka. Inland, upland.

mauna. Mountain.

mawaena. Between, middle, in the middle.

mawaho. Outside, beyond.

me. With.

mea. Thing, person.

mea'ai. Food.

mea he'e nalu. Surfer.

mea pā'ani kinipōpō. Ball player.

mehe. Like, similar.

mele. Song; to sing.

Mele. Mary.

melemele. Yellow.

minamina. To regret, be sorry, cherish.

moa. Chicken.

moana. Open sea, ocean.

moa wahine. Hen.

moe. To sleep, lie down.

moe 'uhane. Dream; to dream.

moho. Candidate.

mō'ī. King.

mō'ī wahine. Queen.

Moke. Moses.

moku. Island, district; ship.

mokupuni. Island.

molowā. Lazy.

momona. Fat; sweet; fertile.

mo'o. Lizard.
mo'olelo. Story.
mo'opuna. Grandchild.
mua. First, foremost, before, front.
mu'umu'u. Gown.

-na. Nominalizing.
nā. The (plural), by, for.
nā'au. Intestines; mind.
na'auao. Learned; wisdom.
na'aupō. Ignorant.
nahele. Forest, grove, trees.
nalowale. Lost, forgotten,
   vanished, disappeared.
namu. To mutter, speak; language.
nāna. By him, her.
nānā. To look at, care for.
nane. Riddle.
nani. Pretty, beautiful.
nāu. Yours, by you, for you.
na'u. Mine, for me, by me.
nehinei. Yesterday.
nei. Here, this.
nīele. To ask questions; inquisitive,
   overcurious.
niho. Tooth.
nīnau. Question; to ask a question.
niu. Coconut.
nō. Concerning, about, for,
   because; very, somewhat.
noho. To live, sit, stay; seat, chair.
noho'i. Really, surely, indeed,
   certainly.
noho pa'a. To dwell permanently;
   established.
noi. To ask for, request.
no ka mea. Because.
nō ke aha? Why?
nō laila. Therefore, for that reason.

nona. By him, her; for him, her.
nou. By you, for you.
no'u. By me, for me.
nui. Big, large, important,
   much, many; very; size.

o. of.
'o. Subject marker.
'ō. There.
'ōe. You (singular).
'ohana. Family.
'ohu'ohu. Bedecked with leis.
'oi. Superior, best, better; sharp.
'oia. He, she.
'oia ala. He, she.
'oia ho'i. Namely, so it is!
'oia mau nō. Same as usual.
'oihana. Profession, occupation, job.
'okina. Glottal stop.
ola. Life, health; living.
'ole. Not, without, lacking.
'ōlelo. Language, speech; to
   speak, say.
oli. Chant (not for dancing), to
   chant.
'olua. You (2).
'olu'olu. Comfortable, refreshing,
   cool; polite, courteous, kind;
   please.
'ōma'oma'o. Green.
ona. His, hers, its.
onaona. Soft fragrance, perfume;
   fragrant.
one. Sand; sandy.
'ono. Delicious; to crave, relish.
'ōpiopio. Young, immature,
   juvenile.
'ōpū. Belly, stomach.
ou. Your (2).

o'u. My.

'oukou. You (plural).

'o wai? Who? *'O wai kou inoa?* What is your name?

pā. Wall, fence, yard, lot, enclosure.

pa'a. Firm, steadfast, secure, learned, memorized, retained.

pa'a hana. Busy, hard-working.

pa'akikī. Hard, difficult, stubborn, obstinate.

pā'ani. To play.

paha. Maybe, perhaps.

pahu. Box, keg, drum.

pā'ina. Supper, dinner.

Pākē. Chinese.

Palani. France; French; Frank, Francis, Frances.

palaoa. Bread. See *lei palaoa.*

palapala. Document, writing.

pali. Cliff, precipice.

pālule. Shirt.

pane. To answer; answer.

paniolo. Cowboy.

Paniolo. Spanish.

papa. Class, board.

papa'ele'ele. Blackboard.

papa he'e nalu. Surfboard.

pāpale. Hat.

papālina. Cheek.

pau. Finished, completed, done.

pā'ū. Sarong.

pehea? How, what?

Pehea la? How about it? What about it?

Pehea 'oe? How are you? How about you?

pēlā. In that way, like that, thus.

pēlā aku. And so forth.

pēlā paha. Maybe so.

pēlā wale aku. And so forth.

Pele. Pele, lava flow, lava.

Pelekane. English; Englishman, England, Britain.

penei. Thus, like this, this way, as follows.

penikala. Pencil.

pepa. Paper; pepper.

pepehi. To hit, beat.

pepeiao. Ear.

pī. Stingy.

piha. Full, filled, complete, full-blooded.

pi'i. To climb, go up.

pilau. Rotten.

pili. To refer to, relate to, apply to, concern, join, be with.

pilikia. Trouble, bother. *'A'ole pilikia,* never mind, it doesn't matter, you are welcome.

Pilipino. Filipino.

Pinamu. Bingham.

pipi. Beef, steak, cattle, cow.

pipi'i. Expensive.

pō. Night; dark.

pō'ahā. Thursday.

pō'akahi. Monday.

pō'akolu. Wednesday.

pō'alima. Friday.

pō'alua. Tuesday.

pō'aono. Saturday.

po'e. People; plural marker.

pōhaku. Rock, stone.

pōhaku ku'i 'ai. Poi pounder.

poi. Poi.
poina. To forget.
pōki'i. Younger brother or sister.
Pokipala. Potipher.
pōkole. Short.
Pokoliko. Puerto Rico, Puerto Rican.
poli. Bosom, heart.
pololei. Straight, correct.
pōloli. Hunger; hungry.
polū. Blue
pōmaika'i. Good luck; fortunate, blessed, lucky.
ponimō'ī. Carnation.
pono. Righteous, right, honest, moral; necessary, should, ought, must.
pono'ī. Self, own.
po'o. Head.
po'ohiwi. Shoulder.
pōpoki. Cat.
pū. Together, together with, entirely; tree consisting of a cluster.
pua. Flower; child.
pua'a. Pig.
puana. Theme, refrain of a song.
pū hala. Pandanus tree.
puhi paka. To smoke tobacco.
pū'ili. Bamboo rattle.
puka. Hole; door; emerge, graduate.
puke. Book
Pukikī. Portuguese.
pule. To pray; prayer, church; week.
punahele. Favorite.

pupuka. Ugly.
pupule. Crazy, insane.
pu'uwai. Heart.

Tsa! Oh!

ua. Rain; to rain; particle preceding verbs, marking completed action or state.
ua . . . la. That aforementioned.
'uala. Sweet potato.
ua . . . nei. This aforementioned.
'uhane. Soul, spirit.
ūi. Hello.
u'i. Beautiful, youthful.
uka. Uplands, inland, area towards the mountains.
'uku. Louse, flea.
'ukulele. Ukulele.
'ula. Red.
uliuli. Blue (of sky), green (of vegetation), dark.
'ulu. Breadfruit.
'umi. Ten.
'umi-kūmā-hā. Fourteen.
'umi-kūmā-hiku. Seventeen.
'umi-kūmā-iwa. Nineteen.
'umi-kūmā-kahi. Eleven.
'umi-kūmā-kolu. Thirteen.
'umi-kūmā-lima. Fifteen.
'umi-kūmā-lua. Twelve.
'umi-kūmā-ono. Sixteen.
'umi-kūmā-walu. Eighteen.
unuhi. To translate; translation.
'u'uku. Little, small.
uwē. To cry, weep, lament.

wā. Period, time, era, age, season, weather.

wa'a. Canoe.

waena. Between, middle.

waha. Mouth.

wahi. Place; some, a little.

wahine. Woman, wife, female, Mrs.

wāhine. Women.

waho. Outside.

wai. Water.

wai? Who?

waiho. To leave.

waiho'olu'u. Color.

wailele. Waterfall.

waiwai. Rich.

wala'au. To talk, speak, shout; language.

wale. So; much, very; for no reason.

wale nō. Only.

wau. I.

wāwae. Foot, leg.

wehewehe. To explain.

wehewehe 'ana. Explanation.

wela. Hot.

wilikī. Engineer.

English – Hawaiian Vocabulary

a. He, kekahi.
able. Hiki.
about. Nō, pili i.
above. Luna, i luna, maluna.
Abraham. 'Apalahama.
accustomed. Ma'a.
action. Hana.
active. 'Eleu.
activity. Hana.
Adam, Adams. 'Akamu.
admire. Mahalo.
adopt. Hānai.
adornment. Wehi.
affection. Aloha.
afraid. Maka'u.
after. Mahope o, pau.
again. Hou.
agree. 'Ae.
ahead. Mamua, i mua.
Alas! Auwē!
alert. 'Eleu.
alike. Like, like pū.
all. Apau.
already. 'Ē.
also. Ho'i, kekahi.
always. Mau.
ancestor. Kupuna.
ancient. Kahiko.
and. A me, a.
and so forth. A pēlā aku, a pēlā wale aku.
anger. Huhū.
angry. Huhū.

animal. Holoholona.
another. Kekahi.
answer. Pane, ha'ina.
are. Ua, he.
arm. Lima.
arrive. Hiki.
artist. Kahaki'i.
as far as. A, a hiki i.
ashamed. Hilahila.
ask. Nīnau (a question), noi (for something).
assist. Kōkua.
associate. Launa (verb), hoa (noun).
astonishing. 'Ē.
at. I, ma.
attendant. Kahu.
awake. Ala.
awkward. Hemahema.

back. Kua. *In back,* i hope.
bad. Maika'i 'ole.
ball. Kinipōpō.
ball player. Mea pā'ani kinipōpō.
bamboo rattle. Pū'ili.
banana. Mai'a.
bashful. Hilahila.
bathe. 'Au'au.
battle. Kaua.
bear fruit. Hua.
beat. Pepehi, pa'i.
beautiful. U'i, nani, maika'i.
beautify. Ho'onani.

because. No ka mea, nō, mamuli, i.
become. Lilo, ua.
bedecked with leis. 'Ohu'ohu.
beef. Pipi.
before. Mua, i mua, mamua.
beforehand. 'Ē.
begin. Ho'omaka.
behind. Mahope.
belly. 'Ōpū.
belonging to. Kō, kā.
below. Iho, lalo.
best. 'Oi.
better. 'Oi.
between. Mawaena, i waena.
beyond. Mawaho, ma 'ō aku.
big. Nui.
Bingham. Pinamu.
bird. Manu.
birth, give birth. Hānau.
bitter. 'Awa'awa.
black. 'Ele'ele.
blackboard. Papa'ele'ele.
bless. Ho'omaika'i.
blind. Makapō.
blood. Koko.
blue. Polū, uliuli.
board. Papa.
Bob. Lopaka.
body. Kino.
bone. Iwi.
book. Puke.
born. Hānau.
bosom. Poli.
boss. Luna, haku.
bother. Ho'oluhi, pilikia.
box. Pahu.
boy. Keiki kāne.
brackish. 'Awa'awa.
brave, bravery. Koa.
bread. Palaoa.

breadfruit. 'Ulu.
bring. Lawe.
Britain. Pelekane.
brother. Kaikua'ana (older of a male), kaikaina (younger of a male), kaikunāne (of a female), pōki'i (youngest).
bundle of steamed food. Laulau.
burn. 'Ā.
busy. Pa'a hana.
but. Akā, koe keia.
buy. Kū'ai.
by. E, nā.
by him, her. Nāna.
by me. Na'u.
by you. Nāu.

call. Kāhea, kapa.
Calvinist. Kalawina.
can. Hiki . . . ke.
candidate. Moho.
canoe. Wa'a.
car. Ka'a.
care for. Mālama, nānā.
carnation. Ponimō'ī.
carry. Lawe.
cat. Pōpoki.
Catholic. Kakolika.
cattle. Pipi.
cent. Keneka.
certainly. Hiki, hiki nō, noho'i.
Certainly not! 'A'ole loa!
chair. Noho.
chant. Oli, hula.
character. 'Ano.
Charles. Kale.
chat. Kama'ilio.
cheek. Papālina.
cherish. Ha'aheo.
chicken. Moa.

chief, chiefly. Ali'i, lani.
chiefess. Ali'i wahine.
child. Keiki, pua, lei.
children. Kamali'i.
Chinese. Pākē.
choose. Koho.
church. Hale-pule.
citizen. Maka'āinana.
city. Kūlanakauhale.
Clark. Kalaka.
class. Papa.
clean. Ma'ema'e.
clerk. Kakau-'ōlelo.
clever. Mākaukau, akamai.
cliff. Pali.
climb. Pi'i.
cloak (feather). 'Ahu'ula.
close. Kokoke, pili.
clothes. Lole, 'a'ahu.
cloud. Ao.
club. Hui (association),
    lā'au (weapon).
coconut. Niu.
cold. Anu, anuanu.
color. Waiho'olu'u.
come. Hele mai.
come back. Ho'i.
come in. Komo.
comfortable. 'Olu'olu.
command. Kauoha.
commoner. Maka'āinana.
complete. Piha pono.
compose. Haku.
composer of songs. Haku mele.
conceited. Ho'okano.
concerning. Nō, pili i.
congratulate. Ho'omaika'i.
continue. Ho'omau, mau.
conversation. Kama'ilio 'ana.
converse. Kama'ilio.

cool. 'Olu'olu.
corner. Kihi.
correct. Pololei, pono (adjective);
    ho'oponopono (verb).
count. Helu.
courteous. 'Olu'olu.
cousin. Hoahānau.
cow. Pipi wahine.
cowboy. Paniolo.
crave. 'Ono.
crazy. Pupule.
cry. Uwē.

dance the hula. Hula.
dark, darkness. Pō.
darling. Ei nei.
daughter. Kaikamahine.
day. Lā.
dead. Make.
deaf. Kuli.
decoration. Wehi, kāhiko.
delegate. 'Elele.
delicious. 'Ono.
depending. Aia. Depending on you,
    aia nō ia iā'oe.
desire. Makemake.
die. Make.
different. Like 'ole, 'oko'a,
    'ē, 'ē a'e.
difficult. Hana nui, pa'akikī.
dinner. Pā'ina.
dirt, dirty. Lepo.
disappeared. Nalowale.
distant. Mamao.
district. Moku, 'āpana.
disturb. Ho'oluhi.
division. Māhele.
do. Hana.
doctor. Kauka.
document. Palapala.

dog. 'Īlio.
dollar. Kālā.
don't. Mai.
door. Puka.
doubt. Kānalua, la.
down. Lalo, iho.
downward. Ihola.
draw. Kaha.
dream. Moe'uhane.
dress. Lole.
drink. Inu.
drive. Kalaiwa.
driver. Kalaiwa ka'a.
drum. Pahu, ipu.
dry. Malo'o.

ear. Pepeiao.
earth. Honua, lepo.
east. Hikina.
eat. 'Ai.
eight. 'Ewalu.
eighteen. 'Umi-kūmā-walu.
eighty. Kanawalu.
eighty-one. Kanawalu-kūmā-kahi.
eleven. 'Umi-kūmā-kahi.
embarrassment. Hilahila.
emerge. Puka.
employer. Haku.
enclosure. Pā.
engineer. Wilikī.
England, English. Pelekane.
enough. Lawa.
enter. Ho'okomo, komo.
era. Wā.
eternal. Mau, pau 'ole.
evening. Ahiahi.
ever. Mau.
exalt. Ho'onani.
Excuse me. Kala mai ia'u.
exhibit. Hō'ike.

expensive. Pipi'i.
expert. Kahuna.
explain. Wehewehe.
explanation. Wehewehe 'ana.
eye. Maka.

face. Maka.
fairly. 'Ano.
family. 'Ohana.
famous. Kaulana.
far. Mamao.
farm, farmer. Mahi'ai.
fast. 'Āwīwī.
fat. Momona.
father. Makuakāne.
favorite. Punahele.
fear. Maka'u.
feather cloak. 'Ahu'ula.
female. Wahine.
fence. Pā.
fertile. Momona.
fetch. Ki'i.
fifteen. 'Umi-kūmā-lima.
fifty. Kanalima.
fifty-one. Kanalima-kūmā-kahi.
figure. Huahelu.
Filipino. Pilipino.
find. Loa'a.
fine. Maika'i.
finish. Ho'opau.
finished. Pau.
fire. Ahi.
firm. Pa'a.
first. Mua.
fish. I'a (noun); lawai'a (verb).
fisherman. Lawai'a.
five. 'Elima.
flea. 'Uku.
flesh. 'I'o.
flower. Pua.

fly. Lele (verb).
food. Mea'ai, 'ai.
fool. Hūpō.
foolish. Hūpō, lapuwale.
foot. Wāwae.
for. Nō, nā.
foreign. 'Ē.
foreman. Luna.
forest. Nahele.
forget. Poina.
for him, her. Nona, nāna.
for me. Na'u, no'u.
fortunate. Pōmaika'i.
forty. Kanahā.
forty-one. Kanahā-kūmā-kahi.
forward. I mua.
for you. Nāu, nou.
foster. Hānai.
four. 'Ehā.
fourteen. 'Umi-kūmā-hā.
fragrance. Onaona, 'a'ala, 'ala.
France, French. Palani.
Frances, Francis. Palani.
Frank. Palani.
fresh. Hou.
Friday. Pō'alima.
friend. Hoa, hoaloha, aikāne.
from. Mai, nō.
front. Mua.
fruit. Hua, hua'ai.
full. Piha, mā'ona.
full-blooded. Piha.
fun. Le'ale'a.

generosity. Lokomaika'i, aloha.
genuine. Maoli.
George. Keoki.
get. Ki'i, loa'a, lilo.
ghost. Lapu, akua.
gift. Makana.

ginger. 'Awapuhi.
give. Hā'awi.
glorify. Ho'onani.
glorious. Hanohano.
glory. Hanohano, nani.
glottal stop. 'Okina.
go. Hele, hele aku.
god. Akua.
good. Maika'i.
good-by. A hui hou aku, aloha.
good evening. Aloha ahiahi.
good morning. Aloha kakahiaka.
Goodness! Auwē noho'i e!
gourd. Ipu.
gourd drum. Ipu.
government. Aupuni.
governor. Kia'āina.
gown. Mu'umu'u, holokū.
grandchild. Mo'opuna.
grandfather. Kupuna kāne.
grandmother. Kupuna wahine,
   tūtū.
grandparent. Kupuna.
granny. Kūkū, tūtū.
grant. Hā'awi.
green. 'Ōma'oma'o, uliuli.
greet. Aloha.
ground. Lepo.
guardian. Kahu.

hair. Lauoho, hulu.
half. Hapalua.
half-past. Hapalua.
hand. Lima.
handsome. U'i.
happy. Hau'oli.
hard. Pa'akikī.
hard work. Hana nui.
hat. Pāpale.
Hawaii. Hawai'i.
Hawaiian. Hawai'i.

he. Ia, ʻoia, ʻoia ala.
head. Poʻo.
health. Ola, olakino.
hear. Lohe.
heart. Puʻuwai, loko.
heaven. Lani.
heavy. Kaumaha.
height. Kiʻekiʻe, lōʻihi.
hello. Ūi, aloha.
help. Kōkua.
hen. Moa wahine.
her. Iāia, kona, kāna, ona, āna.
here. Nei.
here is, here are. Eia.
hibiscus. Aloalo.
high. Kiʻekiʻe.
hill. Kuahiwi, puʻu.
his. Kona, kāna, ona, āna.
hit. Pepehi, paʻi.
hither. Mai.
holiday. Lānui.
home. Home.
honorable. Hanohano.
horse. Lio.
hospital. Hale-maʻi.
hot. Wela.
house. Hale.
house owner. Haku hale.
how? Pehea?
How about it? Pehea la?
How are you? Pehea ʻoe?
however. Koe keia, akā.
how many? Ehia?
hula. Hula.
human being. Kanaka.
human beings. Kānaka.
hundred. Hanele.
hungry. Pōloli.
hurt. ʻEha.
husband. Kāne.

hymn. Hīmeni.

I. Wau, au.
idea. Manaʻo.
if. Inā.
ignorant. Hūpō, naʻaupō.
ill. Maʻi.
image. Kiʻi.
imitate. Hoʻopili.
important. Nui, ʻano nui.
impossible. Hiki ʻole.
in. Ma, maloko.
incorrect. Hewa.
indeed. Nō, hoʻi, nohoʻi.
inland. Uka, mauka.
inquisitive. Nīele.
insane. Pupule.
insert. Hoʻokomo.
inside. Loko.
intelligent. Naʻauao.
interior. Loko.
intestines. Naʻau.
is. He, ua, aia.
island. Mokupuni, moku.
it. Ia.
its. Kona, kāna, ona, āna.

Japanese. Kepanī.
Jean. Kini.
Jennie. Kini.
Jesus. ʻIesū.
job. ʻOihana, hana.
John. Keoni.
join. Hui, pili.
joy. Leʻaleʻa.
judge. Luna kānāwai.
jump. Lele.

keg. Pahu.
killed. Make.

kind. ʻOluʻolu (adjective);
  ʻano (noun).
kindness. Lokomaikaʻi.
king. Mōʻī.
King. Kini.
knee. Kuli.
know. ʻIke.
Korea, Korean. Kōlea.

lament. Uwē.
land. ʻĀina, honua.
landlord. Haku hale.
language. ʻŌlelo, namu, walaʻau.
large. Nui.
last. Hope loa, aku nei.
late. Lohi.
lava. ʻĀ, ʻā Pele.
law. Kānāwai.
lazy. Molowā.
leap. Lele.
learn. Aʻo.
leave. Waiho.
left. Hema.
leg. Wāwae.
lei. Lei.
lesson. Haʻawina.
letter. Leka, hua palapala.
lie (falsehood). Hoʻopunipuni.
lie down. Moe.
life. Ola.
light. Ao.
like. Makemake (verb); like,
  mehe (adverb).
likeness. ʻAno.
like that. Pēlā.
like this. Penei.
line. Lālani.
listen. Hoʻolohe.
little. ʻUʻuku, wahi, liʻiliʻi, iki.
live. Noho.

lively. ʻEleu.
live permanently. Noho paʻa.
living. Ola.
lizard. Moʻo.
loincloth. Malo.
long. Lōʻihi, loa.
look at. Nānā.
look for. ʻImi.
lord. Haku.
lose. Lilo.
lost. Nalowale.
louse. ʻUku.
love. Aloha.
lucky. Pōmaikaʻi.

mainland. Loko.
majestic. Kilakila.
majority. Hapa nui.
male. Kāne.
man. Kanaka.
many. Nui.
Mary. Mele.
master. Haku.
maybe. Paha.
maybe so. Pēlā paha.
me. Iaʻu, aʻu, e aʻu.
meal. ʻAina.
meaning. Manaʻo.
measure. Ana.
meat. ʻIʻo.
medicine. Lāʻau.
meet. Hui, launa.
memorize. Hoʻopaʻanaʻau.
men. Kānaka.
merchant. Kālepa.
mercy. Aloha.
messenger. ʻElele.
middle. Waena.
mimic. Hoʻopili.
mind. Naʻau.

minister. Kahu.
mischievous. Kolohe.
mistake. Hewa.
model. Ana.
Monday. Pō'akahi.
money. Kālā.
month. Mahina.
moon. Mahina.
moral. Pono.
morning. Kakahiaka.
Moses. Moke.
most. Hapanui.
mother. Makuahine.
mountain. Mauna, kuahiwi.
mouse. 'Iole.
mouth. Waha.
moving picture. Ki'i'oni'oni.
much. Nui, wale.
must. Pono.
mutter. Namu.
my. Ko'u, o'u, ka'u, a'u, ku'u.

name. Inoa (noun), kapa (verb).
name chant. Inoa, mele inoa.
namely. 'Oia ho'i.
nation. Lāhui, aupuni.
native. Kama'āina, maoli.
near. Kokoke.
necessary. Pono.
new. Hou.
newcomer. Malihini.
night. Pō.
nine. 'Eiwa.
nineteen. 'Umi-kūmā-iwa.
ninety. Kanaiwa.
ninety-one. Kanaiwa-kūmā-kahi.
no. 'A'ole, 'a'ohe.
noise, noisy. Kulikuli.
none. 'A'ohe.
north. 'Ākau.

nose. Ihu.
not. 'Ole, 'a'ole, 'a'ohe.
number. Huahelu, helu, heluna.

obey. Lohe.
obstinate. Pa'akikī.
obtain. Loa'a.
occupation. 'Oihana.
ocean. Moana.
o'clock. Hola.
octopus. He'e.
of. O, a, kā, kō.
office. Ke'ena.
Oh! Auwē! Tsa! Aloha 'ino!
O.K. Hiki, hiki nō.
old lady. Luahine.
old man. 'Elemakule.
on. I, ma.
one. 'Ekahi, ho'okahi.
only. Wale nō.
opinion. Mana'o.
oppose, opposite. Kū'ē.
or. Ai'ole.
order. Kauoha.
other. 'Ē, kekahi, 'oko'a.
ought. Pono.
our. Kō māua, kō kāua, kō mākou,
   kō kākou; kā māua, kā kāua, kā
   mākou, kā kākou; o kāua, o
   māua, o kākou, o mākou; a kāua,
   a māua; a kākou, a mākou.
outcast. Kauwā.
outside. Waho, mawaho.
oven. Imu.
own. Pono'ī.

paddle. Hoe.
paddle a canoe. Hoe wa'a.
page. 'Ao'ao.
pain. 'Eha.

paint. Kaha.
painter. Kahaki'i.
pandanus. Hala, pū hala.
paper. Pepa.
parent. Makua.
part. Māhele.
part white. Hapa haole.
path. Ala.
patient. Ho'omanawanui.
pattern. Ana.
peace. Malu.
pebble. 'Ili'ili.
pencil. Penikala.
pendant. Lei palaoa (whale-tooth).
people. Po'e, lāhui.
perhaps. Paha.
period. Wā (time).
person. Kanaka, mea.
persons. Kānaka.
picture. Ki'i.
pig. Pua'a.
Piper methysticum, kava. 'Awa.
pity. Aloha.
place. Wahi (noun); kau (verb).
plant. Lā'au (noun).
play. Pā'ani (sport), ho'okani
    (music).
please. E 'olu'olu 'oe.
pleasure. Le'ale'a.
poet. Haku mele.
poi. Poi, 'ai.
poi pounder. Pōhaku ku'i 'ai.
policeman. Māka'i.
polite. 'Olu'olu.
poor. 'Ilihune.
Portuguese. Pukikī.
post office. Hale-leka.
Potipher. Pokipala.
pound. Ku'i.
power. Mana.

powerful. Ikaika.
practice. Ho'oma'ama'a.
prankster. Kolohe, 'eu.
pray, prayer. Pule.
precipice. Pali.
prepared. Mākaukau.
present. Makana (gift).
pretty. Nani.
pride. Ha'aheo.
procure. Ki'i.
profession. 'Oihana.
proficient. Mākaukau.
protect. Mālama.
Protestant. Kalawina.
proud. Ha'aheo, ho'okano.
Puerto Rico, Puerto Rican.
    Pokoliko.
punch. Ku'i (verb).
put. Kau.

quarter, quarterly. Hapahā.
queen. Mō'ī wahine.
question. Nīnau, nīele.
quickly. Koke, 'āwīwī.

race (of people). Lāhui.
Rachel. Lahela.
rain. Ua.
raise. Hānai.
rascal. Kolohe, 'eu.
rat. 'Iole.
read. Heluhelu.
real, really. Maoli.
reason. Kumu. For no reason,
    kumu 'ole, wale.
red. 'Ula.
refer. Pili.
refrain. Puana (song).
refreshing. 'Olu'olu.
regret. Minamina.

relate. Haʻi.
relate to. Pili.
report. Hōʻike.
request. Noi.
resist. Kūʻē.
restaurant. Hale-ʻaina.
retained. Paʻa.
return. Hoʻi.
rich. Waiwai.
ride. Holo.
ride horseback. Holo lio.
right. Pono, pololei; ʻākau (not left). *That's right,* ʻā ʻoia.
righteous. Pono.
road. Alanui, ala.
Robert. Lopaka.
Robinson. Lopikana.
rock. Pōhaku.
room. Lumi.
rotten. Pilau.
royal. Aliʻi, lani.
rum. Lama.
run. Holo.
Russia, Russian. Lukia.
rustic. Kuaʻāina.
Ruth. Luka.

sacred. Kapu.
sad. Kaumaha.
sail. Holo.
Sam. Kamuela.
same. Like, like pū.
same as usual. ʻOia mau nō.
Samuel. Kamuela.
sand. One.
sarong. Pāʻū.
Saturday. Pōʻaono.
say. ʻŌlelo, ʻī, haʻi.
school. Kula.

sea. Kai, moana.
season. Kau.
seat. Noho.
secretary. Kākau-ʻōlelo.
see. ʻIke.
seek. ʻImi.
select. Koho, wae.
self. Ponoʻī, iho.
sell. Kūʻai aku.
semester. Kau.
send. Hoʻouna.
sentence. Māmalaʻōlelo.
separate. Kaʻawale.
servant. Kauwā.
seven. ʻEhiku.
seventeen. ʻUmi-kūmā-hiku.
seventy. Kanahiku.
seventy-one. Kanahiku-kūmā-kahi.
shame. Hilahila.
shark. Manō.
sharp. ʻOi.
she. Same as *he.*
ship. Moku.
shirt. Pālule.
shoe. Kāmaʻa.
short. Pōkole.
shoulder. Poʻohiwi.
shout. Walaʻau.
show. Hōʻike.
Shut up! Kulikuli!
shy. Hilahila.
sick. Maʻi.
side. ʻAoʻao.
similar. Mehe, like.
sin. ʻino.
sing. Mele.
sister. Kaikuaʻana (older of a female), kaikaina (younger of a female), kaikuahine (of a male), pōkiʻi (youngest).

sit. Noho.

six. 'Eono.

sixteen. 'Umi-kūmā-ono.

sixty. Kanaono.

sixty-one. Kanaono-kūmā-kahi.

size. Nui.

skin. 'Ili.

sky. Lani.

slave. Kauwā.

sleep. Moe, hiamoe.

slide. He'e.

slovenly. Kāpulu.

slow. Lohi.

small. Iki, li'ili'i, 'u'uku.

smart. Akamai.

Smith. Kamika.

smoke tobacco. Puhi paka.

soldier. Koa.

some. Wahi, kekahi.

somewhat. 'Ano.

son. Keiki kāne.

song. Mele, hīmeni.

sore. 'Eha.

sorry. Minamina.

soul. 'Uhane.

south. Hema.

Spanish. Paniolo.

speak. 'Ōlelo, ha'i'ōlelo, namu, wala'au.

speech. Ha'i'ōlelo, 'ōlelo.

spirit. 'Uhane.

squid. He'e.

stand. Kū.

standard. Kāhili (of royalty).

star. Hōkū.

start. Ho'omaka.

statue. Ki'i.

stay. Noho.

steadfast. Pa'a.

steady. Mau, pa'a.

steal. 'Aihue.

stick. Lā'au.

stingy. Pī.

stomach. 'Ōpū.

stone. Pōhaku.

store. Hale-kū'ai.

story. Mo'olelo.

straight. Pololei.

strange. 'Ē, 'ē a'e.

stranger. Malihini.

street. Alanui.

strength. Ikaika.

strike. Pa'i.

strong. Ikaika.

stubborn. Pa'akikī.

student. Haumana, haumāna.

subject. Kumuhana.

sun. Lā.

Sunday. Lāpule.

superior. 'Oi.

supernatural power. Mana.

supper. Pā'ina.

surely. Hiki nō, noho'i.

surf. He'e nalu (verb).

surfboard. Papa he'e nalu.

surfer. Mea he'e nalu.

survey. Ana.

sweet. Momona.

sweetheart. Ipo.

sweet potato. 'Uala.

taboo. Kapu.

take. Lawe.

talk. Kama'ilio, wala'au.

tall. Lō'ihi, ki'eki'e.

tapa. Kapa.

taro. Kalo.

teacher. Kumu.

tell. Ha'i, ha'ina.

ten. 'Umi.

ten cents. Kenikeni.

test. Hōʻike.

thank. Mahalo, hoʻomaikaʻi.

that. Kēnā, kēlā, ua . . . la, la.

that way. Pēlā.

their. Kō lāua, kō lākou; kā lāua, kā lākou; o lāua, o lākou; a lāua, a lākou.

then. A laila, ia wā, a.

there. I laila, malaila, ʻō; la, ala.

therefore. Nō laila.

there is, are. Aia, he.

these. Keia mau.

they. Lāua, lākou.

thief. ʻAihue.

thing. Mea.

think. Manaʻo.

thirsty. Make wai.

thirteen. ʻUmi-kūmā-kolu.

thirty. Kanakolu.

thirty-one. Kanakolu-kūmā-kahi.

this. Keia, nei, ua . . . nei.

this way. Penei.

those. Kēlā mau.

thousand. Kaukani.

three. ʻEkolu.

Thursday. Pōʻahā.

thus. Penei, pēlā.

time. Wā, manawa, hola.

tired. Māluhiluhi.

to. i, iā, a.

together. Pū.

tomorrow. ʻApōpō.

too. Hoʻi, kekahi, loa.

tooth. Niho.

top. Luna.

topic. Kumuhana.

torch. Lama.

total. Heluna, nui.

tourist. Malihini.

town. Kūlanakauhale.

trader. Kālepa.

translate, translation. Unuhi.

tree. Lāʻau.

trouble. Pilikia.

true, truly. Maoli.

try. Hoʻaʻo.

Tuesday. Pōʻalua.

tune. Leo.

turn into. Lilo.

twelve. ʻUmi-kūmā-lua.

twenty. Iwakālua.

twenty-one. Iwakālua-kūmā-kahi.

two. ʻElua.

ugly. Pupuka.

ukulele. ʻUkulele.

under. Lalo.

understand. Maopopo.

university. Kula-nui.

unoccupied. Kaʻawale.

untidy. Kāpulu.

until. A, a hiki i.

up. Luna, aʻe.

upland. Mauka.

uplands. Uka.

upright. Kū.

us. Iā kāua, iā māua, iā kākou, iā mākou.

used. Maʻa (accustomed).

vanished. Nalowale.

variety. ʻAno.

various. Like ʻole.

very. Loa, nui, nō, wale, maoli, hoʻi, nohoʻi.

village. Kūlanakauhale.

visitor. Malihini.

voice. Leo.

vote. Koho.

wait. Kali.

waiter. Kuene.

waitress. Kuene wahine.

wake. Ala.

want. Makemake.

war. Kaua.

warrior. Koa.

was. Ua.

waste of time. Ho'opaumanawa.

water. Wai.

waterfall. Wailele.

we. Kāua, māua; kākou, mākou.

weary. Māluhiluhi.

weather. Wā.

Wednesday. Pō'akolu.

week. Pule.

weep. Uwē.

well. Maika'i.

west. Komohana.

what? He aha? Pehea?

what about? Pehea?

What is your name? 'O wai kou inoa?

when. Ke, āhea, ināhea, i ka manawa hea?

where? Aihea? mahea? i hea? 'auhea?

which? Hea?

white. Ke'oke'o.

white person. Haole.

who? 'Owai?

why? Nō ke aha?

wicked. 'Ino.

wind. Makani.

wife. Wahine.

wisdom. Na'auao.

with. Me.

without. 'Ole, nele.

woman. Wahine.

women. Wāhine.

wood. Lā'au.

word. Hua'ōlelo.

work. Hana.

world. Honua.

worthless. Lapuwale.

wrath. Huhū.

write. Kākau.

writing. Palapala.

wrong. Hewa.

yard. Pā.

year. Makahiki.

yellow. Melemele.

yes. 'Ae.

yesterday. Nehinei.

you. 'Oe, 'olua, 'oukou.

You are welcome. He mea iki, 'a'ole pilikia, he mea 'ole.

young. 'Ōpiopio.

you there. Eia nei.

youngest. Hope loa.

your. Kōu, kō, kō 'olua, kō 'oukou, kāu, kā 'olua, kā 'oukou, ou, o 'olua, o 'oukou, āu, a 'oulua, a 'oukou.

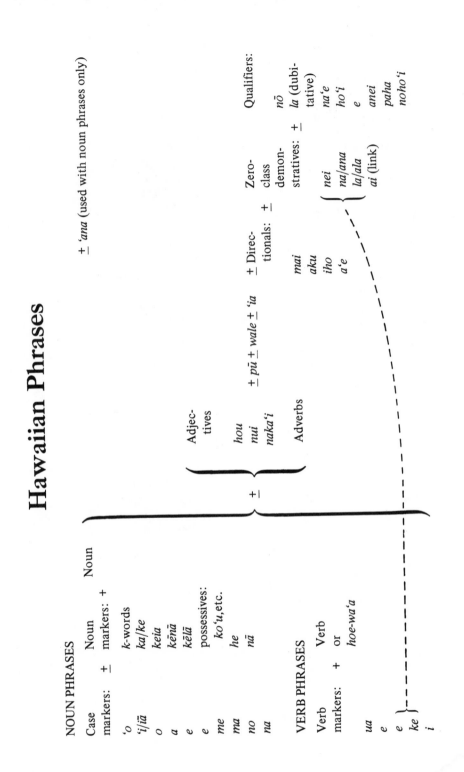

Selected Bibliography

Beckwith, Martha Warren. Introduction and translation to "The Hawaiian Romance of Laieikawai," by S. N. Haleole. In *U.S. Bureau of American Ethnology, Thirty-third Annual Report,* 1911–1912, pp. 285–666. Washington, D.C., 1919.

——. *Kepelino's Traditions of Hawaii.* Bernice Pauahi Bishop Museum Bulletin 95. Honolulu, 1932.

Biggs, Bruce. "The Structure of New Zealand Maaori." *Anthropological Linguistics,* vol. 3, no. 3, 1961.

Elbert, Samuel H. *Nā Mele o Hawaʻi Nei: 101 Hawaiian Songs.* Honolulu: University of Hawaii Press, 1970.

——. "The Unheroic Hero of Hawaiian Tales." *Journal of the Polynesian Society* 69 (1960): 266–275.

Emerson, J. S. *The Lesser Hawaiian Gods.* Hawaiian Historical Society Papers, no. 2. Honolulu, 1892.

Emerson, N. B. *Unwritten Literature of Hawaii, the Sacred Songs of the Hula, Collected and Translated, with Notes and an Account of the Hula.* U.S. Bureau of American Ethnology Bulletin 38. Washington, D.C., 1909.

——. *Pele and Hiiaka, a Myth of Hawaii.* Honolulu: Honolulu Star-Bulletin, Ltd., 1915.

Fornander, A. *Fornander Collection of Hawaiian Antiquities and Folklore.* Memoirs of the Bernice Pauahi Bishop Museum 4, 5, and 6. Honolulu, 1917, 1918, 1919.

Judd, Henry P. *Hawaiian Proverbs and Riddles.* Bernice Pauahi Bishop Museum Bulletin 77. Honolulu, 1930.

Ka Baibala Hemolele o ke Kauoha Kahiko a me ke Kauoha Hou; i Unuhiia Mailoko mai o na Olelo-Kahiko, a Hooponopono Hou ia ("The Holy Bible of the Old Testament and the New Testament; Translated from Ancient Tongues and Revised"). New York: American Bible Society, 1941.

Kahananui, Dorothy M. and Anthony, Alberta Pualani. *Let's Speak Hawaiian: E Kamaʻilio Hawaiʻi Kakou.* Honolulu: University of Hawaii Press, 1970.

Ka Alanui o ka Lani, Oia ka Manuale Kakolika i Paiia ma ke Kauoha o Gulekana, ep. o Panopolis, vic. ap. ("The Path to Heaven, the Catholic Manual Published by Order of Gulstan, Bishop of Panopolis, Vicar Apostolic"). Paris, 1896.

Pukui, Mary Kawena and Elbert, Samuel H. *English-Hawaiian Dictionary.* Honolulu: University of Hawaii Press, 1964.

———. *Hawaiian-English Dictionary.* 3d ed. Honolulu: University of Hawaii Press, 1965.

Index of
Grammatical Rules and Particles

Index of Songs and Chants

Index of Stories and Other Texts

818·729·3333
Rick Burk ♡